HOW TO LIVE IN HIGH VICTORY

HAROLD HILL

Cartoons by John Lawing

LOGOS INTERNATIONAL
Plainfield, New Jersey

Other books by Harold Hill:

How to Live Like a King's Kid
How Did It All Begin?
(From Goo to You by Way of the Zoo)

How to Be a Winner

How to Live in High Victory
Copyright © 1977 by Logos International
Plainfield, New Jersey 07061
All Rights Reserved
Printed in the United States of America
Library of Congress Catalog Card Number: 77-80293
International Standard Book Number: 088270-240-8

Contents

FOREWORD

How to Live in High Victory—this is perhaps the ultimate for the Christian in today's world. To live without frustration, anxiety, worry, fear, stress, or strain—to live the abundant life Jesus came to give—should be the desire of all of us.

The key is to be stewards instead of owners, which is simply to surrender our rights to ourselves to Him. He is the King, and we are His kids—tools in His hands to do with as He sees fit (Rom. 14:7-9). Only then do we reach our full potential in this life, free from disappointments, heartbreaks, and depression, because we know that in all things He works together for good to those who love Him and are the called according to *His* purpose (Rom. 8:28). As King's kids, we know He wants only *His* best for us.

To see everything in our lives as of God (2 Cor. 5:18) and for Him, is to cease struggling to hang onto things and to be grateful that He is able to care for that which is His own.

After all, the only function of the Christian is to be a container for Him. Jesus is *the* all and *in* all. There isn't a single good thing in any of us apart from Him.

We do not seek victory for victory's sake; rather we seek Jesus who *is* our victory. This is *high victory* that is total and complete. In Him, we receive all that His name implies. In fact, we become joint heirs with Him to all of the kingdom of God. To experience this is to enter into the rest of faith—His faith. There will be no fussing or struggling to attain, but simply resting in His finished work and just allowing Him to be all and all in us.

We never will take offense at God for His method of molding us into His image and likeness; rather, we will have perfect confidence in His love for us, being convinced that

v

He is achieving His purpose in us and that His perfect will is being done.

The end result will be a life of high victory expressed in constant praise, which in turn assures us of His continual presence, for the Bible says He lives in the praises of His people (Ps. 22:3).

Dr. Peter Vroom, pastor
Trinity Bible Church
Severna Park, Maryland
February 1977

PREFACE

The purpose of this book is to share with other King's kids in training those things which have produced results beyond the ordinary in my own life as a King's kid these past twenty-three years.

Hopefully, you have read my previous books* in preparation for these deeper truths which have to do with the solid "meat of the Word" (1 Cor. 3:2). If you tend to regurgitate over some of these heavenly T-bones, be comforted to know that I did too—in the beginning.

I offer no new truths and no strange doctrines—only Bible truth as God wrote it, through holy men of old, who faithfully recorded it for us, that we might apply it to our everyday living and thus travel through this life in a state of high victory, to the glory of God and for the blessing of His kids.

"For lack of knowledge my people perish" (Hos. 4:6), God says, concerning the needs of His people today. And "Concerning spiritual gifts, brethren, I would not have you ignorant" is the way God begins First Corinthians 12. In Proverbs 30:5, God says of His own Word, "Every word of God is pure: he is a shield unto them that put their trust in him." In James 1:5, He says, "If any of you lack wisdom [wisdom is knowing what to do next], let him ask of God, that giveth to all men liberally. . . ." "Where there is no vision, the people perish: but he that keepeth the law, happy is he," is the way God states a basic principle involved in King's kid living in Proverbs 29:18.

What this high victory is all about, and the avenue to it, is summed up in Psalm 37: "*Trust* in the LORD" (v. 3); "*delight* thyself also in the LORD; and he shall give thee the desires of thine heart" (v. 4); *commit* thy way unto the LORD; trust

---

* *How to Live Like a King's Kid; How Did It All Begin?; How to Be a Winner.* (All published by Logos International, Plainfield, New Jersey.)

also in him; and he shall bring it to pass" (v. 5); and *"rest* in the LORD" (v. 7). This is the route to high victory, here and hereafter.

God's training is for right now, that we will learn to depend on Him and His power at this very moment. Every experience of life is to glorify God now as well as later through the words of our testimony. "Behold, *now* is the accepted time" (2 Cor. 6:2), is what Paul says about it.

The present has been defined as "a dividing line between our recollections of the past and our anticipations of the future" (Saint Augustine), and it is the only time we ever have to live in and to praise God in. Someone else has said, "Yesterday is a canceled check; tomorrow is a promissory note; today is cash, spend it."

When we abandon to God *now*, detach from ownership *now*, praise Him *now*, then we are *more* than conquerors—literally living in high victory right now, in the midst of all of life's experiences through Him who loved us and gave himself for us (Rom. 8:37; Gal. 2:20). We are super-victors in Jesus!

Simply read the Word of God and do it; then report to others how it works, and please let me hear how it all works out, too.

God bless you,
In Jesus' love,
Harold E. Hill,
King's Kid in Training

INTRODUCTION

Would you like to live in high victory—the kind that never goes away?

You can!

And just what is high victory?

It is that state of "blessed assurance" that God is on His throne and all is well throughout the universe and especially in our little corner. It is that solid state wherein doubt, fear, anxiety, uncertainty, and depression have no part; where we *know* that all things do really work together for good—God's good as well as ours (Rom. 8:28).

Is high victory an unrealistic, euphoric state reserved only for mystics, saints, and holy men? Not according to the Word of God.

High victory is a dwelling place, a promised land, prepared by God for His people who simply dare to enter in by simple faith. It is for those who have learned, or who are willing to learn, to live "by the faith of the Son of God" (Gal. 2:20) and thereby abide in the secret place of the most High, literally under the shadow of His wings (Ps. 91:1; 17:8).

It is truly that "place of rest that remaineth for the people of God" described in Hebrews 4, which becomes ours by entering in. Then the peace of God himself becomes ours, and our hearts and minds are "kept" by it—in perfect peace in the midst of all of life's perplexities, perversities, and problems. Then the "lusts of the flesh"—my rights to myself—are replaced by God's love, and my only rights are my rights to surrender all rights of my own to my heavenly Father for safekeeping. Only then am I free to seek first the kingdom of God where all these other things having to do with my everyday needs are actually added (Matt. 6:33).

How can you begin living that sort of high victory?

By becoming a doer of the Word, according to James 1. Simply read it, do it, and report on how it works—that's God's recommended procedure.

⊕ "But—but—but," sputters common sense. "Don't I have to understand it in order to do it?" Listen to God's reply on that one:

Hearing without doing ends in deception (James 1:22), instability (James 1:6), schizophrenia (James 1:8), and total collapse (Matt. 7:26-27). Hearing and doing produces high victory—the solid foundation to life more and more abundantly, promised by Jesus to King's kids (Matt. 7:24-25).

Just how does all that end up in continuous high victory? By producing that blessed state of childlike trust that our heavenly Father is really in full control of our lives and affairs—our true portion as joint heirs with Jesus our elder brother. Only then and through the practice of continuous praise and thanksgiving will we begin to trust God for who He is instead of for what we think He should be doing for us, for the satisfaction of our carnal lusts.

Lust   Remember, lust is behind all depression, anxiety, fear, uncertainty, and doubt. When lust is denied, disappointment, anger, and resentment end in that awful state of depression, and the gigantic pity party of Psalm 137 results. When lust's demands are met, disillusionment sets in and ends in the same depressed state. You just can't win for losing when the flesh is in control.

Prayer   The purpose of prayer is to maintain contact with God (pray without ceasing) where His abundance is actually ours and where we become intercessors for the needs of others. It never occurs to us to ask anything for ourselves, as our needs are fulfilled in Him who is our high victory. Underneath are the everlasting arms.

The peace of God which Jesus promised in John 14:27 is that special inner foundation of the King's kid who knows his rights and privileges through being a doer of the Word in all his affairs. Then our attitude will be, "As far as I'm concerned—whether it takes a day or a thousand years—I'm trusting God for who He is. What He does about me is entirely His affair."

x

What is the process recommended by God himself for entering into this state of high victory—this rest of God wherein all struggles, stresses, and strains cease to affect us?

Begin right now to start doing the Word of God:

1) Wrap everything in praise and turn it over to Jesus as joint heirs with Him of the results.

2) Refuse to be impressed by appearances.

3) Do the next thing, and trust Jesus for guiding your paths (Prov. 3:5-6).

4) Form the habit of praise in the midst of, in spite of, or on account of whatever is going on (I Thess. 5:16-18; Eph. 5:20; Heb. 13:15).

5) Learn to listen to God. Frequently say, "Speak, Lord. I'm listening for further instructions." But first be sure you've carried out the last instructions He gave you.

6) Don't ask anyone else's opinion about the guidance God gives you. Wait for confirmation from another source if you are in doubt.

7) Stop doubting that God really did speak to you.

8) When God's guidance comes, act immediately, praising Him for results.

9) When doubt enters, tell Him, "I'm going into action, Lord. If I'm on a second-best course of action, it's up to you to block me. But if I'm on the right road, open all doors and benefit everyone concerned."

10) I find this to be a good prayer: "Lord, make me as holy as you can make a sinner saved by grace" (origin unknown).

All this will result in high victory!

"And this is the victory that overcometh the world, even our faith" (1 John 5:4), when it is the faith of Jesus himself (Gal. 2:20), on loan to us!

To King's kids in training
who are willing to say
"Yes, Lord"
instead of
"Yes, but–"

1

How to Live in Victory
over Drinking Too Much

It's after 2:00 A.M., and all is quiet and peaceful in Happytown, U.S.A. The kid next door has finally stopped howling, and Murphy's dog got yanked into the house after two solid hours of baying at the moon.

"Finally," you say to yourself. "Now for some real shut-eye."

That's what *you* think.

But you've overlooked the fact that your next-door neighbor, Harry the Lush (that's your private name for him), is still out on the town.

Just as you're falling off into lullaby-land, the sounds of fun, frolic, and merrymaking come from the distance. But the noise doesn't stay distant. It stops right below your bedroom window. No, all that racket isn't coming from a mob scene. It's only Harry, at it again, winding up another evening of relaxation with the boys. If you weren't afraid of wrecking your petunia bed, you'd throw some old shoes at him.

How does the rest of the neighborhood react to Harry's goings-on?

Harry's boss says, "Harry's a fine worker—when we can

1

catch him sober."

Harry's brother, the deacon, says, "Just a dirty old sinner, that Harry."

Harry's pastor says, "All Harry needs is to use his will power and live the good life."

Harry's co-worker says, "Harry? Why, he's just a no good, lousy drunk."

Harry's teenage son has a handle on the problem: "My pop? I really think he's an alcoholic."

Harry's wife bristles with indignation and tosses a monkey wrench at the diagnosis that could put Harry on the road to recovery: "Harry an alcoholic? Nonsense. He's not that bad. He simply drinks too much."

If you have the effrontery to suggest to her that he ought to try Alcoholics Anonymous, where the sobriety rate is an impressive eighty percent, she'll draw back in super-righteous indignation and shoot you a look that would incinerate asbestos.

"Why, the very idea! Harry might get into *serious* trouble if he associated with *those* people."

And she will continue to aid and abet the sick pride that is leading her beloved Harry directly into total destruction through deliberately ignoring the facts.

Who is right? Is Harry just a heavy drinker? Or is he really *that bad*? Let's check it out with Harry himself the morning after and see what he has to say about the mess he's gotten himself into.

He has stumbled out of bed long enough to gulp a drink of "liquid painkiller," and to tell his wife to fix him an ice bag. While she's doing that, he's crawled back in the sack and buried his bursting head under the pillow. But that isn't sufficient soundproofing to drown out the shrill ring of the telephone on his bedside table. He fumbles the receiver off the hook, and the booming voice of his boss further irritates, his aching head.

"Harry, old man, why did you do it *this* time?"

The overwhelming mass of guilt and self-condemnation already churning in Harry's innards is further aggravated by a fresh batch of remorse as he tries to defend himself with lies, phony alibis and self-justification—classic symptoms of alcoholic rationalization. With throbbing head and quivering frame, Harry replies, "It's not what you think, boss. It's just that old virus of mine kicking up its heels again, so I believe I should stay home today and just rest up.—What? You say you think it's nothing but too much whiskey? Well, I did run into an old friend last night, and naturally we had to celebrate a little, but I had only a couple of beers—" Harry tries to cross the four fingers of his left hand but finds his coordination isn't up to it. "In my weakened condition, those two beers must have gone to my head. —But boss! Everybody takes a little too much toddy for the body once in a while.—*Of course* I promise it will never happen again.—Did you say go to AA?"

He tries to crank out a disarming chuckle, but it sounds more like a decapitating groan instead. It feels like one, too.

"Please, boss, I'm not *that bad*. Why, I can quit anytime I want to. I can take it or leave it. I'll let you know when I need help. Anyhow, next time will be different."

Harry is all wrong, of course, but he is sincere. The trouble is, his problem can't be corrected by will power, determination, pledges, or promises. Harry has a progressive disease. Harry is an alcoholic. How do we know? Like all diseases, alcoholism follows a set of characteristic symptoms, making its identification possible by the patient himself, if he is encouraged to be honest with himself. That's where wives and friends can help or hinder.

Harry's first symptom showed up at age fourteen.

"That first drink of homemade elderberry wine really

3

turned me on," he said in a sober moment, the very memory of it causing him to lick his lips in anticipation. "I felt like my toes lit up. It was such a good feeling, I reached out my glass for a refill."

That's the first symptom of alcoholism—when the first drink demands the second, when the first swig triggers the jug. One sip sets in motion a whole series of drinks, making a belter out of a guy who had nothing like that in mind to start with. An inner compulsion leaves the alcoholic with no choice between drinking or stopping. He has to keep on until something interferes, or until he is downright drunk.

Something interfered at Harry's first encounter with unholy spirits.

"The man holding the bottle refused to give me another drink, and I deeply resented it," he said. Another symptom of an alcoholic in the making.

Nobody interfered with Harry's next bout with booze at a party some years later.

"I drained my glass, then the bottle, then someone else's supply, and ended up in an alcoholic coma for two days," he confessed. "But when I sobered up, I promised myself, 'Never again!' It wasn't worth being so sick."

But Harry did try it again and again, until over the years his weekend drunks turned into nightly benders which resulted in lost jobs, wrecked cars, embarrassing arrests for driving under the influence, sojourns in jails, expensive "vacations" in hospitals, drying-out joints, and all the rest.

Harry's case is not unusual. And the eventual outcome can be predicted with statistical certainty. The record proves that people who are allergic to alcohol and continue in its use ultimately end up with alcoholic insanity or death from alcoholism.

Let's look at some additional symptoms to see how alcoholism may be identified before it becomes fatal. The telltale signs often come forth from the mouth of the victim himself.

"I used to brag about my unlimited capacity for booze—but now I lie about how much I drink."

"In the beginning, I drank for relaxation—now I drink to survive."

"If my wife would quit counting my drinks, and stop her incessant nagging, then I could drink normally."

"It's the pressure of my job that causes me to drink too much."

"I hide bottles all over the house, whereas I used to have them on the sideboard."

"It takes less and less to make me drunker and drunker."

"I have lapses of memory, blackouts, where I have no recollection of what happened the entire evening."

"I find that drinking alone is more to my liking. I just can't stand drinking with those lushes."

All of these are standard confessions of alcoholics in the throes of this progressive disease which strikes the victim in three ways—physically, mentally, and spiritually. Physically, the patient is allergic to the chemical alcohol. Mentally, he is obsessed to drink it. Spiritually, he has had it. Without spiritual help, there is no way to prevent his getting drunk over and over again.

One definition says that an alcoholic is someone who drinks between drinks. He is likely to be an extremist and a perfectionist, someone who is readily frustrated by his never-attainable demands for the impossible. His easy out from constant pressure is the attitude, "If you don't do it my way, I'll get drunk at you." AA's definition: "Anyone who has trouble to *any degree* due to the use of alcohol."

His ready alibi from under the table is, "It's all your fault for not living according to my expectations." That attitude carries him quickly from a position of looking forward to a drink at a certain time each day to the point where he puts his drinking at the very top of his priority list for living.

Another definition says that an alcoholic is a controlled drinker—one who is in complete control until the first drink. Normal drinkers seldom worry about controlling their drinking. They can pretty much take it or leave it. But alcoholics worry about their control, and they do okay—until drink number one hits the brain. From that point, the drink is in control of the drinker.

Folks who have researched these things tell us that seven people out of a hundred are alcoholics, individuals who are allergic to the chemical alcohol. The other ninety-three out of that same hundred can take it or leave it. They may get drunk on occasion, but will power can be effective in controlling their take-it-or-leave-it decisions. That means that out of the 65 million people in this country who drink alcohol, approximately 10 million are alcoholics.

What causes alcoholism? Nobody knows. Back in 1935, the Yale Clinic on Alcohol Studies was begun to try to find an answer. Thirty years later, they gave up. After all their research, they concluded, "We just do not know why alcoholics cannot drink alcohol and remain in control."

Normal drinkers have an alcohol-handling system different from alcoholics. They seem to have some sort of a workable filter, whereas alkys' filters are busted, permitting the alcohol to go directly to the brain. Once there, being a depressant drug, it warps decisions, dulls concentration powers, and "he did it again" is the inevitable, unavoidable result.

More important than trying to determine why alcoholics are like they are is the good news that there is something that can be done about it. There *is* an answer. In 1935, God himself stepped into the problem-solving search and came up with an instant, permanent, and 100 percent effective answer to the problem of alcoholism. Under His direction, two problem drinkers founded Alcoholics Anonymous, a fellowship which today has upwards of a million sober members. (You can read all about it in a book, *Alcoholics Anonymous*, probably available at your public library, or telephone the AA number in your local phone book for further information.)

The first step toward high victory over alcoholism involves a pride-shattering admission: "I am an alcoholic." That's a real toughie, to admit you can't handle your drinking problem yourself. Generally, it's tougher for the friends and relatives who delay the solution by assuring the victim that he's not *that bad*. Of real help in this area is the Alanon Family group.*

Slue Foot effectively prevents many people from recommending or seeking the help of the proven effectiveness of the AA course of treatment by putting in our think tanks a false picture of what an alcoholic has to look like. He keeps us envisioning a dirty, drunken derelict, shivering in a ragged World War I trench coat, with half its

---

*For information write to P.O. Box 182, Madison Square Station, New York, N.Y. 10010. This is Alanon Family Group Headquarters, an activity that provides help for the non-drinking family members whose lives have been adversely affected by the problem drinker in the family.

Classified as an incurable disease by the American Medical Association, it comes as a surprise to some that alcoholism is a family disease affecting the family unit emotionally, spiritually and often physically. Both Alanon for the adults and Alateen for the younger family members can be of tremendous benefit in helping the alcoholic member into a life of sobriety and recovery from his affliction.

buttons A.W.O.L. His bunioned feet are shod with half a pair of tennis shoes, no socks, and he's lying out in a garbage-strewn alley somewhere, surrounded by empty wine bottles, flies, and gnats. Passers-by shudder, turn their heads in the other direction, and sputter indignantly, "He can't blame anybody but himself—he should have used his will power."

Naturally, you don't want to identify your beloved Uncle Harry with such a mess as that, and so when he sobers up the next time, you go to great pains to assure him, "Harry, dear, you're not *that bad.* Of *course* you're no alcoholic, Harry, baby. You just drink too much."

Uncle Harry agrees with you, and stays drunk longer next time. By your very attitude, you are probably hastening the day when the bum in the gutter will cause you to do a double take. You'll back up a few steps, take a closer look at the bleary eyes, the unshaven, sagging jowls, and gasp in horror as you recognize your darling, beloved, dear, sweet Uncle Harry under the raunchy exterior.

Since alcoholism is a disease, just as cancer, TB, diabetes, and heart trouble are diseases, the sooner it is acknowledged and treated, the better the chances for living happily ever after. Alcohol comes from the same sugar molecule which, in its natural state, is murder to diabetics. Sugar in its fermented state is murder for alcoholics. But the disease of alcoholism is more easily treated than diabetes. The diabetic often has to take a shot a day to keep things under control. An alcoholic has only to stay away from a shot a day—the first one—to remain free from all symptoms of his incurable, but treatable, disease.

Of the approximately 10 million "problem drinkers" in the United States, about 1 million are alcoholics who have admitted it. They are in AA, not drinking at all. The other 9 million have assured themselves, and have been assured by friends, families, and doctors, that they simply drink too much, and as a result they are getting progressively sicker.

Are you willing to swallow your pride and lead your beloved one to an AA meeting where he can find instant and everlasting sobriety? That's what happens to eighty percent who go to AA—a record many times better than all other agencies combined!

How do I know it will work for dear old Harry? Because it worked for me. On Good Friday night of 1951, in the midst of my last drinking bout, winding up twenty-nine years of progressive drinking, I said three words: "God, help me." And He did. (You can read all the details in *How to live Like a King's Kid*.)

The following week, I attended my first AA meeting, escorted there by my next-door neighbor who had been without a drink for four years. I looked around the room with the attitude, "What can these peasants do for me? After all, I'm president of my own company. I haven't lost any of my material holdings because of drinking, and I'm really not *that bad*."

It was almost as if they read my mind.

"You don't have to get *that bad* if you'll do what we do. Simply postpone that first drink one day at a time, and you'll have no further trouble with alcohol."

They were right. For twenty-six years now I have been cold sober, by the grace of God, postponing that first drink one day at a time. They also told me something else, something which really blew my mind.

"When you meet God personally," they said, "you won't want to drink anymore."

Being a scientist, and president of my own corporation, I was more than a little handicapped by think-tank-itis skepticism about that. But it happened in spite of me. Three years later, another AA member introduced me to God on a

9

first-name basis. God's first name turned out to be Jesus. And sure enough, He removed from me completely all desire for alcohol. In the bargain, He also took away my guilt, forgave me my sins, gave me eternal life, and installed a super-guidance system by way of a hookup with the head man of the universe. It beats anything electronics can dream up. In this package deal, I was able to exchange a life of increasing wretchedness via alcohol for a life of increasing abundance in the high victory Jesus gives to King's kids.

My prayer is that your alcoholic (or maybe it's you) can become honest with himself, throw his sick pride in the trash can, head for the nearest AA fellowship, and enter fully into God's plan for an abundant life, overflowing with blessings. In Jesus' name, Amen.

2

How to Live in Victory
over Flats, Snowstorms, and Ego Trips

Early in my life as a King's kid, I kept hearing people talk about spiritual experiences, and I wondered what they were getting at. How did they work? I mean, what was a spiritual experience, anyway?

I asked my friend Tom that question one day. He scratched his head for a minute and then came up with a definition so mind-blowing, I was almost sorry I had asked him.

"A spiritual experience," he said, "is a matter of doing something for somebody else and not getting caught at it."

That was about the worst thing a fellow could do to his pride, I figured. Doing something for somebody and not getting caught at it was bound to mean that nobody would give me any credit for it, either. I was still sufficiently interested in Brownie points that I wasn't sure spiritual experiences were for me, but as a scientist I knew it wasn't smart to reject anything on the basis of such scanty information. While I was considering the matter, my friend came up with a "for instance" that showed me unmistakably what spiritual experiences were all about.

"Suppose," he said, "that it was in the dead of winter and you were all comfortably bedded down for the night. Make believe it was snowing and sleeting, the wind howling under the eaves."

He made it so real, I started to shiver.

"Let's imagine that the phone rings at midnight, and when you pick up the receiver, you recognize the voice of a friend who gets kind of deep into the bottle sometimes. It seems he has tried other numbers, but there is no one else able to come to his rescue this particular night. He needs help. Bad."

I stood there shaking my head. I wasn't about to get out of my warm bed and go to anybody's rescue in weather like that.

"Now, it's not hard for you to think of a hundred reasons why you can't go to his rescue," my friend continued, with me nodding my head in full agreement. "But you can't refuse."

"I can't?" I asked in amazement.

"No," he said, "because you're a King's kid, and King's kids are supposed to love one another."

"And to do unto others as we'd have others do unto us," I said, seeing what he was getting at. "Okay, I'll go help him," I agreed, "seeing that it's only a story." I was having such a good time staying high on Jesus in those days that I didn't want to imagine myself being disobedient to His commands.

My friend went on, kind of enjoying the misery he was putting me through. "Let's say you pull your clothes on over your pajamas, drag your overcoat out of the closet, wrap your neck up in a muffler—"

"My wife would want me to wear my overshoes," I put in.

"So okay, you put on your overshoes, and head out, telling your wife you'll see her in a little while. Then you go shovel the snow from in front of the garage door and back the car out."

I hoped he would have me turn the heater on, but he didn't mention that detail.

"By the time you get to the place from which your about-to-be-under-the-table friend has telephoned, he is no longer on the premises."

My heart sunk to my pajama bottoms, then gave a sudden jump as I asked eagerly, "Oh! That means I can go home and crawl back in the sack, doesn't it?"

"Not yet," he said. "You have to look for him for a while."

Well, looking a *few* places might not be too bad—but there was more to it than that. "Your friend isn't at the next place either," Tom informed me. "Or the next."

"Do I keep on looking for him? In that storm?" I asked.

"Yep. The poor fellow has the wandering drunks that night, but after tracking him from one distant place to another, you finally get him localized in the back seat of your car."

I wasn't sure that's what I'd have wanted to do under the circumstances, but the fellow telling me about spiritual experiences wasn't asking me what I'd do about anything.

"It's almost too late," Tom told me. "You recognize that fact while you're shoving his feet in after his legs. Convulsions and delirium tremens (d.t.'s) are about to set in, and you can see he needs medical help, fast."

I caught myself reaching for the telephone to call the rescue squad before I realized it was only a story. By this time, I was certainly eager to learn how it all turned out.

"Well, you get him to the hospital, barely in the nick of time," Tom said. I quit holding my breath, and offered up a little prayer of thanksgiving, but it didn't last long because of the next detail in Tom's story.

"There you learn the unsurprising fact that his billfold is empty, his credit no good."

13

"What do I do next?" I wanted to know. There wasn't such a thing as medicare in those days, and it looked as if I might be left holding the bag. Or maybe there was an alternative—

"You have a choice," my storyteller said, answering my question. "You can take the poor derelict home with you, and maybe have him die on your hands—"

"No, not that!" I wailed.

"Okay, then," he said. "You've made your choice. You can leave him with the competent medical authorities—"

So far, so good, I thought. But once again, there was a catch to it. I sensed a certain delight in Tom's voice as he clobbered my Scotsman's heart with what came next.

"And, of course, you'll leave enough of your green stuff to take care of the bill."

"I will?" I squeaked.

"It's either that or take him home with you and be responsible for the consequences." Then, he rubbed it in. "And from all indications, the bill won't be a small one."

As he talked, something reminded me of the story of the Good Samaritan, and I tried imagining myself, completely out of character, approaching the lady behind the financial desk and quoting some Scripture out of Luke 10:35 to her:

"Take care of him for me," I pretended to say. "And whatever more you spend beyond what I've already given you, let me know, and I'll take care of that later."

I cringed as, in my mind's eye, I saw myself forking over every cent I had. I could hardly believe it. At that point, Tom took over the story again.

"You leave the hospital, fight your way back to your car, brush the new accumulation of snow off your windshield, and start home. From the way the snow is coming down, you calculate it isn't planning to stop until it gets axle-high to a tall ferris wheel."

By now, I wasn't only an icicle, I was exhausted. I could

hardly wait for the hypothetical me to get home.

But the worst was yet to come. Tom increased my misery sevenfold.

"Less than two blocks on your way," he said, "you hear an attention-getting sound above the howl of the gale that is driving the snow so furiously. *Bumpety, bumpety, bump.*"

"Oh, no," I groaned. "Please, Tom, not a flat. Not at this time of night, not in this blizzard, not after all I've been through? Can't you have a little mercy?"

He grinned and shook his head. "You wanted to know what a spiritual experience was like, didn't you?" he chided.

I nodded.

"Well, just hold on a little bit longer and you'll have one." He had me get out of the car to investigate, and sure enough, one of my tires was the spitting image of a very lopsided black doughnut with white frosting.

I was so miserable already, what with getting out of the car, that I decided it might be best to get it over with as quickly as possible.

"Okay," I said. "You can make me change the tire, but please let the spare have air in it. And let the jack be where it belongs."

He was so merciful that not only was the spare properly inflated, and the jack in place, but he had let the car come to its bumpety stop under a street light so I could have plenty of illumination for what I was doing. Still, the job was necessarily an outside one, and I envisioned myself down in the snow and sleet, crawling under the car, getting soaked and muddy in the process.

"All this seems to take forever," he went on, "but you finally make it home. The snow clouds have gone, and the sky is beginning to get light in the east when you turn into your driveway. You crawl out of your car, dig your housekey out of your pocket, and trudge through the snow to the front door. There you thoughtfully take off your soggy galoshes and park them on the porch, opening the door as quietly as possible to keep from waking your wife."

That sounded like such a good idea that an involuntary, "Shhh!" escaped my lips. Tom lowered his voice as he continued, "You tiptoe in, close the door softly behind you, and head for the stairs."

I could feel myself breathing a sigh of relief, but it was cut short by the abruptness of his next word.

"Stop!"

I looked at him, startled, and he explained, "Your eyeballs run into your wife, who is standing smack in front of you, wide awake. No, she doesn't have a rolling pin or a cast-iron skillet in her hand, but her voice makes up for it.

" 'Where have *you* been?' "

I felt my mouth opening to pour forth all the wonderfully exonerating details, but they weren't part of the script.

"Wait a minute," Tom said. "If you give yourself one bit of glory in this, you may never know what a spiritual experience is. Do you want to know? Or don't you?"

I thought it over for a minute.

"Are we getting close to the end of it?" I asked him. "I mean, I'm not sure I can take much more."

"Close to the end," he said, and so I gave him permission to go on.

"Now, you *could* give her all the self-righteous details, have her brew you a perfect cup of coffee, and cluck over you while she tucks blankets and hot water bottles around you. But you don't open your mouth to explain what a saintly fellow you are—"

"I don't? Me? Me waste such a beautiful opportunity for justifying myself?" I stood there, shaking my head, and the strictly out-of-character account drew to a close.

"You just smile at her," Tom said, "button your lip, go up

16

the stairs, and crawl into bed. Unless your wife makes you spend the rest of the night on the couch."

With that, Tom stopped. I didn't interrupt, just waited for him to go on. But there was only silence.

"You mean I don't explain anything?" I protested. "I don't tell her—"

My protest dwindled to nothing, and Tom never had to answer it. All of a sudden, I could see how it would have to be. Why, as soon as my head hit the sofa pillow, heaven would come all over me. I'd forget that I was almost frozen to death, forget my flattened billfold, my ruined tire, my muddy overcoat, my wife's indignation—

I'd have touched eternal things that night. Instinctively, I knew that I'd have experienced the presence of Jesus, and received a heavenly reward, because we can't ever help "the least of these" without somehow encountering Him in the transaction. The literal truth of Matthew 25:40 would have come to roost in my gizzard:

Verily I say unto you, Inasmuch as ye have done it unto one of the least of these my brethren, ye have done it unto me.

As a King's kid for twenty-three years now, in more real situations than hypothetical ones, I have put myself in line for the blessings of "spiritual experiences" every time I have gone about putting the Word of God into action. Doing the Word never leads anywhere but into high victory, and I'm fully persuaded that's what Jesus means for all King's kids to experience all the time. Letting His Word be made flesh in us is what victorious King's kid living is all about.

3

How to Live in Victory
over Vain Philosophy

God says if you want to understand His Word, you'll need to put it in your shoes and go out and try it for size. We are to read it and do it and then report on it, because understanding comes by living experience. After you've had the experience, no one can argue you out of it.

A lot of King's kids, not knowing that, have been in Bible study groups where they've studied ten years, and they're looking forward to another ten years' study to give them an understanding of the Word. Yet they're no further along in bodily health and prosperity, nor will they be until they become doers of the Word.

> For if any be a hearer of the word, and not a doer, he is like unto a man beholding his natural face in a glass: For he beholdeth himself, and goeth his way, and straightway forgetteth what manner of man he was. But whoso looketh into the perfect law of liberty, and continueth therein, he being not a forgetful hearer, but a doer of the work, this man shall be blessed in his deed. (James 1:23-25)

What is the reaction of a normal man beholding his natural

face in a glass? If I can judge by what I see around me, after he has showered and shaved in the morning and gotten all spiffed up for the day, he looks at his reflection and purrs, "You lover boy, you. You beautiful hot lips. Man, am I glad you're not like other men." He continues his Pharisee-like attitude with the clincher, "You've really got what it takes, man."

He might not admit that to other people, but that's about how it goes. And when the preacher preaches on love, he sits back, relaxed, comforting himself with the thought, "Man, am I glad I'm a lover."

All that exalted opinion of self comes from deception. People are so squirreled up in their heads that they can readily deceive themselves into thinking they're some kind of good guys. But that's not what the *Manufacturer's Handbook*, which is never wrong, says about man here. It says that when he looks in the mirror, he forgets what kind of man he really is. He's persuaded himself, "I'm not all bad. Why, I know at least a dozen guys worse than I am."

But a King's kid isn't deceived like that. He hears the Word and goes right out and does it, so he won't forget what it's all about.

Doers of the Word are always in trouble, about to get out of trouble, or on the verge of getting into more trouble. That's how doers of the Word operate, knowing that what the world calls trouble is just raw material for God's glory.

A woman in attendance at a Faith at Work conference in New York City went shopping one afternoon. New York is full of people who like to take other people's property. One such person snatched the woman's handbag and flew down the street with it. Well, the woman was sold out to Jesus, and instead of chasing after the purse-snatcher or calling the police, she reached down in her gizzard for the sword of the

Spirit, which is the Word of God. She got hold of one of the psalms in the process, the one that says,

> Surely he shall deliver thee from the snare of the fowler, and from the noisome pestilence. He shall cover thee with his feathers, and under his wings shalt thou trust, his truth shall be thy shield and buckler. Thou shalt not be afraid for the terror by night, nor for the arrow that flieth by day; nor for the pestilence that walketh in darkness; nor for the destruction that wasteth at noonday. (91:3-6)

Sooner than it takes to tell it, the woman saw that the Scripture was her guarantee that God would protect her from the thing that had just happened to her, so she reminded Him of it. It came out a little paraphrased, but the origin was clear to anybody who knew the Scripture.

"I'm covered with feathers!" she yelled at the top of her voice.

The purse-snatcher was so addled that he dropped the purse and took off at double his former speed. I guess he didn't want some feathered monster to gobble him up. And so the Word of the Lord delivered the woman from her enemy, according to His promise, because the woman didn't just hear it, she acted on it.

In the midst of trouble, the doer of God's Word acquires experience to give him hope for the next time. It's a constant and glorious regenerative process. A hearer, on the other hand, is exercising only his hearing mechanism. His ears get bigger; the rest of him atrophies. His feet go to sleep and stay there, and he deceives himself by saying, "Well, I know my heart is right, so I don't have to be a doer of the Word. I'll just let other people tend to that. I'll stay where I'm comfortable." When a man has that attitude, he's not benefited, and God is not glorified.

How can we minister to the needs of others when we don't have faith for our own needs? We sit back in our Bible study group and nitpick: "What does this mean, what does that mean?" Because you don't find out what it means unless you do it, soon everybody is acting like an expert theologian and nobody is acting like a King's kid.

In our Bible study groups, we need to talk about what the Bible says, then go and do it, and report on what happens when we take God at His Word. That approach will save a lot of bickering, argument, and theological nonsense.

Religion points out what God is no longer capable of doing. And theology explains in great detail why He can no longer do it. These two subjects—religion and theology—are man's idea of God, but the Bible is God's idea of himself.

Who needs man's ideas when the whole head is sick? (Isa. 1:5)—unless that head is enlightened by the Holy Spirit. God doesn't take a dim view of our intellect or our education, but He says that people who hear the Word and speculate about it without ever doing it are in danger of deceiving themselves (James 1:22) and becoming philosophers. The *Manufacturer's Handbook* warns us about them:

> Beware lest any man spoil you through philosophy and vain deceit, after the tradition of men, after the rudiments of the world, and not after Christ. (Col. 2:8)

For the most part, the world has not noticed that warning, and vain philosophy has deceived men time after time.

A question in Greek philosophy was discussed pro and con for many centuries. It went like this:

"Why is it that you can take two fish of the same weight, one of them alive, one of them dead, and drop them into a full bucket of water, and the live fish will not cause the water to overflow, but the dead fish will?" Philosophers enjoyed

21

arguing that question. But one day some stupid servant who didn't know any better came along and spoiled their fun. He got a live fish and a dead one, dropped them into identical buckets of water, and found that both buckets overflowed.

The ancient philosophers would never stoop to perform a practical experiment. They would argue and debate for centuries, write learned dissertations by the score, but never go to the laboratory. That was beneath their dignity. One of the questions of speculative philosophy on which they wrote many learned papers was, "Why do men have more teeth than women?"

Again, one day a peasant came along. He wasn't ranked as a philosopher. He was just a peasant who wasn't expected to know any better than to question authority. His curiosity was aroused by the philosopher's discussion, and so he went home and said to his wife, "Open your mouth, dear. I want to count your teeth."

Being a properly submitted spouse, she opened her mouth, or kept it open as the case might have been, and he counted. That done, he said, "Now, woman, count mine." He opened his mouth, she counted his teeth, and the rest is history: Men have the same number of teeth as women.

More recently, modern eggheads have written all kinds of learned treatises about principles they find in the *Manufacturer's Handbook*, without checking out their conclusions by actual experience. Speculation about any of these things is vain. Trying them is the only way to find out if they work or don't work. And King's kids who try the principles of kingdom living find that God knows what He's talking about.

When we become doers of the Word and not hearers only, we never find ourselves dying of boredom in a rut somewhere. Being King's kids in action is lively business. It can get you thrown out of some interesting places, but it can introduce the power of God in some interesting places too. It's worth the risk. When the power of God is manifested through a King's kid in action, it's natural that some theologians would be disturbed, but that's their problem. Jesus doesn't let their reaction bother Him, and we shouldn't let it bother us either.

When it happened to me, I felt as if maybe I would never touch the ground again.

4

How to Live in Victory
when You Don't Feel Like It

Do you feel like a King's kid? Do you know that you are one whether you feel like it or not? One of the first things that King's kids need to realize is that feelings are not reliable. They are likely to change with the weather. It is by faith that we accept our positions as members of the body of Christ, and the Scripture indicates that we are to walk by that faith, not by our feelings.

Nevertheless, when we first come into the fullness of the Holy Spirit, we're likely to feel different from how we felt before. When it happened to me, I felt as if maybe I would never touch the ground again, and I complained about it just a little.

"Lord," I suggested, "please turn it back just a tiny bit, enough so I can get some traction, so I can get down close enough to see what's going on."

During those days, I *knew* I'd never again have any fear or anxiety about anything. But one day, much to my surprise, I woke up and discovered that all my juicy glory feelings were gone. I felt deserted. I panicked, crying out, "Lord, why did you leave me? Where are my feelings?"

I banged the doors of heaven, but the only answer I could hear in the midst of my fear and distress was coming from the other place. Satan was in there pitching.

"You see?" he leered at me. "You were just too much for God to handle. He's given up on you already. You might as well quit while you're behind. You don't fit into this new life anyhow."

That's Satan's standard approach, I've learned since. And it's all a lie. But in those days, I didn't know that, and as I listened to his lies, I sank lower and lower. Finally I got miserable enough to really go to the Lord about it.

"Lord, I admit that I'm pretty bad material, but I've known some who claimed they were worse than I was. Paul carried on like he was the chief of sinners, and yet you stuck with him, somehow. I'm not going to believe that you've given up on me, because I understand you never start something that you don't finish. But what about my feelings, Lord?"

At that point, I heard from God. I didn't hear Him speak audibly, but by a strong impression in my mind. And this is what He got across to me:

"You miss those feelings, don't you, Hill." It wasn't a question, it was an incontrovertible statement of fact.

"I sure do, Lord. They were delicious. If it's all the same to you, I'd like to have them back."

"What does John 1:12 say?" He seemed to be asking me next.

I'd gotten that verse solidly into my gizzard by that time, so I quoted it to Him.

> But as many as received him, to them gave he power to become the sons of God, even to them that believe on his name.

As I said the words, I picked up the understanding that as a son of God, a King's kid, I was expected to grow up. Next,

He referred me to the Romans passage where Paul wrote,
For as many as are led by the Spirit of God, they
are the sons of God. (8:14)
That verse sounded as if it had something to do with a transition from babyhood to adulthood, too, and so I was all set to understand and accept what He said next:

"Your feelings have served their purpose, Hill," He said, ever so gently. "Now it's time for you to get on your spiritual feet and really begin to walk by faith. You'd never learn to do that if I let you depend on your gooey feelings all the time, would you? Waiting for feelings can dissipate your energy and invite the enemy to come in while you wait. He works in the area of the soul, and that's where your feelings are. Whether you ever feel my presence again or not, I'm with you. And I promise that I will never leave you nor forsake you."

The Lord taught me in all this that babies always want to be feeling something. They need feelings, they demand attention, they crave amusement—toys, rattles, pacifiers, and other gadgetry to play with. They have to have something new going on all the time—a new revival meeting, a new preacher, a new teacher, new chill bumps. But when King's kids are getting themselves established to walk in faith, they have to know that Jesus is in full charge whether or not they feel any Fourth of July fireworks going off inside them.

The Lord further enlarged my understanding of feelings by giving me the parable of the bathtub. That parable is not in your Bible, but it is written in the living epistle that God is writing in this King's kid. I'm slow to learn, and so He has to bring rather vivid pictures to my think tank so I'll get the point.

He seemed to say to me that the kingdom of God is like a bathtub full of hot water. When you first stick your

27

big toe in, the contrast between your normal temperature and that of the water in the tub is quite noticeable. The hot water may feel intensely uncomfortable at first. But as you gradually lower one foot into it, and then the other foot, and then your whole carcass, your body begins to adjust to the new environment. After you sit there a few minutes, getting good and relaxed, things begin to equalize somehow. After a little, you don't even feel the water unless you move about and slosh around in it, because the surface of your body has taken on the same temperature as the water. In that same way, after you've walked in the Spirit for a while, and the gooey feelings have gone away, it's partly because your old "normal" temperature has been exchanged for the temperature of heaven.

It's natural for us to enjoy good feelings. When Peter and the other boys experienced good feelings up on the Mount of Transfiguration, they wanted to stay there forever (Mark 9:5).

"Let's build three tabernacles and stay up here on the mountaintop above the ordinary level of life," Peter suggested. "We can really be religious full time up here, without the interruptions and frustrations of the world to bother us."

It sounded very appealing, but Jesus had a better idea.

"If you walk by feelings all your life," He indicated, "you'll be way up above ordinary folks, the needy ones who are crying out for help even now. We can't stay on the mountain with tabernacles and goose bumps. We belong down there in the valley where sick folks need healing, where the darkness needs the light. Let's go."

Peter and the rest of them understood, and they got on their spiritual feet and began to walk by faith.

It took me three years to get to that point. For more than a thousand days after my feelings left me, I didn't have one

28

thrill or chill, one bit of a gooey feeling to make me aware of the presence of God in my life. During that time, I became solidly persuaded that our Christian life has to do, not with feelings, not with having faith in God for what He can *do*, but having faith in Him for who He *is*. All that brought me to faith in God, period. My confession went something like this:

"All right, Lord. If I never feel your presence again, if I never see you do a cottonpicking thing, I'll know you're with me just because your Word says you are. I'm going to believe that you meant it when you said, 'I'll never leave you nor forsake you.' That's good enough for me. Let's go."

We went, and I forgot the feelings. I just walked by faith.

Oh, I still like the chills and thrills, but I'm aware that Satan can produce counterfeits of them at the drop of a hat if that's what we're after. And he'll let us sit and thrill and chill and twitch and jump and jerk and yell and roll for hours. That's no threat to him, because when we're doing that, we're not adding anybody to God's kingdom. We might even be subtracting a few by being so intent on amusing ourselves. In babies, it's cute. In adults, it's pretty icky.

There *is* a certain amount of energy involved in every anointing of the Holy Spirit. Energy plus action equals power—the power to change something, the power to create, the power to produce. And if we receive the anointing power of the Holy Spirit and dissipate it by the manipulations of the flesh, we'll have that much less divine energy to minister to the needs of people. Satan is never interested in ministering to people, he's interested in getting you to make a spectacle of yourself, somehow getting you to think you'll look more religious if you're twitching like you were on a giant vibrating machine. Such antics *do* make people look more religious—but less spiritual. And religion is not where the glory of God is.

When God saw that He had brought me to the place where

I would not depend on feelings but on Him, then He began to drop a few goodies my way from time to time, sort of as a little bonus. I still enjoy feelings as much as anyone, but I'm no longer impressed by them. When we're walking by faith, we cannot become discouraged, because faith looks at God and not at ourselves. And God never fails. Looking to feelings, or anything else in the soulish realm, can lead to discouragement. And God can't use a discouraged Christian.

Feelings are the realm where the enemy operates to the greatest degree to rob us of our inheritance in Jesus. I'm interested in living up to the level of my inheritance, as outlined in the *Manufacturer's Handbook*. That means I have to walk by faith, not by feelings.

The Bible is the Word of God. And all His promises are yea and amen on a permanent basis in Jesus (2 Cor. 1:20). God says, "I am God. I change not. I will never leave you nor forsake you" (Heb. 13:5).

King's kids take the Word of God, act like it might be true, regardless of their feelings, and find that it really is.

5
How to Live in Victory
over Unbelief

What is faith? Faith is being willing to believe more than you can understand. Faith is not being limited by what your top ten inches can figure out. Faith is the new guidance system that God has instituted in this life which will carry on over into the next life, if I understand His Word correctly.

Faith has to do with believing a thing for only one reason—because God said it. Faith leaves no room for quibbling.

Unbelief is not lack of faith. Unbelief is something you pump up by refusing to do what God says or refusing to receive what He has done for you.

God's chosen people had a massive dose of unbelief. They simply would not believe the Word of God when He said, "Look. I've set up the Promised Land for you. There it is. All you have to do is walk in and possess it."

The Israelites quibbled.

"Wait a second," someone suggested, "we'd better hold a committee meeting first, to see if God knows what He's talking about."

That's where they goofed the whole assignment. The

31

committee was glad to take full responsibility.

"Don't worry," they assured the people, "we'll work this thing out. Just leave everything to us."

The first action of the committee was to send spies into the Promised Land to check up on conditions there. The spies were expected to come back with a report based on their common sense. The results of anything that you do on your own have to be limited by the capacity of your five senses to receive the information, put it together, work out an answer, and come up with a workable conclusion. That's the way "normal" life functions. (It's only when we're in the Spirit that our common senses can be augmented by the nine supernatural senses or gifts of the Holy Spirit. Then we can make decisions based on having the same mind in us that was in Christ Jesus.)

Well, the spies went out, and ten out of twelve of them came back shivering in their sandals.

"D-d-d-don't go," they stammered. "Th-th-th-there's g-g-giants."

God never said anything about whether there were giants or not. He just said they were to walk in, and He would take care of whatever was in the way. But the people weren't willing to trust Him that far.

Two of the spies, Joshua and Caleb, were God's men, however. They stood firm and said, "Let's try it God's way. We've always been able to trust Him up to now."

The people shook their heads. They thought they were letting the majority rule when they decided to follow the counsel of the ten scared spies. They hadn't realized that even one with God is a majority, and so they settled for second best. And God let them have their own way.

Because of their unbelief, they could not enter the Promised Land. Their unbelief was a negative power generated by the human mind which said, "I refuse to move.

I know more than God."

"Have it your own way, then," God told them. "You don't have to enter in. You can die in the desert if you'd rather do that than to trust me." And that's exactly what they did. The whole generation died in the wilderness.

When the Hebrews opened their mail one day, centuries later, they were told not to goof it as their ancestors had done. And God uses the same passage of Scripture to speak to us today:

> Take heed, brethren, lest there be in any of you an heart of unbelief, in departing from the living God. . . . Let us therefore fear, lest, a promise being left us of entering into his rest, any of you should seem to come short of it. For unto us was the gospel preached, as well as unto them: but the word preached did not profit them, not being mixed with faith in them that heard it. For we which have believed do enter into rest. . . . They to whom it was first preached entered not in because of unbelief. . . . There remaineth therefore a rest to the people of God. For he that is entered into his rest, he also hath ceased from his own works, as God did from his. Let us labour therefore to enter into that rest, lest any man fall after the same example of unbelief. (Heb. 3:12; 4: 1-3, 6, 9-11)

"Labor" strikes us as a strange word in this Scripture. Is God saying, "Work your head to the bone trying to enter that rest?" But how can this be accomplished, since we know already that our own labors can't get us there? Did God's secretary make a mistake?

No, God's secretaries were always faithful to put down exactly what He wanted them to record. What Jesus said about this labor, the kind of work God wants us to do, is plainly spelled out in John's Gospel.

Then said they unto him, What shall we do, that we
might work the works of God? Jesus answered and
said unto them, This is the work of God, that ye
believe on him whom he hath sent. (6:28-29)

When we have reached that point in our lives where we are
depending on Jesus, we are ready to enter the promised land
of perfect rest that remaineth for the people of God, rest
from our own labors about everything!

This dependence on Jesus is accomplished as we soak
ourselves in the Word, believe it, and let it become an active
part of our lives.

For the word of God is quick, and powerful, and
sharper than any two-edged sword, piercing even
to the dividing asunder of soul and spirit, and of the
joints and marrow, and is a discerner of the
thoughts and intents of the heart. (Heb. 4:12)

There are three real areas of life dealt with in this passage
of Scripture—the spirit, the marrow, and the intents or
motives of the heart. It deals also with three counterfeit or
unreal areas—the soul, the joints, and the thoughts. God is
telling us that His Word is the only instrument powerful
enough to cut a dividing line right down the middle, between
the natural man and the spiritual man.

The soul is not life, but it provides a read out of the real life
which is in the spirit. The joints are equivalent to the
busy-busy-busy of religion, as opposed to the marrow which
is life, because the red blood cells are manufactured in the
marrow of the bones. The thoughts, the ideas, and the
mental capacity of a human being are in the soul, while the
intentions or motives of the heart are in the spiritual realm.
Through the writer of Proverbs, Jesus said that the real
issues of life come from the heart (4:23). No man knows his
own heart unless the Holy Spirit reveals it to him.

The unreal, soulish, area of life is always trying to run the

34

show, to get into the act, to demonstrate the big-shot-itis that's programmed into us at birth, insisting, "I must excel; I must win; I must have the best for me." Every spirit of competition, dissension, division, and other striving spirit is opposed to the real life where Jesus is, in the spirit, the marrow, the motives.

No pagan psychiatrist can show a man the depths of his heart. He can scrape around on the surface, dredge up a whole bunch of muck, and ask you what you're going to do about it. But it's against his ethics to tell you what to do, to give you any constructive advice. And while you go out and quietly—or noisily, depending on your particular preference—shoot yourself, he collects his fees and adds to the suicide statistics.

Once pagan psychiatrists tell you that you are problem case number so and so, and that you are what you are because of something else you can't do anything about, they've done all they can. And it hasn't helped you a bit. They are powerless to correct the situation. The blood of Jesus is the only thing that can get down in there and scrub the record, and the blood of Jesus is simply not listed in this world's pharmacopoeia. Neither is the agent that puts it into action, His Word and His Spirit, as indicated in numerous Scriptures. Among them are:

Now ye are clean through the word which I have spoken unto you. (John 15:3)

But we all, with open face beholding as in a glass the glory of the Lord, are changed into the same image from glory to glory, even as by the Spirit of the Lord. (2 Cor. 3:18)

By simply accepting Jesus' finished work for us, we enter into that rest, whereas otherwise we would have to keep on struggling to maintain our position. When we are resting in Jesus, we don't have to excel in anything, because He is the

Excell-ent One. We don't have to prove anything; He has triumphed over all. And we don't have to assert out own rights. As real King's kids, we have given up self-ownership and turned it over to Jesus so that we might become stewards of all that He is in us. If that's not hallelujah ground, I've never seen any. Perfect rest in Jesus.

A whole lot of the world's population past the age of fifty is making retirement plans, but King's kids have nothing to retire from. Once we enter the rest of God, at whatever age, we're automatically retired from all the pressures of life. But we never get bored, because we're not retired from the activities. We can stay right in the midst of things, where the exciting action is, but never suffer for it. We can live it up, have a ball, and there are no detrimental effects on our physical systems when we're in the rest of God. His peace is in the eye of the storm.

In the fullness of the Spirit of God everything is at rest because it's in perfect equilibrium with all forces balanced out. This power of the Holy Spirit is the spiritual counterpart of what Dr. Albert Einstein foresaw many years ago in the realm of the physical world. In his theory of relativity, which was so far out in his day that people shook their heads and said, "The man has flipped his lid," he told how it is possible to interchange energy and matter at the speed of light. And that's exactly how God does it and has done it from the beginning of time.

"Furthermore," Einstein said, causing his critics to shake their heads even more furiously, "I believe that the speed of light is the turnover point. If we can go beyond that point, we can reverse history."

Today's scientists have discovered that Einstein wasn't way out at all. He was right on. Whether we knew it or not, he was seeing what God does. I'm a case in point. God took me beyond the speed of light, reversed the history of my past, and restored the years that the locusts, the caterpillars, and the cankerworms had eaten, just as He promised to do in the Scriptures.

And I will restore to you the years that the locust hath eaten, the cankerworm, and the caterpiller, and the palmerworm, my great army which I sent among you. And ye shall eat in plenty, and be satisfied, and praise the name of the LORD your God, that hath dealt wondrously with you: and my people shall never be ashamed. And ye shall know that I am in the midst of Israel, and that I am the LORD your God, and none else, and my people shall never be ashamed. (Joel 2: 25-27)

God is always as good as His Word. He gave the locust-eaten years back to me better than ever. And He came to live in me to keep all future locusts away so that I wouldn't have to be ashamed again.

The laws of physics and science and the Bible fit perfectly together, because our God is the overall designer. He can run history backward for His people so we don't have to get old. The Bible says that Moses lived 120 years, at the end of which he did not show the ravages of time:

And Moses was an hundred and twenty years old when he died: his eye was not dim, nor his natural force abated. (Deut. 34:7)

When we're resting in the rest that remaineth for the people of God (Heb. 4:9), it's as if we're living in victory at the fountain of youth.

One day as I was meditating on Hebrews 4:12, I asked the Lord, "How can anything be sharper than a two-edged sword?" He showed me, in the Spirit, a big old two-edged sword, sharp as a razor, but only on two edges. The other two sides were flat. They could slap you, but not cut you. They could make you smart a little bit, maybe inflict a painful bruise if the sword was wielded by a real muscleman, but there was no way they could be surgically useful at all.

"Well, Lord," I suggested, my think tank being in motion, "how about a four-edged sword? Is your Word sharper than that?" He showed me, again in the Spirit, that a four-edged sword would have four flaps, each interfering with the action of the cutting edge. It wouldn't be very useful—a museum piece. Only fifty percent of the sword, used in the conventional manner, could cut at any one time. It would be slow going.

"Lord, is there some shape that would make possible an instrument that would cut in all directions so nothing could evade it? So that however a guy moved, it would grab him? It seems to me that your Word must be something like that if it's sharper than a two-edged sword."

He showed me a laser beam.

Lasers produce light beams so concentrated that they can be used as surgical instruments for the most delicate operations, such as eye surgery to stitch detached retinas back in place, restoring vision. God was showing me that He uses His heavenly laser, the Word of God, to literally open our eyes to His truth, putting our sin-detached spiritual retinas back in place, restoring them to proper use and focus. It is the laser beam of God, suturing as it goes, that cuts between the real and the phony, revealing truth in the light of God's presence. Under those conditions, darkness has no choice but to take off, and we are cleansed from the tendency to think we can do anything about our own sinfulness. As we give up, acknowledging to God that we don't have what it takes, the Word of God accomplishes the cleansing in us.

For today's King's kids, as well as for the Israelites of old, the gospel mixed with faith produces the best that God can provide. We are to receive His Word, mix it with faith in our think tanks, and put it into action. If we mix it with unbelief, as the children of Israel did, we'll blow it every time, goofing the whole thing. But if we mix the Word with faith, we'll see it happen. We'll move into high victory in Jesus.

6
How to Live in Victory
over a Blown Mind

God has given us a book of directions, the *Manufacturer's Handbook*, not to take away our fun, but to tell us how to enjoy maximum benefits from this life and the life to come.

A lot of people believe we are born with a free choice and a free will. But it's not true, not since Adam's fall. Without our having made any choice at all, we're born with a will that's bound up by Satan. When we "do our own thing," we're actually doing Satan's thing. He's deceived us into thinking we're having our own way, and that deception is as old as the human race.

You recall that way back in the Garden of Eden, man was created in the image and likeness of God, which means he had a free will to do his own thing or God's thing. And God said to Adam, "In the garden here, you can have almost free reign, but there is one particular tree that's a no-no. In the day that you eat of that fruit, it'll wipe you out. You'll be totaled."

Automatically, the no-no fruit became highly desirable. Anytime there's a no-no, it doesn't matter what it is, we have to try it—just because it's a no-no. That's a good enough reason for the spirit of rebellion, which is standard equipment in the children of disobedience.

Naturally, when the shiny green gentleman came along with his sales pitch, knocking at the back door and telling Eve how ravishingly beautiful she looked that day, she was ready to listen to him.

"Look over my wares, lady. I've got some gorgeous fruit here, fresh off the tree."

Instead of saying, "There's the old man in the hammock. Take it up with him," as she should have done, Eve took it upon herself to deal with the fast-talking peddler, and he was mighty persuasive. When she told him about God's prohibition against their eating any of the fruit from the tree of the knowledge of good and evil, he reasoned with her.

"Now look," he purred. "You don't mean to tell me you think God *really* means what He says. You can't *really* think He'll kill you if you eat that fruit."

Slue Foot made the whole thing sound so preposterously ridiculous to Eve that she fell for snake talk in preference to God talk.

The whole head of the whole human race has been sick ever since. Whenever anything appeals to your think tank, watch out. That top ten inches, riding on your shoulders, your Educated Idiot Box, is guaranteed to keep you in trouble. Thanks to heredity, when Adam and Eve blew their minds with the no-no fruit, the effects were destined to be felt even until now. So the handicap with which we're saddled at birth goes right back to the original act of disobedience in the Garden of Eden.

"You can handle it without God" is still the enemy's greatest trick today. I ran into it as soon as I got saved. I went to my pastor and asked him, "Now that I'm a Christian, how do I go about living this Christian life? I don't know a thing about it, and I'm starting strictly from scratch."

"Well," he said, "for one thing, ask God to help you with all the big things. Don't bother Him with the little things. He's too busy for that, and after all, you can handle the little things yourself."

"All right," I said, not knowing any better at the time. "That sounds reasonable enough." So I started out by asking God to help me with the big things, and the first thing I knew, lots of times I forgot all about God. That happens invariably if we don't go to Him about everything. There's a gradual, insidious progression in it. And finally, there is nothing too big for us to handle according to the dictates of our own ego. God fades out of the picture, and the dreary, drab, empty frustrations of life begin to creep back in.

When I found that my former misery was slithering back, I suspected that my pastor's recommendation was a bum steer for me.

"Well, Lord," I confessed, "please forgive me for being so stupid. From now on, instead of me being head man and inviting you to be my helper only in the big things, how about letting us be co-partners in everything?"

He seemed agreeable, and so we tried that for a while, but to tell the truth, the new way wasn't a whole lot better than the old way. One of the problems was that I was never really sure which part was His responsibility and which was mine. It was hard to divide up. Eventually, after some struggle again, it got through my thick skull that God has set it up so that if I would be the weak one—in everything, great and small—He would be the strong one! His strength would actually be manifest through my weakness! That was a mind-blower for sure.

When I began to try that, fantastic things began to happen, and as long as I stick with that way of doing business, they keep on happening.

What we call our strength is what God calls weakness.

Compared with His strength, weakness is all we ever have to offer.

Once when he was writing to the Corinthians, Paul was relating how he had had an experience with the Lord that, in the natural, would have tended to make his head too big to go through doorways (you can read about it in 2 Corinthians 12). But he said God did something to prevent his being "exalted above measure" (v. 7) ("to prevent big-shot-itis" is the way we would say it today). He gave Paul a "thorn in the flesh" (v. 7). And that thorn was so bothersome to him, that Paul asked God three times to take it away (v. 8). But God didn't take it away; He did something better: He gave Paul grace to bear it, saying,

> My grace is sufficient for thee: for my strength is
> made perfect in weakness. (v. 9)

That seemed to be good enough for Paul. He said, "Okay, Lord, if that's the way you want it,

> Most gladly therefore will I rather glory in my
> infirmities, that the power of Christ may rest upon
> me. Therefore I take pleasure in infirmities, in
> reproaches, in necessities, in persecutions, in
> distresses for Christ's sake: for when I am weak,
> then am I strong. (v. 9-10)

Using human wisdom to figure it out, people have come up with all sorts of definitions of Paul's thorn in the flesh. Some have said he was an epileptic, others that he had bad eyesight, a horrible mother-in-law, or malarial fever. But verse 10 above makes it clear to me that none of these is the answer. The "thorn" referred to *any* adversity that might come into Paul's life, anything that would tend to offend him or disturb his peace of mind if he was trying to tough it out on his own strength (weakness) instead of on Christ's.

By accepting all "infirmities, reproaches, necessities, persecutions, and distresses" as from His heavenly Father,

43

Paul let God work through the thorns of the flesh of his human weakness to show the glory of God.

When I began to try that attitude in my life, one of the first things I learned was that I didn't have to go out of my way to ask Him to send infirmities or distresses or any of the rest of it. They seemed to be automatically present, integral components of the package called life. When one of these icky items came my way, I'd swallow hard and say, "Lord, I don't see any benefit in this for me at all. But I'm no longer impressed with what I can see. I'm impressed instead with the fact that you're my heavenly Father. And since you say that you're going to work everything together for my good (Rom. 8:28), I'm going to believe it and act like I believe it."

How does a King's kid act like He believes God is working all things together for good for him? Why, he praises God for everything that comes.

"That's ridiculous! That's stupid!" my idiot box protested. But I began to try it, and it began to work. I have yet to say, "Lord, please send another affliction for me to try out," but I can highly recommend the praising-God-for-everything route.

Afflictions are guaranteed to come with regularity, invited or not. Just plain living puts you in a state of having either awful problems or glorious adventures. If you are strong in your own strength, you get problems; if you know your weakness, and are willing to let God's strength be manifest through you, you will have hair-raising, spine-tingling adventures. The difference is in your attitude toward them.

When Paul wrote to the Philippians, he said it like this:

It is God which worketh in you both to will and to do
of his good pleasure. (2:13)

The Amplified Bible translation brings out the fuller meaning of the words with,

It is God Who is all the while effectually at work in you—energizing and creating in you the power and desire—both to will and to work for His good pleasure and satisfaction and delight.

Now, if God is working in me to cause my will to conform to His will, to motivate me to conform to His perfect plan for my life, there is never any instance when I should find fault with anything. When that concept got down in my gizzard, it revolutionized my life!

Is God unaware of anything that comes my way? Does He miss anything? Every now and then it looks like it. I tell him, "Lord, it looks to me as if you missed that one. I think it must have sneaked right on past without your noticing. But in line with our agreement, I'm going to reserve judgment until I know for sure."

Every single time so far it has turned out that He has been in full charge all along, never asleep at the switch. And the results have been out of this world.

Some principles having to do with God's strength being made perfect in our weakness are further delineated in Paul's first letter to the Corinthians:

The foolishness of God is wiser than men; and the weakness of God is stronger than men. For ye see your calling, brethren, how that not many wise men after the flesh, not many mighty, not many noble, are called: But God hath chosen the foolish things of the world to confound the wise; and God hath chosen the weak things of the world to confound the things which are mighty; And base things of the world, and things which are despised, hath God chosen, yea, and things which are not, to bring to nought things that are: That no flesh should glory in his presence. But of him are ye in Christ Jesus, who of God is made unto us wisdom,

45

and righteousness, and sanctification, and
redemption: That, according as it is written, He
that glorieth, let him glory in the Lord. (1:25-31)

Jesus is made to be for us the things that we lack without
Him. Here He does not offer to make us wise or to sanctify
us, but He offers to be our wisdom and our sanctification
within us. It is only when we acknowledge our
weakness—that we don't have what it takes—that He can
become these things for us within us. He is ever changing my
will to conform to His will, and He is furnishing both the
power and the motivation to do it (Phil. 2:13).

All this happens when we stay in the position of a tuned-up
King's kid, in the solid state of perfect coordination, total
alignment with His will so that all parts of us are doing their
thing for the common good by being in a high state of
praising God, acknowledging Him in every situation.

Trust in the LORD with all thine heart; and lean
not unto thine own understanding. In all thy ways
acknowledge him, and he shall direct thy paths.
(Prov. 3:5-6)

We are not to look to our common sense—ever. The reason
it's called common is that there's so much of it, and it's not
worth anything. Common sense will mess up every time.
But as we acknowledge God to be in charge, He will direct
our paths. Notice that in this Scripture, the word *paths* is
plural. He's not talking about some narrow, restricted way,
but promising that in whatever way we go, He will direct us,
because we're acknowledging Him. Victory is the
irreversible outcome when we acknowledge our weakness
and invite Him to be strength in us.

7

How to Live in Victory
when the Egyptians
Are After You

The Lord has shown me that there are three basic areas of reliance that King's kids have to unlearn before they can experience the best God has for them. These three areas are self-reliance, thing-reliance, and reliance on other people. Each of these can become a false god in our lives, obscuring the true and living God.

There's an illustration of reliance on other people in the experience of the prophet Isaiah:

In the year that king Uzziah died, I saw also the
Lord sitting upon a throne, high and lifted up, and
his train filled the temple. (6:1)

The prophet is telling us that he saw the Lord for the first time after King Uzziah died. It was if he could not see the heavenly King until the earthly king was out of the way. Perhaps Isaiah had been so concentrating on his earthly king before that time that he had almost worshiped him. That kind of reliance on other people is something that has to go if we are really to know the King of kings and Lord of lords and walk in the victory He bought for us.

There was almost an Uzziah in my own life. Ed, the man

47

who introduced me to Jesus, became almost an idol to me. I was probably more conscious of his reaction to my behavior than I was to how the Lord felt about it. It seemed that I was more bent on trying to please Ed than on trying to please Jesus. I thought there was no way I could ever live without this earthly friend. But there came a day when I had to tell him goodbye, the day the Lord moved him to Hawaii. And on the day that Ed left, I too saw the Lord, high and lifted up, where He had been all along. With Ed out of hollering distance, I learned to holler to the Lord.

At some time in their Christian experience, most people have a King Uzziah or an Ed in their lives. There is an ever-present danger that we'll settle for reliance on a fallible human being instead of reliance on an infallible God. For that reason, counselors and others who lead people to Jesus have, at some point, to divorce themselves from folks who keep on coming to them for advice instead of learning to seek the help of the Lord for themselves. King's kids have to come to dependence on God and on God alone. The fruit of our heavenly obstetrics are not to remain under us; they are to go on with the Lord without being limited by our limitations.

In Psalm 138, God says:

> The LORD will perfect that which concerneth me. (v. 8)

God himself is capable of finishing the work He has begun in us without the help of any human person if He chooses to do it that way. "Forsake not the works of thine own hands," the psalmist prays in the same verse. If I am the work of His hands—and what else could I be?—then He will not forsake me, but will finish what He has started.

If Jesus is "the author and finisher of our faith" (Heb. 12:2), we are to look to Him and Him alone. Furthermore, Jesus himself declares,

> Be not called Rabbi: for one is your Master, even

Christ; and all ye are brethren. And call no man
your father upon the earth, for one is your Father,
which is in heaven. Neither be ye called masters:
for one is your Master, even Christ. (Matt. 23:8-10)

Reliance on other people or things instead of on God is not
the way to live the victory in Jesus. Faith in anyone or
anything other than God is bound to lead to some kind of
disaster sooner or later. The experience of Pharaoh and his
mighty hosts when they went after the escaping children of
Israel is a good example.

Pharaoh had agreed to let the Israelites go, time after
time, being persuaded by plagues of flies, fleas, frogs, hail,
locusts, and other undesirable house guests; but he had
always gone back on his word before the Israelites could
make their getaway. It was only after the death of his own
first-born son, as prophesied by Moses, that Pharaoh saw
that he had better get rid of the Israelites fast—men,
women, children, cattle, and all. Once again, however, after
he'd had a little time to think about it, he changed his mind.
It was too late to refuse to let the Israelites go—they were
already on their way—so he and his hordes saddled up and
took off in hot pursuit.

The Egyptians caught up with the children of Israel just
as they were approaching the banks of the Red Sea.

When the Israelites glanced over their shoulders and saw
the soldiers gaining on them, it looked like the chosen people
were in for a losing battle. They complained to God, of
course. They had had a lot of practice in complaining in
Egypt. This time, the complaint came out in the form of a
railing against Moses:

"Did you let us survive the trip just to get us out here and
kill us all? Take us back to Egypt—we never had it so good as
when we were there."

Short memories, those Israelites had, but Moses looked to

the Lord for help, and God enabled him to take charge of the water. It opened up before them, and they went right through on dry ground. You can read all about it in Exodus 14.

The Egyptians still hadn't learned their lesson. They figured that anything the Israelites could do, they could do better. Exercising faith in their ability to match the supernatural ability of the living God, they wheeled down into the Red Sea. Their hot pursuit immediately became a chilly one, as God pulled the wheels right off their chariots, bringing the whole procession to a soggy halt. They began to bog down in mud that suddenly appeared out of nowhere, and then the walls of water crashed down upon them, wiping out men, chariots, horses, Pharaoh, and all. Meanwhile, the children of Israel were safe and dry on the opposite bank. They hadn't even gotten their sandals wet.

The difference in results was inevitable because of the difference in what the opposing forces relied on. Moses was relying on God's supernatural ability; Pharaoh's faith was in himself and his soldiers.

The victory dance the Israelites had on the opposite shore must have been something to see. And the victory dance is always ours when our reliance is on God.

If the clay has a mind of its own, it's a waste of time for the potter to work on it.

8
How to Live in Victory
over Mud Ball Origins

In the *Manufacturer's Handbook,* God gives us many different practical illustrations to show us how King's kids are formed out of ordinary pagans. One of the most striking illustrations is the one God mentioned to the prophet Jeremiah one day.

When God first called Jeremiah to the ministry, He told him, "Before you were ever born, I chose you for this particular ministry." In the face of words like that, Jeremiah still tried to talk God out of the assignment.

"But, Lord, I'm just a little kid," he protested. "I can't minister. Why, I wouldn't even know what to say."

"Wait a minute," God told him. "Don't say you're just a little kid. Get busy and go where I tell you to go and say what I want you to say. You won't have to worry about getting up a message for the people. I have already put My words in your mouth (Jer. 1:9). Just be yielded to me. I don't need you to be a creative genius. I just need you to be an empty vessel I can use."

Jeremiah later testified, "God touched my mouth, and from there on out, the words that came forth were strictly

53

from Him." All it took on the part of Jeremiah was submission to God's desires in place of the rebellion of his own desires.

Later, after Jeremiah had been preaching, "Thus saith the Lord . . ." for seventeen chapters, God told him,

Arise, and go down to the potter's house, and there
I will cause thee to hear my words. (18:2)

I imagine Jeremiah was just a little bit insulted at that.

"What does a potter know about Scripture," he might have mumbled to himself. But he went down to watch the potter anyway, and there God showed him an indispensable principle of the Christian life by the simple illustration of a mud ball in the hands of a master potter. The illustration was especially meaningful to me, because for a number of years I had dabbled in pottery making as a hobby.

The pottery-making process begins when the potter digs out of the ground a mud ball that has already been processed for many centuries through glacial action and other environmental factors. The makers of Ming and other famous Chinese porcelains use clay from a specially prepared clay pit, rich in calcium. The calcium comes from the bones of dead pigs thrown into the clay pit every few years.

You can imagine what the finest clay smells like—and what a drink of tea out of a fine china cup would taste like—if there wasn't a way to get rid of the smell of dead pigs' bones.

After getting a ball of clay that has the properties he wants, the potter has to throw the ball of clay on the wheel. Literally. The clay will not behave itself until the potter shows it who is the head man. He has to slam it down in the middle of the wheel as hard as he can. That slamming down looks cruel, but it is a loving act, putting down rebellion. The clay will not stick any other way. It's impossible to paste it down, to coax it down, to stick it down with glue, or by persistence to push it down enough times to make it stay. It has to be slammed down—hard. That's an essential step in pottery making.

If the clay does not possess the quality of submissiveness or plasticity, if it has a mind of its own, it's a waste of time for the potter to work on it. And plasticity can't be produced in clay by any kind of chemical formula we dream up. It's either there or it's not there, an intrinsic, innate quality put there by the hand of God. If this quality is not present, the clay will have to be reworked.

Another element that could appear in clay, causing the clay to collapse, is an air bubble. We see a parallel in God's people. When they are full of the hot air of their own self importance, they will collapse every time. Motor-mouthing and complaining are readouts of this spiritual condition. Murmuring, the Bible calls it, and God cannot stand that quality in His people.

If the mud ball wants to go in big circles right from the start, it is likely to fly right off into space, knocking things over as it goes, causing destruction. But if the mud ball is content to just sit and spin around in small circles on the wheel, becoming nothing in its own eyes, the potter can begin to shape it to usefulness. The clay never questions the process, just succumbs to whatever the potter has in mind. Resistance would only result in its being smashed into a formless ball again so the potter could start over.

But there is more to becoming a vessel than simply being formed into a bowl or cup or vase. After it is all shaped up, the clay object is still a hunk of mud, looking so slimy and smelling so bad it wouldn't appeal to us for dinnerware or a container for a bouquet of flowers. It has to be put through the fire and baked before it can be used.

In all this, the potter must continue to have a free hand to do his thing in spite of what the pot thinks about it. When the pot is completely formed and set in the kiln for the first time, the fire is turned up, and the heat begins to build. Already the pot begins to consider itself a pretty rare and valuable article. Everybody can see it's just a shaped-up mud ball, still reeking, but it's saying, "Lord, use me. Send me. I'm ready now."

Then the fire gets hotter, and the pot starts to smell so bad the whole neighborhood notices it. The vegetable matter is burning out. All the impurities that are not wanted in the finished product go up in smoke. It belches forth from the kiln, and people have to open windows, turn on ventilating fans, and spray deodorizer all over the place.

And when the pot gets so hot that it begins to glow red itself, it really has a bad time. "That crazy potter. He went to all that trouble to make me, and now it looks like he's going to shrink me down to nothing and burn me up in the process."

But the potter doesn't stop even there. He turns the fire up and up until when he peeks through the peephole of the kiln, the pot has disappeared. It's invisible because it has taken on the same temperature as the fire itself. By then the pot has stopped complaining, because it's certain it is headed for total destruction and there's no sense in protesting.

"It's all over now," he says to himself. "The potter has given up on me. I was too much for him to handle."

About then, old Slue Foot starts his whispering campaign in a King's kid's ear. "God didn't really mean to use you in the first place. He just ran a test run, found you weren't fit for anything, and He's burning you up to get you off the scene."

The accuser of the brethren can always be counted on to give us some such discouraging news as that, and if we don't understand something about the workings of the Master Potter, we might be tempted to agree with him. But whether we agree or not, the Potter goes on with His job.

If the maturing fire is properly done, the pot may sit and soak for a week. Then, when he think it's all over for him except for scattering the ashes somewhere, the potter turns the fire off. The cooling-off process is deliberately slow, so the pot won't go *Zing!* and fly into a million pieces. But after a week or ten days has passed, the potter opens the kiln and there sits a pot—beautiful and useful. Still that's not the end of it.

The first firing process has produced something of value, but the pot is still just earthenware. It will hold dried beans, but it won't hold water. It can be a showcase item, but if it wants to be more useful, it has to go through additional firings. We do, too, if we want to be made into vessels that can hold the treasure of Living Water (John 7:38-39).

"Oh, Lord, I thought that first trial by fire was going to be it. You mean there's more?"

"Yes, there's more. That was only the beginning. But don't worry. I've never lost a pot yet."

The Lord's batting average as a Potter is considerably better than mine was, I have to admit. As an amateur potter, I was in a hurry one night. I had the kiln loaded with a number of pieces that I had spent many hours in preparing. Eager to get through with it, I figured the directions in the handbook were probably more conservative than they had to be. I decided I would speed the process by turning the burners up a little bit faster. Feeling satisfied about my efficiency, I went upstairs to read while the kiln was firing.

At first, everything was quiet and peaceful. Then a resounding *Boom!* nearly knocked me off my rocker. I didn't know if there was an earthquake, the city was being bombed, or what, but it seemed to make sense for me to take shelter in the basement and check on my pottery while I was about it.

When I opened the kiln, my sneaking suspicions were

57

confirmed.

I should have followed the directions.

Instead of beautiful pots, drying out at a very efficient rate of speed, I had a kiln full of broken pieces. Everything inside had exploded. All my work was blown to smithereens by the steam pressure that built up in the clay from the too sudden high temperature of the firing.

I was far from being a master potter. In straining to make it happen faster, I had produced a bunch of psycho-ceramics, cracked pots.

There are a lot of psycho-ceramics, cracked pots, running around loose for the same reason. That's what happens when we try to do things our own way, at our tempo, instead of waiting patiently for Him to accomplish His will for us in the fullness of time. His perfect timetable is always better than anything we could dream up, but psycho-ceramics don't know that. They go running around, doing this, getting into that, trying to help God. The result is a delay in the game, making it necessary for us to have to go through the same process over and over.

When we acknowledge that we have blown it, time after time, God has to say to us, "Okay, now that you're ready to let Me do it in my time-tested, proven way, get back in the fire, and I'll take care of your perfection myself."

In fine china, some of the multiple firings have to do with adding decorations, uniting quality improvements to the vessel. And every firing refines the surface as well as the crystal structure of the piece. It becomes stronger, more resilient, better able to cope with stresses.

You can take a well-seasoned, matured piece of fine china or porcelain made by a master potter and drop it on a concrete floor and have it bounce back almost to your hand. It can receive shock and give it back. The master potter knows exactly how to condition the piece of china so that it will not fly to pieces under stress and strain. It does not absorb the stress—stress bounces off from it. If you tried the same trick with my amateur stuff, you'd have to get the broom and sweep up a million scattered pieces.

The last bit of firing is at a very critical temperature, just below red heat. It is at this stage that the banding of gold is put on. Too much heat, and the gold will blacken, ruining the whole thing. And heating it to too low a temperature will result in gold that can be rubbed off the china. That's no good either. The firing has to be exactly right.

By the time this stage is reached, the pot has generally learned a few things, and is now ready to keep his good advice to himself, and to say, "Lord, do it your way. Turn the burners up or not, just as you see fit."

A worldly master potter never puts his hallmark, his personal signature, on a piece until he is assured of its perfection. It may be that a flaw will come to light at the fourteenth firing, and he will scrap the whole thing, destroying it or putting it on the market without his name on it.

But God handles that in a different way. Every piece that He makes is destined to be a masterpiece, and He puts His mark on us in the mud stage. He knows e has never yet rejected the stinkiest mud ball who has come to Jesus and said, "I am your property, a mud ball in your hands. I don't want to try to do anything on my own; I just want to be a vessel to hold the treasure that you are. I'm going to look to you to shape me up by the power of your Holy Spirit."

That attitude puts us in a position to cooperate with the Holy Spirit instead of struggling against Him. We can rest in Jesus while the molding and firing processes are going on, knowing that His plan for us is perfection.

As we submit and let Him have His way, He brings us from glory to glory, from firing to firing, until we come to the perfect measure of the stature of the fullness of Christ himself (Eph. 4:13) in every atom of our being, saturated with the fire of the Holy Spirit, ministering life instead of death wherever we go. Completed vessels, fulfilling the Scripture,

> We have this treasure in earthen vessels, that the excellency of the power may be of God, and not of us. (2 Cor. 4:7)

The Potter and the clay—God's picture of the kind of humility He wants in Jeremiah and in us, in order for Him to get the best results.

Clay that begins as a stinky mud ball, slammed to the Potter's wheel, submitted to the Potter's plan, and tried by fire, winds up as a transparent vessel revealing the glory of the great treasure of heaven—Jesus himself.

9
How to Live in Victory
over Condemnation

Did Slue Foot ever tell you that you were a worse person after you became a Christian than you were before? He's told me that plenty of times, and before I got wise to his tricks, I was inclined to agree with him. But then I became aware of Romans 8:1, the part of the Word of God which says we don't have to put up with condemnation. And Slue Foot took off when I began to throw the Word at him.

I knew I wasn't worse than I used to be, because no one will ever be worse than he was the day he was born. By nature, we're born slobs, with perverted natures, on account of all that Adam-and-Eve business back in the Garden of Eden. It doesn't take too many years for us to learn to act like slobs, to live it up according to our fouled-up natures.

Take any baby and look at his vocabulary. Maybe "ma-ma" and "da-da" are the first words he learns to say, but the third one is "no-no." That's because of the inborn disobedience in him, the law of sin and death that was part of the curse that God put on all His creation. But that law is not meant to reign and rule for eternity. Jesus is. And when we let Jesus have His way in us, He sets us free from the law of sin and death.

Where King's kids are acting like it, the dead are raised and the sick are healed according to the power of the Holy Spirit working in us. We are ministering life instead of death when we're walking in the Spirit. And so what Paul wrote to the Romans has special relevance for us when Satan comes at us with his accusations.

> There is therefore now no condemnation to them which are in Christ Jesus, who walk not after the flesh, but after the Spirit. For the law of the Spirit of life in Christ Jesus hath made me free from the law of sin and death. For what the law could not do, in that it was weak through the flesh, God sending his own Son in the likeness of sinful flesh, and for sin, condemned sin in the flesh: That the righteousness of the law might be fulfilled in us, who walk not after the flesh, but after the Spirit. . . . But ye are not in the flesh, but in the Spirit, if so be that the Spirit of God dwell in you. (8:1-4,9)

When Satan comes at us, trying to make us feel condemned, accusing, "Look what you did. You acted just like a pagan," we're lost if we deny it, trying to protect our reputations. But victory from condemnation is ours if we agree with him saying, "I know I acted like a pagan. But I'm not one. I'm a King's kid, and if Jesus doesn't change me some more on the inside, I'll continue to goof it on the outside. But Slue Foot, you know what 1 John 1:9 says about goofing it. There God promises that if I confess my sins, He is faithful and just to forgive my sins and to cleanse me from all unrighteousness. And Slue Foot, I have already confessed the sin you're hammering me about. The record is scrubbed. Take off."

When we do that, Satan has to leave the premises. He has no ground in us when we know our rights and privileges as King's kids.

The Bible tells us that if we say we have no sin, we deceive ourselves and the truth is not in us (1 John 1:8). And if we take that road of deception, it'll rot our socks, ruin our bone marrow, and give us all kinds of other physical readouts—arthritis, cancer. . . . But if we acknowledge who we are and keep our confessions up-to-date, we have the victory.

King's kids never have to feel guilty. Jesus has taken care of all our sins, and He keeps on taking care of them. There *is* no condemnation to us who are in Him.

The Bible never said that all Christians always live pure and holy lives. They don't. Furthermore, they can't. But when we allow God to have His way in us, we, like Paul, are living by the faith of the Son of God who loved us and gave himself for us (Gal. 2:20). Jesus said we are to be perfect as our heavenly Father is perfect (Matt. 5:48), and we reach that perfection when we allow Jesus to operate fully within. The perfection is never us; it's always Jesus.

We could sign up for all the self-improvement courses in the world, and in spite of our herculean efforts to act more pure, they wouldn't make an iota of difference in us. Unless we got worse. But when Jesus is living His life in us and through us, we have total victory. His offer to be our perfection, our patience, our righteousness, our everything (1 Cor. 1:30), is the best offer in the universe.

Knowing these things are so, why do we find ourselves struggling to make it happen faster, or bigger, or better? It's the old spirit of do-it-myself, and hurry-it-up competition working in us. We think we can get on with our perfection faster than God can. But the Scripture says plainly that we're to run the race with patience, looking not to other racers, but to Jesus, having our attention glued on Him (Heb. 12:1-2). And as we lift Him up so all men can see Him, He'll be glorified in their lives, too. Instead of fruitless struggle, there'll be victory everywhere we look.

10
How to Live in Victory
over a Judgmental Spirit

Suppose you are going along, and God is making a lot of progress in turning you into the kind of person you'd like to be. Why, you act almost saintly a lot of the time, and if it weren't for a couple of people who bug you, you'd never backslide. You'd live in victory all the time. How are you supposed to get rid of those stinkers in your life, the goons who keep getting in your way, making you lose your temper, messing up your perfect relationship with the King of the universe by causing you to react in ways unbecoming to a citizen of the kingdom?

The *Manufacturer's Handbook* anticipates this problem in the lives of King's kids and prescribes a troubleshooting technique guaranteed to eliminate the stinkers from your life. I'll tell you how to go about it, and then I'll give you the Scripture for it.

First of all, take a long piece of paper (maybe you'll need a whole tablet) and a bunch of sharp pencils. Think of the worst stinkers you know, the creeps you can't stand, the ones who are so repulsive your innards begin to churn at the thought of them. Pick up your pencil and make a list of everything that's obnoxious about them: grasping, tight, liars, profane, dirty, narrow-minded, cheats, gluttons, opportunists, opinionated, know-it-alls, selfish, proud, arrogant, boastful, bigmouths, raunchy, snobbish, jealous, greedy, unforgiving, blabbermouths . . .

Write it all down. Take a couple of weeks if necessary. It's important to make this job complete, putting everything down in detail.

Then, read Romans 2:1, the verse which reveals the mirror principle of human relationships:

Therefore thou art inexcusable, whosoever thou art that judgest: for wherein thou judgest another, thou condemnest thyself; for thou that judgest doest the same things.

Ouch! But I didn't say it, God did. And since He's always right, you might just as well take the inventory list you've compiled and sign your name to it. The *Manufacturer's Handbook* says flatfootedly you never would have seen those things in the other person if they were not in you.

When you've recovered from your embarrassment, you can get on your knees and pray for the stinkers and for yourself, and you'll both improve. The stinkers who kept fouling up my life changed so radically once I got to using that arrangement, that I hardly recognized them.

I've learned to be grateful to those stinkers for showing me myself, because once I knew my sin, I didn't have to be stuck with it anymore. I could pray to be delivered from my miserable character defects that I saw reflected in other people. Jesus changed the other people while He was changing me, so they were grateful too. When there's changing to be done, we can't do it, but Jesus can do it in wholesale batches. After the stinkers have served their purpose, they usually turn into your best friends.

Now when I see something in someone else that bothers

me, I say, "Praise the Lord! Thank you for showing me what I'm still like. I thought I was better than that, but I see that I'm not. Keep on working on me, Lord." He always hears that prayer and answers it.

God has given us this very helpful mirror principle because we're all such phonies, liars, cheats, and connivers, that we refuse to admit the truth about ourselves until we face it in the mirror.

Once we have learned to recognize our own faults in one another and to pray for one another, we move into a new dimension of life in the Spirit. Our condemning judgment of others, which was a perversion of God's original plan, becomes discernment for the needs of others. We still see the faults of other people, maybe even with heightened intensity, but no longer as a reflection of our own raunchy selves. God gives us the discernment of spirits so we can be God's channel for blessing, delivering God's gifts to the needy. Paul explains it this way:

> He that is spiritual judgeth all things, yet he
> himself is judged of no man. For who hath known
> the mind of the Lord, that he may instruct him? But
> we have the mind of Christ. (1 Cor. 2:15-16)

The judgment of the spiritual man, who judges with the mind of Christ, is given to enable him to pray for others and to teach them what God's Word says about how to walk in victory over the sins that beset them.

11

How to Live in Victory
in the Perfect Will of God

How can you know that you're in the center of God's will at every moment, no doubts about it? The answer to the great question is clearly given in Paul's first letter to the Thessalonians:

Rejoice evermore. Pray without ceasing. In every thing give thanks: for this is the will of God in Christ Jesus concerning you. (5:16-18)

These verses are perfectly plain, without any Greek interpreter. They guarantee that we are in the center of God's will at all times when we're rejoicing, praying, and giving thanks.

We protest, "That's too simple; I've got to louse it up somehow." But it's right there in the Word of God, crystal clear.

An important part of doing God's will has to do with the use of a very small organ of the body, the tongue. The tongue has everything to do with the course of our life. In the Book of James, God says,

If any man offend not in word, the same is a perfect man, and able also to bridle the whole body.

Behold, we put bits in the horses' mouths, that they
may obey us; and we turn about their whole body.
Behold also the ships, which though they be so
great, and are driven of fierce winds, yet are they
turned about with a very small helm [the lever or
wheel for controlling the rudder of a ship],
whithersoever the governor listeth. Even so the
tongue is a little member, and boasteth great
things. Behold, how great a matter a little fire
kindleth! And the tongue is a fire, a world of
iniquity: so is the tongue among among our
members, that it defileth the whole body, and
setteth on fire the course of nature; and it is set on
fire of hell. (3:2-6)

Here God is saying that the tongue directs the course of
our lives much as a rudder does a ship, or a bit in the horse's
mouth guides the horse.

A couple of ounces of steel in a thousand-pound horse
doesn't sound very important, but that's how you steer him.
And a relatively little rudder on the back end of a huge ocean
liner doesn't look as if it would do a thing for it, but that's
what guides its path. The tongue is to the body and to the
Christian's life, as the rudder is to the ship, and the bit to the
horse. When the tongue is used negatively, as "a world of
iniquity," it produces a lot of things that are second best.

If I'm a Christian and I'm complaining and grumbling, the
world doesn't know that I'm any different from pagans. My
spirituality is gone, my testimony has departed, and my
effect in dispelling the world of darkness has flown the coop
because I've chosen to magnify the problem by
motor-mouthing about it instead of magnifying the answer
by praising Jesus.

When, right in the midst of whatever is going on, I say,
"Lord, I'm going to thank you for one reason, because you

said to," immediately I enter a new dimension.

Do you think it sounds spooky, altogether crazy, to praise God when things are falling apart all around? That's all right. Nowhere does God say that praising Him will make any sense to finite minds; He just says, "Do it. And then you can know that you're in my will." When we're in His will, we're in line to experience perfectly answered prayers.

God burned a couple of Scriptures into my consciousness near the beginning of my Christian life as a license to ask for anything and know I will receive it for His glory:

> And whatsoever we ask, we receive of him, because we keep his commandments, and do those things that are pleasing in his sight. (1 John 3:22)

> And this is the confidence that we have in him, that, if we ask any thing according to his will, he heareth us: And if we know that he hears us, whatsoever we ask, we know that we have the petitions that we desired of him. (1 John 5:14-15)

John's Gospel spells the same truths out in a slightly different way:

> If ye abide in me, and my words abide in you, ye shall ask what ye will, and it shall be done unto you. (15:7)

Right away I saw that to be in a position to receive the answers to my prayers, I had first to keep His commandments and do the things that were pleasing in His sight. It was a tall order. Obedience doesn't come naturally to the human race.

"Lord," I protested, "I can't keep your commandments."

"It's a good thing you know that," He answered. *"Of course* you can't keep them. You aren't expected to. But you can elect to do it. And when you decide you *want* to keep them, then I'll come in and take over and keep them for you" (Phil. 2:13).

That was certainly a relief. It meant I wasn't going to be responsible for doing everything that was pleasing in His sight all on my own. But I knew something I *could* do. In the Thessalonians Scripture and in a number of other places scattered throughout the *Manufacturer's Handbook*, I saw that the one thing that pleases God more than anything else is that we praise Him. I could do that. I could be obedient to the Psalm that says,

Oh that men would praise the LORD for his goodness, and for his wonderful works to the children of men! (107:8)

I was more than ready to praise Him. "Lord," I said, "I thank you for keeping the commandments for me. And thank you for showing me the one thing I can do. By your grace, I will praise you without stopping. I know I can't do even that on my own, of course, because on my own, I'd go right back into the nit-picking, griping, complaining, grumbling, and gossiping at which I've become so proficient. I've been geared for these things all my life and have practiced them continually. But from now on, if you'll take over my tongue, I'll praise you continually instead."

All this came about before I knew anything about the gift of tongues, but instinctively I somehow tied the disciplining of my uncontrolled tongue with putting myself in a position to have my prayers answered all the time.

Our tongues provide an accurate read out of the condition of our souls, and our souls prosper only when they're under the dominion of the Spirit of God instead of under our own self-control. Our souls are admonished:

Bless the LORD, O my soul: and all that is within me, bless his holy name. Bless the LORD, O my soul, and forget not all his benefits: Who forgiveth all thine iniquities; who healeth all thy diseases. (Ps. 103:1-3)

71

When the soul is blessing the Lord, it is prospering, paving the way for prosperity and health in line with God's will for us:

Beloved, I wish above all things that thou mayest prosper and be in health, even as thy soul prospereth. (3 John 2)

How can you tell whether or not your soul is prospering? God has given us several checkpoints so we can know for a certainty about these things. Soul prosperity is a natural result when we are rejoicing, praying, and giving thanks, because these actions keep us on the wavelength of heaven where God dwells in the praises of His people (Ps. 22:3). We are abiding in Jesus, and His words are abiding in us, when we are hearing His words and doing them.

When the soul is in an ownership position, it will never prosper. It will be in a state of disorder, out of tune with God, because God never intended for us to be owners. When He set Adam in the middle of the garden, He said, "Be my steward. I'm putting you here to take care of my creation. You are delegated to name the animals; you can be a steward of the whole business. But keep your cottonpicking fingers off the ownership. Stay loose."

A steward has no responsibility except one thing—faithfulness. An owner has to give it all he's got in order to protect his rights. But a steward has only to be faithful to the boss. When trouble sets in, he's entitled to holler, "Hey boss! We've got a problem here. What are you going to do about it? I admit I got us into this mess, but I'm counting on you to come to the rescue."

A steward has it easy, no ulcers, because he never has to decide anything. All he has to do is report to headquarters for further instructions after he has carried out the ones he just received. The consequences of his Spirit-directed actions are none of his business. He is free, as only the Son

72

can make a man free. Owning nothing, he can enjoy all of God's possessions.

That freedom was lost in the Garden of Eden through the inversion of human nature when it listened to snake talk in preference to God talk. That perverted the whole thing, and stewardship in which there is liberty became ownership in which is bondage and misery.

God never said that giving up our soulish ownership position would be easy. But it can be done. Here's an illustration of it from the Gospel according to Matthew:

> And Jesus, walking by the sea of Galilee, saw two brethren, Simon called Peter, and Andrew his brother, casting a net into the sea: for they were fishers. And he saith unto them, Follow me, and I will make you fishers of men. And they straightway left their nets, and followed him. (4:18-20)

Here were some fellows, making a living by catching fish. When Jesus came along with an invitation to them to give up their ownership and become stewards, they left their nets right away. They didn't say, "Let's take inventory first, and count this catch," or "Wait till we sell the fish," or "At least let's have a fish fry first so this catch won't all go to waste." They just dropped everything and followed Him. They gave up ownership instantly when they saw Jesus.

Any time your feelings are hurt, that's a direct indication that you are acting like an owner. Nobody can violate your rights to yourself unless you have some self rights to be violated. Any time you pop your martyr pills and throw a pity party, lamenting, "Pore little ole me, nobody understands," you're on a wrong road. When you're in the midst of these things, your soul is doing everything *but* prospering. Prosperity, health, and all the other hallmarks of abundant living in Jesus will be far from you.

73

King's kids never react against anything when they're walking in the Spirit. They respond all the time to the needs of others. Reaction or response? That is the barometer by which we can tell in which dimension we are living: the dimension of ownership—in the soul, which is Slue Foot's domain, or the dimension of stewardship—in the Spirit, in which everything is moving as God ordains.

12
How to Live in Victory
over Self

The principles that have to do with successful King's kid living are usually what the world calls failure. In an ordinary race, there's only one winner, and the rest are all losers. There are no losers among King's kids who are acting like it. King's kids recognize their true status, that Jesus within is their only strength. As weak vessels, they have one thing to brag about—their weakness, because therein is God's strength made manifest. The letter to the Hebrews gives us some insights into this King's kid race and how we're to run it.

> Wherefore seeing we also are compassed about with so great a cloud of witnesses, let us lay aside every weight, and the sin which doth so easily beset us, and let us run with patience the race that is set before us, looking unto Jesus. . . . (12:1-2)

What weights hinder our Christian life if we do not lay them aside? Anything we have regarded as our strength, any point where we have been tempted to rely on ourselves instead of on God hinder our Christian life. On the other hand, our weaknesses are our points of victory, because in them we acknowledge that we can't do anything, that God will have to do it all.

Every situation in life is an opportunity for us to either show forth our strength, our ownership, our possessiveness, and become losers, or to recognize our weakness, turn it all over to God, and become winners through His power.

When we think we're strong, we have to guard our position.

When we are wise in our own conceits, we have to be careful that some other wise guy doesn't outsmart us.

When we are rich in our possessions, we have to be on the alert against rust and moths.

When we are the head of any situation, we have to labor twenty-four hours a day to hold onto our position.

When we have an image to protect, we have to tailor all our actions to conform to it.

All these defensive precautions will take the energies we might otherwise be expending in going ahead as King's kids.

This makes no sense at all to an unregenerate mind. Our unsanctified common sense is programed to direct us into a losing situation every time. Oh, it might not always look like it at first, but after we have "won" a particular point through our own efforts, it's never satisfying for long. There's a surprising lack of satisfaction in achieving worldly accomplishments in a worldly way.

This was extremely baffling and frustrating to me as I went up the ladder of success in my chosen profession. Every rung of the ladder promised fulfillment, but never provided it. When I reached the pinnacle that had looked so shining from the bottom of the ladder, I found myself yawning and saying, "So what else is new?" Until I met Jesus, I was never satisfied with anything. The reason is that we are created to be spirit, soul, and body people—three-dimensional beings. King's kids.

76

Each of our three dimensions has its own peculiar hungers, and these hungers are always trying to be satisfied by the things of the world until our minds become reoriented by our entering into training for kingdom living.

The first letter of John talks about these three areas of life:

For all that is in the world, the lust of the flesh, and the lust of the eyes, and the pride of life, is not of the Father, but is of the world. (2:16)

The "lust of the flesh" refers to the body, which is always trying to be satisfied with physical thrills.

Have you ever eaten too much and wondered why? Your body was craving something to satisfy the total person. But you can eat enough to become a blimp and your inner craving will not be satisfied. Or seeing that overeating doesn't work, you can diet until you become a sliver, and you'll still have a gnawing dissatisfaction, because it's not through the flesh that satisfaction for the whole being can come.

The "lust of the eyes" has to do with soul-cravings. The soul, like the body, is always seeking to be fed to the point of satiety with bigger and better possessions. But the soul is always left hungry, no matter how much it acquires of worldly possessions, honor, or fame, because for all their cost, these things are nothing more than empty husks.

The third area John mentions here is the "pride of life." That's the real killer—the human ego trying to satisfy itself by human accomplishments, by insisting on its own rights. The big battleground comes into the picture whenever you have any self rights. Just as sure as you have self rights, someone is going to violate them. And you'll have to stick up for your rights. That means war. And therein lies the path of the loser.

"You mean I should lie down and be a doormat?" people argue back at me.

It's not what I mean; it's what God means. He guarantees

that those who are willing to become heavenly doormats are the ones who will live in high victory. Does it sound familiar? It should. Jesus said it:

> If any man will come after me, let him deny himself, and take up his cross, and follow me. For whosoever will save his life shall lose it: and whosoever shall lose his life for my sake shall find it. (Matt. 16:24-25)

This giving up of self rights hurts, right down where you live. As a matter of fact, the giving up of self rights is something nobody in his right mind ever contemplates—unless he happens to be a King's kid, interested in following the King's instructions for victorious living.

Quite a while ago, I said to the Lord, "Why is it that I am intermittently in turmoil? Why is it that every now and then I still get disturbed? I am a King's kid, and I know my position in the kingdom: I am completely and totally and eternally saved. You bought me and paid for me. My record is clear in the books of heaven. I will never have to account for my sins because my past record is under the blood of Jesus. I am right with God because you made me right. You even gave me your righteousness.

"Knowing all that, and knowing that this world is a training ground for something so much better, why should I ever be disturbed about anything? What is it that prevents me from completely, totally, and permanently resting in what you have done for me?"

The Lord gave me a one-word answer: "Possessiveness."

"Lord, I didn't realize that," I told Him. "I thought I had given up all my rights to you."

"Of course you didn't realize it," He agreed. "That is the trick in the trap of the enemy, to get you to thinking that you had given up everything to me."

I didn't understand.

"But Lord," I argued, "I started tithing, then went to double tithing, triple tithing, quadruple tithing, and now I'm tithing fifty percent. That's murder for a Scotchman like me, so it has to be your grace. As a matter of fact, all I have is yours. I'm just a steward, You are the owner. What more can you possibly want? What more is there?"

"Hill, that's fine—as far as it goes," He acknowledged, leaving me more mystified than ever.

"As far as it goes? You mean I can go farther than that?" I had visions of standing in a shivering soup line somewhere, stripped to my skivvies. But that's not what He had in mind.

"You can go farther than that," He affirmed. "You have given me all rights to your possessions. Now you can give me all rights to yourself."

That nearly blew my mind.

"You mean that I can no longer stand up for my own rights? Is that what you're trying to tell me?"

"That's exactly it," He said.

"But Lord, surely you don't want me to become a vegetable?"

"No, just a pauper, poverty-stricken in the area of your own rights."

That sounded like an echo of something I remembered reading in the Book of Matthew: "Blessed are the poor in spirit . . ." and I wasn't sure it sounded altogether good.

The Lord knew my thoughts, as usual. He always does.

"Hill, do you want to keep your ragtag rights to yourself, or do you want to live like a King's kid ought to—in total, continuous victory, as a continuous winner, without that occasional turmoil you were just telling me about? Which do you want most? First best or second best?"

I had to swallow hard on that one, but the choice seemed clear-cut. If I couldn't have victorious living *and* my own rights at the same time, I'd have to let my own rights go.

"Lord, that constant victory bit sounds best to me. So how do I go about giving up my rights to myself?"

I didn't see my self rights as something tangible I could just hand to Him on a silver platter. But when I came to that point of relinquishment, the Spirit began to show me. Foremost, I had to give up my leftover "religious" thinking that by doing a lot of "good works" I could make Brownie points to guarantee my admission to heaven. I had to admit that God's Word was plain on the subject. All my best righteousness would never be anything more than filthy rags in God's sight (Isa. 64:6).

God let me see this principle in my physical system. For many years my blood pressure had registered a whopping 90/50. That's practically the vanishing point. It was barely enough to kick a corpuscle through my arteries. I didn't have the strength to stand up to do anything. I had to learn to lean on Jesus and draw all my energy from Him—or else stay horizontal all the time.

God used all that to teach me that by myself, even loaded down with vitamins, I was unfit for anything. Unless I was drawing on His strength, I would fall flat on my face. As I learned that, in situation after situation, I gradually experienced release from ownership of my self rights, too.

It's true that I have not yet arrived. I still flare up and demonstrate my ownership of some self-held right. Anytime I *react* to a situation, trying to protect "my rights," I am showing that I am still handicapped by ownership. Whenever I *respond* instead, praising Jesus and asking, "What's in this for you, Lord?" I am evidencing stewardship.

Walking in the Spirit, victorious King's kid living, can be done successfully only by one who has given up ownership of everything and become a steward of God's riches in glory in the here and now.

Back in the days when I was an owner, I was always

having to add to my holdings to increase my so-called security. If the stock market went up a point, I had a fit because it would probably come back down sooner or later. People who are hanging on to worldly things for security are really down the tube these days. The market is eroding—that's what the brokers call it. God calls the process rust and moths. It amounts to the same thing in the end. When you're hanging on to soulish satisfactions, they always evaporate one way or another. They're never big enough. But looking unto Jesus as the owner and myself as the steward, I can say, "Lord, I really blew that one. How are you going to rescue me from this disaster, Lord? I admit I got us into this colossal goof-up, but because I'm just a dumb steward, I can't figure the way out. I'm looking to you for that."

The requirements for stewardship are not great intelligence or wisdom, but faithfulness to the Lord. If I'm being as faithful as I can be, when I fail, I can say, "Lord, I goofed even though I was doing the best I knew to do. Furthermore, if you don't remove from me the tendency to do my own thing to a greater degree, I'll probably do it just as poorly the next time. But I am offering myself as a container for your perfection. And if you'll consent to forgive me one more time and do your thing through me, it's got to get better."

Sure enough, it does get better. Every time I give up. And I'm learning to do that sooner and oftener.

As I do that more and more, I begin to experience the blessedness of the life of continual high victory in Jesus.

I've learned not to try to persuade billy-goat Christians...

13
How to Live in Victory
over Billy-Goat Christians

The *Manufacturer's Handbook* tells us how King's kids are to live in victory, but it is not a do-it-yourself manual. Instead, in it, God says to us, "Here's the way it's got to be for best results. But I know you can't do it on your own, kids. So, because I want you to experience my best for you, I'm going to send my Son Jesus to live in you and do these impossible things for you."

That takes out all the struggle and strain, which were never part of the master plan. The master plan is for us to rest in Jesus and let it happen. That's the way it has to be, because if we could struggle to make it happen, we'd be entitled to a little pinch of the glory.

The life style of a Christian, which means "little anointed one," is impossible unless we're anointed with His presence. There's no such thing as a plain ordinary believer, because each one is hand-picked, according to Jesus. He said,

Ye have not chosen me, but I have chosen you, and ordained you, that ye should go and bring forth fruit, and that your fruit should remain. (John 15:16)

This choosing of us for His purposes wasn't done after He saw what good guys we were, with our white socks and all that. He chose us before we were even in existence! Before our goodness—or even badness—had even happened. Scripture for this is found in Paul's letter to the Ephesians:

According as he hath chosen us in him [in Jesus]
before the foundation of the world, that we should
be holy and without blame before him in love. (1:4)

Not only has God chosen us, but He has provided all the power and equipment necessary for us to use in fulfilling the great commission. It is up to us to ask for it and to receive it.

When I first became a King's kid, I was ignorant of these things. I thought that just because I had invited Jesus to come into my heart and be my Savior, I had all I needed to live a victorious Christian life. But very early in the game, I found that there was no way I could keep His commandments. One of the commandments that I found spelled out over and over again in the *Manufacturer's Handbook* was the commandment to love one another (John 13:34-35; 15:12,17). Well, I tried. And I tried. I'd tie my stomach muscles in knots trying to psych myself up to love. But it didn't work, and I had to confess it to God.

"Lord," I told Him one morning, "your Word says I am to love one another and that I am to love you with everything I've got." I said that out loud, but I kind of whispered the next words, because I was half afraid He might belt me.

"Lord, there's no love in me for anybody," I confessed. I thought about how I had been sitting among the brethren with a fake toothpaste smile glued on that made my jaws ache.

When He didn't say anything immediately, I got real honest and came out with more of it.

"Lord, I don't even love you."

I wanted to hide under the table or behind a wall

84

somewhere so the bolt of lightning wouldn't hit me, but the lightning never came. God always seems to appreciate our honesty, even when the things we have to confess to Him are so raunchy they make our insides shrivel.

"Well! Finally! It's about time you got honest about it, Hill."

Since He felt that way about it, I decided it was time to let it all hang out.

"Furthermore, God, I don't think I will ever love you unless you do something about it yourself. There's just no love in me."

I fancied I heard all heaven cheering, the angels letting out a whoop of hallelujah joy: "Praise the Lord! Hill is leveling with himself for the first time!"

Well, God showed me that the love He wants to come forth from us is not supposed to be human love. It's the love He provides, the love He was talking about when He and His secretary put this in the Scripture:

> The love of God is shed abroad in our hearts by the
> Holy Ghost which is given unto us. (Rom. 5:5)

Since love wasn't being shed abroad in my heart, or in any of the rest of me, I began to suspect that the Holy Ghost was somehow missing from my life. I had run across other Scriptures, too, that indicated the same thing. One of them was a promise of Jesus in the Book of Acts:

> But ye shall receive power, after that the Holy
> Ghost is come upon you: and ye shall be witnesses
> unto me both in Jerusalem, and in all Judaea, and in
> Samaria, and unto the uttermost part of the earth.
> (1:8)

I didn't see any power operating in my life, and I knew I wasn't being a witness in my own backyard, much less in any of the faraway places the Scripture talked about. If I was to have love, power, and be a witness, after the Holy Ghost had come upon me, I was ready for Him to come upon me. And I was even readier after I found in First Corinthians 12 the list of gifts that the Holy Spirit had to offer: wisdom, knowledge, faith. . . . They sounded good; they sounded made-to-order for me. I wanted them all.

When I went to my pastor and told him my need and showed him these exciting passages promising God's provision to meet my need, he shook his head.

"Sorry, Hill," he said. "You received all the Holy Spirit you'll ever have at the moment you were born again."

According to my *Manufacturer's Handbook*, that was either a lie or else Jesus didn't know what He was talking about, because He said in Luke 11:13 that if we wanted the Holy Spirit, we could ask God for it and He would give it to us. That didn't sound to me like He was saying we have it already and we have to go struggling along on our powerless way and hope for the best.

I consulted other religious people, who were supposed to have all the answers, and they said that God had canceled all His supernatural arrangements when the disciples died off.

"God's power petered out when Peter petered out," they told me. As authority for their position, they cited an awesome twosome, Dr. Tinkling Cymbal and his co-laborer, Professor Sounding Brass. Somehow, I was not impressed, even though they had more degrees than a thermometer. I knew thermometers were competent to talk about the weather, but I doubted their authority in spiritual matters.

I found a lot of good churchgoers who claimed to believe the Bible, from cover to cover, but they didn't believe in getting too personal about what was written *between* the covers. They preferred not to talk about the supernatural. They had adopted a series of religious doctrines to protect them from the embarrassment of possible failure if they went crawling out on a limb and took God at His Word.

86

I had done some investigating on my own, and so I said, "Look, folks. Right here God says it, I believe it, and for me that settles it."

It didn't seem to settle it for them, however. They wanted to nitpick and hedge, smiling indulgently at my ignorance as they did so.

"Well," they agreed disarmingly, "of course He *said* it and it *used* to work, but it doesn't have to work any more because God has given us something better than supernatural means. More dependable. I mean, we have doctors, and wonder drugs, and hospitals—"

I quit trying to persuade them, and I decided to check these things out by trying them. If they were for today, they would work. If they were not, they wouldn't. It was that simple. Any laboratory technician knows how to check the validity of a formula. He puts the ingredients together and looks at the results. And I did that with the Word of God, taking it literally, trying it, and watching what happened.

For starters, I asked for and received the baptism in the Holy Spirit. When that Holy Ghost love began to be shed abroad in my heart, I lost my worst enemy. Before I received the baptism, just the thought of a certain man's initials would set my motor racing. Afterward, I wanted to go hug his neck.

The baptism brought new power and an ability to witness into my life, too, and the supernatural gifts came into operation, exactly as He had said they would.

Before many months had passed, I knew that casting out devils was for today, because I had seen it happen. I knew that speaking in tongues was for today, because I spoke in tongues myself. I knew that when believers laid hands on the sick, the sick recovered.

I carried that testimony in the middle of my back. In a 1954 tent meeting, Oral Roberts, a believer, had laid hands

87

on me, and I had recovered from a painful spinal ailment. Got a new spinal disk while I waited.

I hadn't accidentally taken up any snakes nor drunk any poison, but I didn't think I had to check out those signs. Jesus had kept His Word on the first three out of five of the Mark 16 signs that I had checked out, and I believed that if the occasion arose, I could count on His reliability on the others.

As I began to move in the flow of the Spirit, experiencing more and more of the joys of King's kid living, I saw some of the reasons why many Christians fail to enjoy the life style Jesus intends for all His children. Some of the roadblocks to the blessings of a more abundant life—ignorance, unbelief, impatience, unforgiveness, and false teaching—are solidly entrenched inside our thick skulls which are biased by our own thinking.

Bias is a principle that can be used to good advantage in electronic circuits. A little bit of negative energy can stop all flow of positive power. In the same way, a little bit of bias in the human mind can block everything positive. Blockheads are people who have let their minds be blocked by the negativism of false teaching or ignorance. Ignorance of the things of God comes through initial lack of information or through a biased, closed, unteachable, "religious" mind that has been brainwashed into thinking that God is less able and less capable today than He was in the beginning, when He made it all and set it into motion.

When bias comes into the mind, learning ability ceases, and the sound that comes off the tongue is a dead giveaway: "Yes, but—" That's the sound of a billy-goat Christian in action. Other bias signs are, "Don't you think . . . ?" and "What about this? What if that?"

Some King's kids try to straighten such people out and tell them how they really ought to think, what they really ought to believe, but invariably they get nowhere because they're dealing with unspiritual persons in terms of spiritual principles, and the two are incompatible (1 Cor. 2:14).

I've learned not to try to persuade billy-goat Christians or theologians of the truth of God's Word. I had heard that Dr. Tinkling Cymbal was claiming that God's arm of power had shriveled up into a little knot. Professor Sounding Brass had said that God was so weak He could no longer crush a strawberry. Instead, I put them on my icky prayer list.

"Lord, they're your problem. I'm glad I'm not required to straighten them out and make them believe like I do. I'm turning them over to you, asking that whenever they open their mouths to teach a false doctrine, you'll make them so miserable they can't stand it. Whenever they go out to tell people that you are weak in power, and that your arm is shortened and shriveled, clobber them with your truth. Make them so miserable that they can't tell a lie one more time."

That kind of prayer has been resulting in theologians getting saved right and left, and the saved ones are even coming into the fulness of the Holy Spirit, the only place where a victorious life is possible.

14

How to Live in Victory
over Footnote Theology

The normal supernatural life style of King's kids is described by Jesus himself in the closing verses of the Gospel according to Mark:

> And these signs shall follow them that believe; In my name shall they cast out devils; they shall speak with new tongues; they shall take up serpents; and if they drink any deadly thing, it shall not hurt them; they shall lay hands on the sick, and they shall recover. (16:17-18)

Is this passage in small print in your Bible? It doesn't matter. The Word of God works just as well in the small print of footnotes as it does in billboard-size letters at the top of the page.

Have you heard that these verses aren't in *all* the early manuscripts? Don't worry about that either. Being a researcher, I've checked these things out, and I've found that the verses are present in ninety-eight out of a hundred of the early manuscripts. It takes only one time around for God to say a thing, and I imagine the omission of those verses in a few manuscripts happened something like this:

Abie and Jakie were hard at work, copying the Scriptures, when the lunch whistle blew. It had been a long time since breakfast, so they knocked off to eat, leaving all their writing materials on their desks. While they were gone, one of Abie's kids came into the workroom and gave a little turn to the scroll of the Scripture they were copying. He knew he wasn't supposed to touch it, but boys will be boys.

The result of his mischief was that when Abie and Jakie came back from lunch, the last few verses of Mark that hadn't been copied yet were covered up. Not noticing that anything was wrong, they picked up their goosequills and started copying again at the place to which the scroll was turned, never dreaming that someone had tampered with their business. And so they missed the last words of Jesus as reported by Mark. Their manuscripts were incomplete, lacking Jesus' description of the signs that would follow King's kids when they were believing His Word and acting upon it.

Let's give a closer look at what these signs are. The first one Jesus mentions is casting out devils.

Casting out devils is an assignment that scares some people off, but it shouldn't, not if they're all prayed up. And it doesn't have to be a rowdy proceeding either. God can get rid of devils decently and in order if we're in tune with Him.

At a meeting recently, some folks introduced me to a woman who was in terrible condition. "She's demon-possessed," they said. "She really needs help. Will you go to work on her?"

"Hold it a minute," I told them. "How many people have already 'gone to work' on her?" They named many.

"You want me to work on her after all those have prayed for her without apparent results? I have a better idea," I said. "Let's all get together in Jesus' name and see what He wants to do about it."

I could see disappointment written all over them.

"But doesn't she have to throw up the demons?" they wanted to know.

"I couldn't tell you about that," I said. "Has she heaved some up already?"

"Oh, yes! Buckets and buckets full."

"And she still has demons to spare?"

"Apparently so."

Well, I admitted that could be possible. The Bible records one instance where Jesus cast two thousand demons out of one fellow, exactly the right number to fit into a herd of pigs grazing nearby (Matt. 8:28-32). The demons turned them into sub-aquatic pork chops in a hurry. It stands to reason that if a person has two thousand demons to start with, heaving up a few dozen into buckets hardly reduces the population enough to be noticeable. Maybe it gives the remaining demons more elbow room to romp around and increase the misery level of their host. It was clear that in the case before us, there was no use in our dabbling in demons by the bucketful.

"Tell you what," I suggested, "let's all go to lunch and claim God's promise about how if we agree on earth about anything, He'll do it for us in heaven (Matt. 18:19). Let's just ask Jesus to handle this situation."

We were in the midst of a CFO camp where not everybody understood about these things yet. I didn't want to scare any of them off before they had a chance to meet Jesus as Baptizer. That ruled out any heavy exorcism session such as the woman's friends seemed to be counting on so they could whistle, stomp, holler, and carry on without regard to the effect it might have had on the newcomers present. We need to be mindful of the needs of others.

The Bible tells us that a believer can tell a mountain to go jump in the lake and it will obey, but a King's kid who is sensitive to the needs of others will stop and consider the fact that somebody living on the other side of the lake might get wet if the mountain's nose-dive raises the water level a few feet. There's no glory for God in a spectacular sideshow if the work can be accomplished around a quiet lunch table.

Well, the woman's friends seemed to understand. They swallowed their disappointment at being cheated out of a chance to sell tickets for a real performance, and joined hands with me. We agreed that Jesus could handle the whole thing. I was counting on God's power going into action according to the Scripture that promises,

The accuser of our brethren is cast down. . . .
They overcame him by the blood of the Lamb, and
by the word of their testimony. (Rev. 12:10-11)

When we were seated at the lunch table, I took a good look at the sister with all the problems. She was wild, looked like she might fly into orbit at any minute. The other women were praying in the Spirit, and I began simply speaking to the demon-possessed woman as the Spirit gave me utterance, quoting verses of Scripture, giving her a simple word of testimony. Her ears were taking it all in, while her eyes darted around the table, trying to identify the source of the power coming against Satan within her. Slue Foot was angry and tormented because he couldn't get a handle on what we were doing. He'd had plenty of dealings with motor-mouth Christians, and he knew how to avoid them, but this was all such undercover warfare, so quiet and peaceable, he didn't know who was fighting him.

All this went on for about ten minutes, and suddenly I could see something like a black veil being removed from the woman's face. She started to glow as the glory of God came over her, and she opened her mouth to say, "What happened?"

She had been delivered, completely delivered from the

demons that were oppressing her, and apart from our table, not another person in the place knew that anything had been going on. We had broken the powers of darkness simply by interceding in the Spirit. Jesus was victorious, as always.

We don't necessarily have to make a big scene to cast out demons. Sometimes people do, because they think it makes them look religious. Satan probably gets a laugh out of such ineffectual carryings-on, and God waits patiently for them to grow up.

Can Christians be possessed by demons? Do you have demons—or do they have you? I hear these questions argued a lot in King's kid circles. I don't care what you call it—possession, oppression, or what—but I know that if you do anything to encourage the operation of the boys in black in your life, the results are highly detrimental. While you're arguing about terminology, I'll be dealing with the demons, which is much more beneficial, in addition to being obedient to Jesus (Mark 16:17).

Because the casting out of devils is the first thing Jesus mentions in the Mark 16 passage, someone could argue that that's the first thing King's kids ought to do when they come on the scene, before they do anything else. The implication is that demons are to be found almost everywhere, and that's why we get rid of them first. Sometimes, I admit, it takes more than just serving notice on Slue Foot to get rid of him, but that's a starter.

For this kind of spiritual warfare, it is vital that we keep a clear channel open to God for His instructions to come through, and for all His gifts to be operating through us. If the channel isn't clear, we're likely to get taken apart. Don't get into heavy caliber warfare unless your equipment is in good working order.

Jesus is not talking about some kooky "deliverance ministry." He is not telling us to make a witch hunt of our

94

Christianity. He is simply telling us that He has given us such authority, that when we walk on the scene we can serve notice on Slue Foot that his lease is up and that he will have to look for greener pastures somewhere else. It's a principle of physics and of life that where light is, no darkness can stay. Darkness has to take off if it doesn't want to be wiped out.

Back in 1954, in the beginning of my King's kid days, I had more ignorance about these things than should have existed on the entire face of the earth. To get rid of Satan, I didn't know I could just tell him, in Jesus' name, to take off and he would have to do it. I must have thought he was deaf or something. I'd rant and rave and try to stomp his tail. I couldn't see him, of course, so I didn't know where his tail was, but I'd try to visualize his long red underwear and stomp in the direction of the buttons on the back seat. But I've learned many things since those days, among them that the Bible doesn't talk about Satan in terms of long red underwear, but in terms of an angel of light. That's why God gave us the Holy Spirit gift of discernment (1 Cor. 12:10), so we could pick him out of a crowd.

I've also learned that not every sickness, ailment, or problem in human life is caused by evil spirits. A whole lot more of them are caused by our failure to believe the Word of God and follow His instructions.

The second sign that would follow believers, according to Jesus, is that they would speak with new tongues. They would get on the hot line to heaven, reporting for duty in the only language the devil can't wiretap.

Some people won't pray in tongues because they say, "Brother So and So prays in tongues so pretty, and I don't want to pray in tongues until I can pray as pretty as he does." One sister complained, "All I have is two grunts and a squeak," but if she'd go ahead and use what God has already given her, He'd give her more. I've heard of a tribe whose entire language for either praising God, or saying, "Pass the biscuits," and everything else, has only ten grunts for a total vocabulary. But they get by.

One sister said, "All I can do is cluck."

"Hallelujah!" I told her. "Go ahead and cluck. That's all a mama hen has to bring up her chicks with, and some of them turn into pretty healthy flocks. Don't complain about what you have, use it. If God finds you faithful over a little, maybe He'll give you a whole bunch more."

The bit in this Scripture about picking up snakes and drinking deadly poison bothers believers sometimes. A young man came to me at a conference one day where we were talking about some of these things. He asked me, "What about picking up snakes?"

"Feel free," I told him. "Do you happen to have any with you?"

It turned out that he didn't. The way I read the Bible, I find that Paul took up a poisonous snake accidentally one day when he was picking up firewood. The snake fastened itself to Paul's hand, but instead of dropping dead, Paul flipped the snake into the fire where it got dead instead (Acts 28). Paul just kept on about the Lord's business.

I don't see that Paul or any of the rest of the disciples ever deliberately picked up poisonous snakes. So in the light of Scripture, I take this part of Mark 16:18 as God's promise that if I encounter anything deadly when I'm on the King's business, it won't be able to harm me. King's kids don't fool with snakes, but if snakes fool with them, they'd better watch out. We can do them in, in the name of Jesus.

Many who call themselves believers refuse to have anything to do with these signs that Jesus himself said would follow wherever they went. Why do they hang back from being doers of the Word once they've heard it? There are several reasons. Unbelief, always encouraged by Slue Foot, is one. Another is the deadly sin of pride.

Pride keeps some of us from laying hands on the sick. We're afraid we might spoil our religious image. "Well, but what if I lay my hands on the sick and they get sicker or maybe even drop dead? What would happen to my reputation as a great healer?"

It's not our reputation that's at stake. Our reputation is already below zero. Jesus made himself of no reputation (Phil. 2:7), and He tells us to follow Him (John 21:19). When we have no reputation to protect, we're more likely to do what He tells us to do, and He will do the rest. He tells us to lay our hands on sick folks in His name, and they'll recover. Pride has no place in that transaction.

What if you lay hands on someone and he dies the next day? That's not your responsibility. Just lay hands on the next one, and if you keep on doing that, eventually you'll catch one who will live through your prayers.

Act like it and you'll begin to feel like it; and the more you feel like it, the more you'll act like it. It's regenerative, cumulative, increasing all the time, and finally you get the message, "We *are* King's kids! This is what it's all about. The King of the universe is within me, and I'm going to show Him forth without. I'm going to live the victory."

The first time I laid hands on a sick person, everything within me screamed, "Don't do it! Who do you think you are?"

The right answer came from me, for once: "I'm a child of the King, that's who I am. And I have it direct from God that I'm to lay hands on the sick." Then I threw Slue Foot's question back at him: "You're the big loud mouth hollering in my ear; who do you think *you* are?"

I knew my rights and privileges as a King's kid and watched him get run off the premises.

Everything God gives us is for one purpose—to give away as rapidly as possible to serve the need of another person. That makes room for more, and when we learn to give away fast enough, we become a flowing channel of His grace, a pipeline for His blessings to minister to the needs of others. Being a doer of the Word is being such a pipeline. If you've never laid hands on the sick, it's about time you started. In this passage, Jesus doesn't even say that we have to pray for them, He just says we are to touch them and the work will be done. If we're following His instructions, we're praying without ceasing already (1 Thess. 5:17).

One day I was considering the order of the "signs following" in these verses, and I saw that we generally do everything backward. The order specified is: (1) cast out devils, (2) pray with new tongues, and (3) lay hands on the sick. We're far more likely to romp in, lay hands on the sick first, pray with tongues next, and then try to get rid of the devil. But we've already telegraphed our punches to him, and he's far more deeply buried than ever. Next time, try it frontward and see if the results are improved. Tell Satan to take off, then pray in tongues on the hotline to heaven. It may be that God will give you further instructions, a word of knowledge or wisdom in terms of a revelation of the true state of affairs. Next, He will give the gift of faith to glue it all together. And when you lay hands on the sick, maybe they'll be healed already because you've been faithful to follow God's procedure. His way is worth trying. And it's the only way with guaranteed victory built in.

15

How to Live in Victory
over Deadly Dispensationalism

Many times people are not healed because the enemy talks folks into believing that the Scriptures promising healing are not for today. I encountered a situation like that one day in Knoxville, Tennessee. I had gone up there for a weekend of bragging on Jesus, and I stayed in the home of a local family who were staunch Methodists.

At the end of our first session together, I noticed that the lady of the house was having a good bit of difficulty in getting out of her chair. I can recognize back trouble at the creak of a vertebra, because I was in misery with a disintegrated disk until Jesus gave me a new one.

I said to the woman, "Excuse me, but do you have a pain in your back?"

She smiled and nodded her head.

"All the time," she admitted. "I was in a car accident some years ago, and my nerves, my bones, and my muscles were left all churned up together in my spine. Doctors have done all they can, and they tell me that without morphine, I'll be in pain the rest of my life. Since I'm a Christian, I refuse to put morphine in my body, so I guess I'll just have to bear the pain."

She didn't look as if pain was a hobby she wanted to pursue that long.

"I don't know what your theology says," I told her, "but I can't go along with it because of what Jesus said in Mark 16:17-18. Have you ever noticed those verses?"

Well, she didn't remember that she had, especially, and so we opened the *Manufacturer's Handbook* and took a look at them.

> These signs shall follow them that believe; In my
> name . . . they shall lay hands on the sick, and they
> shall recover.

The Scripture said some other things, too, but at that moment our needs tuned us in to the healing portion of the promise.

"Had you ever noticed that?" I asked her.

"Well, now that you mention it, I do recall having heard that Scripture before. That was wonderful for the early church. They really had it good, didn't they?"

"Yes," I agreed, "but that Scripture is for today, too."

"Oh, no," she laughed. "You can't believe that. Why, such things don't happen today. At least I've never heard of them happening. That Scripture was canceled out when the disciples died out."

She looked at me as if she was giving *me* the good news. But I didn't buy it, because I knew better.

"How do you know the Scripture won't work for today?" I asked her. "Tell me, have you ever tried it?"

"Well, er—ah, no, of course not," she stammered. Being interpreted, those words were an evasive, "I wish you hadn't brought that up. It bugs my doctrine. My theology is at stake, and I must defend it at all costs." Her theology left no room for spiritual growth.

"I've heard that Scripture interpreted in all kinds of

ways," she said, and she proceeded to give me a few of them. But I didn't listen past the first one—an oldie. She'd heard that that passage was missing from some early manuscripts and therefore it appeared only in a footnote in some modern translations of the Bible.

"What's the matter?" I said. "Don't you think God's Word can work from the small print of a footnote?"

She didn't have a ready answer for that one. No one had asked her in quite that way before, and I could see she was giving the matter a little thought. Since she was a housewife, I figured maybe a kitchen analogy would help.

"Do you have a cookbook in your home?" I asked her.

"Oh, yes, several of them," she acknowledged, brightening because she thought I had changed the theology-threatening subject to one with which she was on more familiar ground.

"When you read a recipe on how to make an apple pie," I said, "do you read the list of ingredients and ask, 'Now, how should that be interpreted? I wonder what they mean when they say "Two cups of flour." ' Or do you just measure out the flour, dump it in the bowl, and proceed from there?"

"Why," she said, laughing kind of nervously, "I just follow the recipe."

"Even if the cookbook is kind of old? Or the print is rather small?" I crowded her a little. "Do you take it for granted that the same ingredients will produce the same results they used to?" She nodded rather hesitantly, and I could see she knew what I was getting at.

"Did you ever think of following the Mark 16:17-18 recipe for healing with the same unquestioning faith and obedience?"

"Well, no—" I could tell from the tone of her voice that she was weakening.

The Holy Spirit gave me permission to move in for the kill.

"Look, lady, is pain your hobby?"

"No."

"Would you like to get rid of it?"

"Yes."

All the theory was shoved aside for the moment.

"All right. Sit in the prayer chair and we'll pray for you according to the directions."

At that point, I could see that while she didn't want to subject herself to something so foolish looking, her live pain had suddenly overcome her dead dispensationalist doctrine.

I kept the Book open so she could follow along and see that we were following the instructions exactly.

"First, let's see if we have all the necessary ingredients: 'These signs shall follow them that believe.' Do we have any believers here?"

Her husband and her son held their hands in the air, so we checked that off.

"They shall lay hands on the sick," I read on. "We have several pairs of hands," I said. "Do we have anybody sick?"

The woman was entering into the spirit of the thing now, and she stuck her hand up in the air.

"All right, we have a sick person. And we've got the name of Jesus because He gave us power of attorney to use His name."

There was some talk then about how she didn't have that much faith. I explained to her that her faith level was probably not too far below the faith level of Lazarus when he had been dead four days. Jesus raised him anyway, and since He told us we would do the same things He had done and even greater things (John 14:12), we could probably make do with the measure of faith that God has given every man—and woman (Rom. 12:3).

The woman gave us permission to proceed then, and the three of us laid six hands on her and prayed the simplest

102

prayer we could think of:

"Lord Jesus, in obedience to your Word, and in the power of your name, we're laying hands on this sick person. We thank you for healing her according to your promise. Amen."

Healing doesn't have to be an emotional deal, but for some reason, that woman got emotional all of a sudden. She erupted from her chair shouting, "I felt it! I felt it! I'm healed, I'm healed! Glory to God!"

She was so stirred up, I thought we might have to take some measures to calm her down. But eventually she quieted down on her own. She's still so impressed by how perfectly God's Word works today when we apply it to the appropriate situation that she and her husband call me up every now and then to rejoice over the phone at the goodness of God.

"Brother, I'm still healed!" she exclaims.

"Of course you are," I tell her. "When God does a thing, He does it to last. No temporary messing around. He always does a permanent, perfect, foolproof job."

All we did was take the recipe for healing and put together the active ingredients called for, and God did the work. We acted on His Word, did our part, and watched Him do His.

God's instruction to King's kids is, "Put your action where my Word is, and you'll see it happen. Show your faith by acting as if what I say is true. The world will be a different place because of it."

Our God is vitally interested in the things that glorify Him and bless His people. When we follow His directions, we get the best. God's Word works when we try it, and it always brings victory.

103

For three years he's been stumbling around blind as a bat.

16
How to Live in Victory
over Eyeball Ailments and Other Imperfections

It is thrilling to read the promises of God and know they're written by one who is absolutely dependable. His promises can be read and acted upon with the full assurance that they'll produce results. God is truthful.

Why is it then that we don't always see things happen as soon as we ask for them? Many are puzzled when they pray about a thing, have full assurance from God, a witness of the Spirit with goose bumps galore, but nothing happens as far as they can see.

I have thought a lot about these things and wondered why it was that sometimes when I prayed for a person, I could see that they were instantly healed. At other times, they were dead twenty-four hours later. But I've not come up with any pat explanations to satisfy my educated idiot box. The results have to remain God's department. If God wants me to know why, He'll tell me. Otherwise, maybe it's none of my business. It *is* my business to follow Him.

Nevertheless, I have encountered a few principles about these things which seem to apply in some cases.

Right after I was saved, I was red hot. I always expected

people to want to be healed, and I always expected to see them healed on the spot—as soon as I, and whoever was praying with me, had said Amen.

One of the first things I learned about healing is that not everybody wants to be healed. Lots of folks enjoy the fringe benefits of poor health. There's no better way to throw a pity party and have everybody for miles around commiserating with you than to be under the weather with a physical ailment or affliction. Some people can get a lot of mileage out of an ingrown toenail. They can let it be known that they're bearing their cross.

Some even say they believe it is God's will for them to be sick. Of course, if they really believed that, they wouldn't call the doctor and try to get well through his skill and training. They wouldn't take medicines designed to correct their condition.

Jesus used to ask people, "Wilt thou be made whole?" (John 5:6). That's a key in many situations. Wholeness is not the same thing as healing. Wholeness has to do with the total person—soul, spirit, and body. Healing has to do with patching up the old garment of the body. When Jesus told the lepers to go and show themselves to the priests (Luke 17:14), their healings were manifested when they were on their way. When He told the man who had palsy, "Arise, take up thy bed, and go unto thine house" (Matt. 9:6), He was requiring action of him, too, and as his body responded in obedience, the healing was made manifest. To be well, we have to be willing to do the things that health would require of us.

Another principle that became very meaningful to me in all this healing business is the one Jesus described in these words:

Verily I say unto you, Whatsoever ye shall bind on earth shall be bound in heaven: and whatsoever ye

shall loose on earth shall be loosed in heaven.
(Matt. 18:18)

Anything I bind on earth, by my anxiety in trying to force it to happen *now*, is unlikely to happen at all. Trying to push God, to force Him to do something, is the pattern of the glory glutton, who is trying to steal the glory from God. It never works. God doesn't need our help, He needs our surrender. He works in the midst of the need we can't meet with what we term "our own resources."

Sometimes we make the mistake of trying to make it happen, trying to help God so that His image won't be tarnished. I've seen that sometimes where men say they are "claiming the promises."

One of the members of our fellowship in Baltimore said, "God told me He's going to heal my eyes," and he threw away his glasses. For three years, he's been stumbling around blind as a bat. He can hardly shave himself without putting a tourniquet around his neck. He can't even read his Bible. Maybe that's all right for him, but it's not good enough for me. Who needs to be tripping over people all the time, having to be picked up off the floor. I keep my glasses on so I can read my Bible every day. And part of what I read says that when believers lay hands on the sick, they shall recover (Mark 16:17-18). But it doesn't say how soon after the laying on of hands the perfect recovery will come. We know it will show up sometime, since God says so. But there's a fullness of time factor in His dealing with men that has to be left in the equation if we don't want confusion to result.

Have you ever thought that it would be advantageous for God's people if we saw miracles immediately every time we prayed? Have you thought it would convince more people of the presence and power of God if miracles popped out every time Christians opened their mouths?

Well, think again. Miracles happened continually in Jesus'

day, and they didn't persuade everybody. The Pharisees kept telling Him He was out of line to do such tricks on the sabbath day, and they got Him killed for His trouble.

In the Old Testament, when God was leading the children of Israel through the wilderness, every mouthful of food was a miracle of manna straight from heaven. And their clothing lasted for forty years without wearing out. They walked the whole way, and nobody got a hole in his shoe or a blister on his heel. When they ran short of water, God let water flow out of a rock. When they got tired of manna, He sent quail by the carload. Everything they asked for, He gave them instantly. But it never satisfied them. Nitpicking and complaining were their constant activities; motor-mouthing against Moses, which was the same as motor-mouthing against God.

Instant answers to prayer require no faith at all, and so their faith was never exercised during a waiting period. They prayed the prayer; they ate the answer. Just like that.

"So what else is new?" became their attitude before long. And eventually, they couldn't do anything but complain about the service.

Finally, God got disgusted with them, He said, "Drop dead." And they did. Thousands of them dropped dead in the wilderness.

"One thing I can't stand," God said, "is murmuring, complaining Christians." God didn't want to kill off His people, but He had no choice. When we begin to complain, find fault, or react in other negative ways to every blessing of God, we drain the life right out of ourselves. A goof-proof recipe for do-it-yourself destruction is: gripe your head off, complain your heart out. The Israelites dropped dead by their very best efforts to straighten Moses out, which was the same thing as telling God what to do, because Moses was getting his instructions from the one on high all along.

God says over and over again in His holy Word, "If only my people would rejoice and praise me for my goodness to them, then I could work through their praise and thanksgiving to give them the good things they want." But the Israelites were fearful instead, afraid that God was going to fail them. They could never enjoy the full victory of kingdom living until they learned the faith and patience that could develop when they experienced something other than instant answers to prayer.

God has shown me at least one other benefit of healing miracles that are delayed:

In connection with a laboratory experiment, I shot the vision out of my left eye with a high-intensity light beam, similar to a laser beam. It wasn't a direct hit, or it would have cooked my brain, but it was direct enough and powerful enough to disintegrate the retina in my left eye. The peripheral vision is still there, but I have no vision at all in the middle of it. Doctors at Johns Hopkins in Baltimore have declared the eye medically hopeless. I'm on the records in the state of Maryland as having 20/200 vision in that eye.

When I show up before the board of medical examiners with 20/20 vision in both eyeballs, Jesus will get all the glory. If it had happened immediately, people would have said, "Oh, wrong diagnosis, huh?" and He wouldn't have been glorified at all. I'm in no hurry, if God isn't.

The insurance people came to me one day and said, "We're ready to handle your claim for loss of vision in that left eye of yours. We can settle out of court without any further discussion, because it's obvious that you're medically incurable."

I was ready to go along with them, but the Spirit of the Lord checked me.

"No, Hill. I want you to go to court. How else are a lot of pagans to hear your testimony of what I'm going to do? An out-of-court settlement won't be good enough in this case. Go through the whole procedure so I can glorify my name. This is an opportunity for someone to hear about me."

Well, I did what He said, and the affair is all settled—for now. I'm looking forward to the day when I'll go back to them and say, "Here's a refund on that insurance payment. I can't keep it legally, because you see, I'm not blind any more. Test my eye if you don't believe it." I can just see them keeling over like a row of dominoes when my vision tests 20/20 in both eyes.

God's fullness of time varies in every situation. When you plant the seed of an oak tree, a little acorn, five years later you won't see much more than a little stem poking out of the ground. It won't look as if it can ever amount to anything. But a hundred years from now, the beams that have come from it could be holding up a country barn. Plant a poplar seed, and in five years you'll have a big tree. But there will be no strength or resilience to it. Any little storm will snap it. Knowing these things, I have no interest in rushing God. His timetable suits me better than my own.

Since I have been prayed for about my eye situation, and I know God wants me to be perfect, which has to include perfect eyes, I thank Him every day for my healing. I know "these signs will follow" because His Word says so. Since His Word doesn't specify exactly *when* it will happen, I'm waiting. Some morning I'll start to put on my glasses and realize that I don't need them anymore. Until then, I praise God for the glasses that help me see.

Recently I heard about a man who praised God for everything he had, including a capped tooth that gave him trouble from time to time. One day the cap popped off, and there was a God-made filling out of natural materials underneath. The man didn't need the cap anymore.

A cap on a tooth is a usable arrangement, but a brand-new

tooth underneath it is even better. Now that person didn't pull off the cap and throw it away and sit down to wait until he got a new tooth. He just went about his business, which happened to include a lot of praising the Lord, since he was a King's kid. He let the new tooth happen in the fullness of God's time.

God will do what He wants to do. If we try to help Him do it, so we can get a little credit ourselves, a little pinch of glory, He won't do it. If He works too quickly, I might fall into the trap of thinking that *God and I* can do something. Pretty soon, I'll think that *I and God* can do something. The next step will be to think that *I'm* the indispensable partner in the arrangement and that God is helpless without me. Finally, I'll be thinking, "Who needs God?" That's the progression that tends to develop when our prayers are answered too quickly. God may employ delaying measures sometimes just to keep us in line.

Sometimes healing results are not in the offing because somebody has the idea that the signs mentioned in Mark 16:17-18 shall follow only those believers who are especially anointed for particular ministries among God's people. That's not what the Bible says, however. All believers are King's kids, assigned to special duty to go and represent God in every area of life, in every experience, in every situation. When we apply the Word of God to the situation, we can watch Him happen—in the fullness of time.

Another common mistake among King's kids who want "these signs" to follow them is one I committed frequently in my early King's kid days, the sin of condemnation.

If you were wearing glasses, I'd go up to you and say, "Brother, you must have some kind of sin in your life." I was a walking menace of condemnation because I had fallen for a devilish doctrine that says sinners never have anything good happen to them, and people without sin never have anything bad happen to them. Of course, it isn't true, but people made up the doctrine just the same, way back in the Old Testament, and it's still hanging around.

Remember Job's friends? They came to him and suggested that if he would quit his sinning, things would get better for him. Because he didn't know any sin to quit, things stayed worse instead of getting better. Finally his wife got so disgusted with him, she said, "Why don't you curse God and die?" (2:9).

Job didn't understand what was going on, but he resolved to hang in there with God if it cost him his life:

Though he slay me, yet will I trust in him. (13:15)

In the end, Job was thoroughly vindicated, and God gave him prosperity beyond anything he had had before.

God seems to be trying to get us all to the point where we'll depend on Him no matter what happens. And since He is sovereign God, He is free to do exactly what He chooses. And to do it the way He chooses.

Some people say that a sick person can't be healed unless he himself has the faith for it. But this is not what I find in my *Manufacturer's Handbook*. In some cases, the faith of the sick person is mentioned, in some cases the faith of an intercessor is mentioned, in other cases faith—or lack of faith—is not mentioned at all.

In his first book, Doctor Luke reported an interesting case history involving a man with a physical ailment:

And, behold, men brought in a bed a man which was taken with a palsy: and they sought means to bring him in, and to lay him before him. And when they could not find by what way they might bring him in because of the multitude, they went upon the housetop, and let him down through the tiling with his couch into the midst before Jesus. And when he saw their faith, he said unto him, Man, thy sins are forgiven thee. (5:18-20)

When Jesus looked up and saw the faith of the men on the roof, He healed the man who was before Him. Apparently He paid no attention to the faith—or lack of faith—of the person on the couch. This is just one of a number of scriptural instances of healing where the faith of a sick person is not so much as mentioned. The faith of the man's friends was sufficient to get the job done.

After it happened, the scribes and the Pharisees began to reason among themselves (v. 21). It hit their think tanks, and that's where trouble usually sets in. When anything spiritual gets into the human mind, and is allowed to roam around there, it usually gets mixed up with unbelief. Anything mixed with unbelief instead of with faith is likely to produce something second best, such as, "Yes, but—" "Don't you think—" or "Healing was for back in those days." Well, I'm glad it was for those days, too. Praise God that it was, but healing hasn't been canceled out yet, because ailments haven't been canceled out yet.

The unbelief of the Pharisees was expressed like this:

Who is this which speaketh blasphemies? Who can forgive sins, but God alone? (v.21)

The Pharisees knew that if sickness had to do with sin, healing would have to do with forgiveness. They never questioned the fact that sin was behind the man's palsy. But they couldn't buy the fact that Jesus was so one with God that He could do things only God could do, things like forgiving sin. As always, Jesus knew what they were thinking:

When Jesus perceived their thoughts, he answering said unto them, What reason ye in your hearts? Whether it is easier, to say, Thy sins be forgiven thee; or to say, Rise up and walk? But that ye may know that the Son of man hath power upon earth to forgive sins, (he said unto the sick of the palsy,) I say unto thee, Arise, and take up thy couch, and go into thine house. And immediately he rose up before them, and took up that whereon he lay, and departed to his own house, glorifying God. (vv. 22-25)

Faith and obedience were the two stages of this healing. There was the faith of the man's friends in bringing him and letting him down through the roof into the presence of Jesus. There was the obedience of the sick person to get up and put his healing into action. If he'd said, "Now, er, ah, I'm a dispensationalist. These things just aren't being done anymore," he'd still be on his couch. But he mixed the good news with a faith that, like Abraham's, was manifested in obedience, and he got up and went home a well man, leaving the Pharisees sweeping up their eyeballs.

17
How to Live in Victory
over Divisive Disagreements

Another principle of healing is suggested in the Scripture where Jesus promises,

> Again I say unto you, That if two of you shall agree on earth as touching any thing that they shall ask, it shall be done for them of my Father which is in heaven. (Matt. 18:19)

Among the human race, even among those who have experienced miracles of His healing power, we often find the disagreements that divide instead of the agreement that is a channel for further blessing.

Examine the case of two men who met outside a church one morning. One of them said to the other, "How long have you attended this church?"

"This is my very first time," the second man replied. "How about you?"

"It's my first time, too," the first man acknowledged. And then he asked a further question: "Where did you attend church before you came here?"

"Never went before today. This is the first time I've ever gone to any church."

"That's amazing! I've never gone to another church either. How come you never went before?"

"Well, you see, I was born a blind beggar, and people don't take blind beggars to church much. They park us out somewhere along the road and give us a cup of pencils so we can beg for our living. How was it with you, brother?"

The other guy was shaking his head, marveling that they had so much in common, because he had been a blind beggar, too. The men shook hands, patted each other on the back, and rejoiced together before they continued sharing their stories.

"By the way," the first beggar began, "would you mind telling me what happened? You said you were born blind. How did you get healed?"

"Well," the second beggar told the first, "part of this is hearsay, because of course I couldn't *see* what was going on, but they tell me that a man named Jesus was coming along the road. When He got to me, He stopped and reached down on the ground and picked up a handful of dirt. Then He spit into the dirt, stirred it around a little, plastered it on my eyes, and the next thing I knew, light was streaming in. I could see!"

The first beggar was jumping up and down excitedly, bursting with eagerness to tell how it was with him.

"What a coincidence!" he shouted. "That same man, the one they call Jesus, is the one who came along and touched me, too, and all of a sudden I could see!"

Both men had a glory fit right then and there on the sidewalk. Two formerly blind beggars restored to 20/20 vision rejoiced together at the goodness of God, hugging, crying, and carrying on for a good while, apparently not worrying about the other people streaming past them on the sidewalk. But then a faintly puzzled look came into the eyes of the second beggar, and he stopped rejoicing to peer

116

intently at the other guy.

"Tell me again how it was with you." He listened very carefully as the first beggar repeated his story, then asked, "You mean this Jesus just touched you? He didn't put mud in your eyes or anything like that?"

The first beggar interrupted his rejoicing to say, "That's right. He just touched me. No mud, no medicine, just His touch, and I was well all over."

The second beggar backed away, a disgusted look replacing the joyful smile that had been on his face.

"I hate to tell you, man," he said, "but if Jesus didn't put mud on your eyes, you're not really healed. It's just your imagination. A case of wishful thinking. By tomorrow morning, you'll probably be blind as a bat again, just the way you were before."

After a few minutes of heated argument, the beggars parted, enemies for life. And since the church they had attended that morning didn't believe that Jesus could heal, the men who had received their sight started two new denominations—the Mudites and the anti-Mudites, emphasizing healing techniques instead of the Healer. That's a pretty good illustration of what invariably happens when folks insist on being religious, trying to explain the things of God instead of just reporting on them.

King's kids aren't required to explain anything. They just report, as witnesses to what Jesus has done. They don't set up doctrines that divide; they dwell in the rejoicing which unites. And because they don't tell God how to work His signs and wonders, they have the joy of seeing more of them than anybody else.

18
How to Live in Victory
with a Tiny Bed and an ENORMOUS Bedmate

Nearly two thousand years ago, Jesus sent the seventy out by twos (Luke 10:1), and when they returned, they reported joyfully that even the demons obeyed them when they used His name (Luke 10:17). Jesus promised that there would be unlimited power available to be channeled through two King's kids when they were about His business:

> If two of you shall agree on earth as touching any thing that they shall ask, it shall be done for them of my Father which is in heaven. For where two or three are gathered together in my name, there am I in the midst of them. (Matt. 18:19-20)

I myself have had the opportunity to travel about as half of a pair sent out by Jesus. It has gotten me into some highly interesting situations.

It was my privilege to travel one time with Tommy Tyson. He was a pretty well filled-out man back then, about as wide as I am tall. One day we arrived in the area of Grand Rapids, Michigan, where Tommy was to preach a revival. I was to be with him for a week there. Upon our arrival, the pastor said, "One of the church families has offered to put you fellows

118

up."

That was fine. We appreciated accommodations being prepared for us.

The pastor took us out to the farmhouse that was to be our home for the week. The lady of the house led us upstairs—and then up another pair of stairs, into the attic. By the time we reached the top, I had begun to disbelieve that warm air rises, because the higher we climbed, the icier my bones got. It was somewhere around twenty-eight below zero outside, and considerably chillier than that inside, it seemed to me.

When we reached the top of the flights of stairs, our hostess shoved open a door, and pointed into a corner of the attic.

"There's your bed," she said. "I do hope you'll be comfortable here." I pegged her right then as someone who believed in miracles. She turned, closed the door on us, and went back downstairs to thaw out by the fireplace.

I looked at Tommy, Tommy looked at me. We both stared in disbelief at the bed we were to share. King-size beds hadn't been invented yet, as far as I know, and queen-size was still unheard of. If we had been giving the matter any thought, we'd probably have expected to have a twin bed apiece or maybe a regulation-size double bed to share.

We'd have been wrong in either case. What there was, shoved over against the well-ventilated eaves, was the tiniest three-quarter-size bed I've ever seen.

There's nothing that will teach you cooperation with your traveling partner more quickly or more thoroughly than the privilege of sharing such a bed under such circumstances. Early in the week I learned that if I didn't turn over every time Tommy did, in perfect synchronization, holding onto the covers for dear life, I'd be left naked and shivering in my pajamas. By the second night, I was a past master at the kind of cooperation that was necessary if I was to survive the week.

I learned another thing, too. If I didn't go to snoring first, it would be almost impossible for me to get to snoring at all.

I began to understand that Jesus sent them out two by two for a purpose—so they would learn to work together in harmony. In the midst of our perfect agreement about the wisdom of bedtime harmony (my very survival depended on it), we were having the joy of introducing others to Jesus. It made the unluxury of a crowded bed in a polar-bear climate seem hardly worth mentioning by comparison.

Maybe one reason Paul learned to be so content in the midst of otherwise raunchy circumstances (Phil. 4:11) had something to do with all the fruit-bearing that resulted when he praised God, no matter what.

19
How to Live in Victory
over Spiritual Drought

The first psalm contains about the best instruction for
fruit-bearing that I know of in any part of the Bible:
> Blessed is the man that walketh not in the counsel
> of the ungodly, nor standeth in the way of sinners,
> nor sitteth in the seat of the scornful. (v. 1)

This first verse contains what could be an accurate
description of the people all around you in a denominational
church. Some congregations are pretty messy, filled with
saints and ungodly people—sinners and scorners. A
mixed bag. It's a lot more fun to belong to a little hallelujah
100-percent-saved group, but there's not much potential for
bringing forth fruit in a mutual admiration society. True
disciples can stay in whatever church God has placed them,
and be blessed to bring forth fruit for Him right where they
are.

God so delights in one sold-out King's kid in the midst of a
fouled-up, miserable, unbelieving congregation, that if he
stays there and does as God directs, he'll begin to see things
happen. That doesn't mean that God might not lead someone
out of a church for a season, to teach him something, but

chances are He will be sending him right back where he came from after he's learned a thing or two.

But his delight is in the law of the LORD, and in his
law doth he meditate day and night. (v. 2)

A blessed man is one who is in an enviable position. According to the psalmist, this is a man who so delights in the law of the Lord that he meditates on the pure Word day and night. He thinks about God's Word more often than just between programs, or on his way to the kitchen during commercial breaks. If he mixes that meditation with any other additive—pills, tranquilizers, chemicals in the system, the boob tube—he won't get the same effect. The benefits will be diluted to some level below the point of blessedness.

Many people find the Bible such a drag that it practically kills them to spend fifteen minutes a day reading it because they have spoiled their appetite for good food by partaking of so much junk from the world—TV, movies, worldly books and magazines. They are like the little kid who eats so many cookies and so much candy that he can't enjoy vegetables and fruits that are good for him. And so he stays anemic and sickly instead of vigorous and victorious.

When a person finds his delight in the law of the Lord and meditates in that law day and night, that doesn't mean that he keeps his nose in the *Manufacturer's Handbook*, tripping over dogs and people, running into lampposts, colliding with doors, fireplugs, and all that. He takes a good bite of the Scripture in the morning, chews on it all day long with his eyes open, and thinks about it all night with his eyes closed. In the midst of that meditation, God begins to show him some things he hadn't seen at first glance.

When I follow this directive, I have Scripture sloshing around inside of me and oozing out my pores to meet the needs of the people around me. And sometimes I wake up in the night spouting Scripture and praying in the Spirit.

If you aren't yet finding your delight in the law of the Lord but in the things of the world, don't ask God to make you His disciple. When Jesus said we were to count the cost, He didn't mean that there would be no cost. Letting all second best go is one of the costs of the kind of commitment that will bear fruit. You can pray, "Lord, I see that I'm not ready for full discipleship to you. Lord, I confess there is sin in me and ask you to make me ready. Make me prefer your Word to all the distractions that have been keeping me from it. I will probably never have any more fun, but that's all right, too, if that's the way you want it."

The psalmist indicates that if we're made willing to delight in His law, we'll get the best results.

Many Christians to whom I speak complain, "I never receive signals from God like you do. I don't ever get readouts on the powers of darkness. I don't get the diagnosis of a situation by a word of knowledge. Why not?"

God says that all gifts are for all believers to deliver to the needy, so when believers are not functioning up to par, when they're not bringing forth fruit, there has to be a reason for it. For the first five years of my life in the Spirit, I had rather sporadic results. They weren't consistent at all, and I used to wonder why. Then one day, I found this psalm and realized that fruit was guaranteed to come forth from the ministry of one who stuck to God's Word twenty-four hours a day. Once I saw that, and began to do it, there was an immediate increase in the fruit of my ministry. It quit stagnating and began to bear fruit for His kingdom when I trained my attention on Him by spending time in the Word to the exclusion of other things. The Lord was keeping the promise of this psalm in my life:

> And he shall be like a tree planted by the rivers of
> water, that bringeth forth fruit in his season; his
> leaf also shall not wither; and whatsoever he doeth

shall prosper. (v. 3)

If we dare to do it God's way all the way, by day and by night, He promises that we will be like a tree planted by rivers of water. Not just one river, a whole bunch of them. If one of them is running a little bit low, there are plenty of others backing it up to provide the water, which is the Spirit. Rivers of living water would flow from the inmost being of anybody who believes in Him, Jesus said (John 7:38). And here in the very first psalm, He assures us that we will bear fruit. That was His purpose in choosing us in the first place (John 15:16).

Are you getting off the beam? Are you failing to bring forth fruit? That is a checkpoint God has provided to keep us on His wavelength. We can know the quality of our Christian life by looking at the fruit that is coming forth. If there's no fruit in evidence except for a few shriveled-up prunes, maybe we need pruning ourselves. His Word is pretty plain about some things.

Giving up second best is pretty cheap when you consider all the first best you get in exchange. The pearl of great price is worth far more than the sum total of a whole bunch of little pearls.

When the man found the field that contained the great treasure, he sold all that he had, and bought acres of dirt just to get the thing he wanted (Matt. 13:44). He willingly put up with the withdrawal pains for the things that had been so habitual in his life, things that had seemed so significant, "educational," and important.

When I came to Jesus, I gave up torment, fear, agony, anxiety, uncertainty, and a death wish in exchange for victory in Jesus over everything. Pretty good swap, all things considered, and I wouldn't trade back for anything.

Actually, when we begin to do it God's way, the pains are not so bad, because the peace that comes with His way is so great. When we major in God's Word, not only will we bring forth fruit for His kingdom, but our "leaf will not wither." We'll never look dry, never feel dry, never be dry.

Do you feel dry and unproductive in your Christian life at times? Well, check over the input to see what's wrong with the output. If the input is worldly garbage instead of the vitamins of God's Word, the output is going to reflect it. The computer world has a term for this principle: GIGO. That means, "Garbage in, garbage out." In other words, you can't put garbage into a computer and expect to get good sense out of it. The product is necessarily related to the raw material. LILO, "Life in, life out," is preferable to GIGO. God's Word is the word of life, and when that's what we feed on, that's what we convey to others.

The punch line of the psalm is in this third verse: "And whatsoever he doeth shall prosper." The life of King's kids whose attention stays on the King is prosperity and total victory, no matter what the surrounding circumstances might look like. Kingdom living is a full-time job, and so is staying in condition for fruit bearing. Pruning has to go on as long as we grow.

The psalmist goes on to compare the blessedness of King's kid living with the wretchedness of life among pagans:

The ungodly are not so: but are like the chaff which
the wind driveth away. (v. 4)

Now, chaff is a very necessary thing in the business of wheat production. If the wheat didn't grow at the top of three feet of straw, we'd have fat rabbits and squirrels and skinny kids, because we'd never be able to bake a loaf of bread. If the straw wasn't so flexible, waving in the breeze, the birds would light on it and have a continual feast while we starved to death waiting in vain for the harvest. It would be already consumed by our feathered friends. God didn't do it wrong when he made the wheat and other grains to grow at the top of a slender stalk. He was looking out for our interests. If we try to get rid of the chaff before the harvest, we'd be depriving ourselves of groceries for months to come.

The straw makes good cattle bedding because each piece is ventilated by an air column through the middle. When the cows are ready to have their sheets changed, you can plow the secondhand chaff into the soil to get it in better shape for planting something. Nothing in God's economy is wasted.

In the same way, the Christian who is settling for the boob tube or the ball game or the bridge club will find that they have to go when he's ready to be useful for the Lord. Sometimes these things are not bad, anymore than straw is bad, but they get in the way when it comes to feeding His sheep. A Christian who decides to go part way only and then stops to do his thing, trying to divide his attention between the things of God and the things of the world, will find his Christian life stagnating and the ways of the world becoming increasingly attractive.

When we look at it this way, we don't condemn ourselves for all the extraneous, frivolous things we have gone through to get to our present stage. Everything that has been part of our life had a part in bringing us to where we are now. Knowing that, we can make allowances without condemnation for the chaff in our lives while we are being prepared for the time of fruit bearing. The chaff will have to go when maturity comes, but it'll hang around till then.

While the grain is growing, coming to maturity where it can be used to feed His sheep, every breeze causes a reaction. The young grain waves in the breeze, saying, "Hallelujah," "Praise the Lord," "Glory to Jesus." Then as the heads of grain get a little heavier, and the straw starts to mature, you can hear it clap its hands, rustling and carrying on at a great rate when the wind sweeps through it. For a while, it's disturbed by winds of doctrine, some of it broken down even. But after the harvest, when the wheat is separated from the chaff and sacked in hundred-pound bags, even a hurricane can't disturb it. It's stable, ready to be made into broken bread, the final sacrifice to feed God's people and to remind them of who He is and what He has done for them. If the seed was good, the harvest will be good. In the fullness of time.

The temptation from the enemy is for us to get impatient with God's fullness of time, and rush in and try to make it happen all by ourselves. We want to see it happening now, and when we try to harvest the crop ahead of God's timing, it dies on our hands. God says we're to be patient, to stay where we are and be the catalyst whose very presence makes things happen that could not happen without us. And the things happen because we are keeping our eyes on Jesus and not on the hopelessness of the material with which He is working.

Do you recall reading in the Scriptures about Moses coming down from the mountain where he had been with his whole attention on God? His face was so aglow with the reflected glory of God, he had to put a veil over it so he wouldn't sunburn his congregation when they saw him. He was radiating nuclear energy.

In detecting nuclear energy, scientists use a device called a scintillation meter. It's coated with a material that glows, and Moses' natural skin must have been coated specially by God for that appearance so he wouldn't be destroyed by all the radiation of God's presence. Moses actually scintillated.

Because I was trained to be a scientist, I think in terms like these, and God can give me revelations in such terms. In every instance, He makes me think of Jesus. And He may give you revelations in the area of your special training, too, whether you're a coal miner, a housewife, a student, a doctor, or an Indian chief.

127

Jesus so delighted to do the will of His Father, that every time people caught up with Him they found Him teaching the Word, teaching the teachers of Israel. The anointing of the Lord was so upon Him, it came out His pores. It should come out of ours. But it never will, unless we give His Word our priority attention.

The last verses of the psalm contain a strange statement that used to puzzle me until I received God's interpretation of it:

> Therefore the ungodly shall not stand in the judgment, nor sinners in the congregation of the righteous. For the LORD knoweth the way of the righteous: but the way of the ungodly shall perish.
> (vv. 5-6)

I used to wonder what had happened to the sinners and the ungodly folk to make them so they wouldn't stand in the judgment. I had figured they *would* stand to be judged while we King's kids had front-row seats for the drama. I read the thing five hundred times, I guess, never seeing what it really said. I had a superior attitude toward all those folks and was conditioned to condemn them, thinking, "It serves them right to be obliterated when the day of judgment comes. They should have had sense enough to get smart like I am and get lined up with Jesus so they wouldn't have to perish."

But one day in the midst of my self-righteousness, God showed me what He had in mind, and I hallelujahed for days over His plan which was so much better than mine.

It seemed as if He asked me, "Hill, where do you think the King's kids get the fruit of their ministry, the new baby Christians? Out of thin air? No, they come from those who were formerly ungodly scoffers and scorners. They turn into the fruit of born-again believers in me according to the obedience of the one sold-out member of the local group who is willing to delight in my Word in the midst of the congregation."

Well, I didn't need any prodding to rejoice over that. In my mind's eye, I could see the final windup before the white throne of judgment. There would be folks there who would go up to the sold-out ones and say, "I praise God for you. You showed me the way. I know Jesus, too, and I'm going along with you into gloryland. I doubt this blessing of eternal life would have come to me if you hadn't stayed there in the congregation and showed me the way."

The sold-out one will be amazed.

"I don't remember ever talking to you about Jesus," he'll say. "When did I show you the way? When did I say anything to you about salvation?"

"Oh, you didn't say anything, exactly," the beaming heaven-bound soul will explain. "But you seemed to be living in the midst of the rest of us in a different dimension, or something. You made your life so attractive and unruffled before me and some of my friends here, that we went looking for what you had and found Jesus in the process."

The Lord was telling me that if I would be true to my calling—and if all other King's kids would be true to theirs—there wouldn't be any ungodly folks left over at the day of judgment. They would have become our fruit—new creatures in Christ Jesus, according to His promise, and we'd all be rejoicing together.

The way of the ungodly would have perished. It would have been transformed into the victorious way of King's kids living it up for the King.

How do we live it up for the King? We look for God in the midst of every situation. We expect Him to be working in every life. We don't consider the problems people bring to us; we consider Jesus in the midst of them, and praise Him for everything. We don't try to sort out the good from the bad according to our feeble minds. We don't waste time

129

trying to judge everything and figure everybody out. "Lord, is that ungodly person a backslidden Christian or a front-slidden Christian? Or is he really a pagan?"

We don't have to know these things. Judging is God's department. But when we're sold out to Jesus, praising Him, rejoicing in all things, we will bear fruit.

Go and talk like a King's kid, and walk like one, and see the kingdom of heaven come forth right before your very eyes. The sick will be healed, the dead raised, and demons will leave the premises. Christians are made out of pagans, and from the ungodly, the scoffers, and the scorners will come our fruit. Hallelujah.

20
How to Live in Victory
over Green-Marble Grapevines

I ran a test on fruit bearing one season with my grapevine.
I said, "I wonder what would happen if I didn't trim it back,
prune it, purge it. I'm going to let it grow and find out."

That year, my grapevine ran down the arbor and back up
again. It made growth like I'd never seen before. It must
have had fifteen-foot shoots on it. Then the buds came out in
abundance, and the blossoms followed in great profusion. It
looked so good, I congratulated myself.

"Well, I guess I've discovered something that maybe the
Bible doesn't know about. I'm going to have the best grape
harvest in town."

Pretty soon, the grapes began to form—zillions of them!
Sure enough, I was headed for a bumper crop. I watched the
grapes as they grew from tiny seed-like nubbins on up to the
size of small green peas.

But there they stopped. And there they stayed. Green.
Pea-sized. They never matured.

The best test of a grape crop is the reaction of the bees. If
they come in swarms, you know the fruit is good. That year,
the bees didn't come close to my vineyard. They were too

131

smart for that. A hungry bee wouldn't lower himself to look at my grapes. He'd sooner perch on a ball bearing. The most efficient bee can't make honey out of sour green marbles, and that's all my grape crop amounted to, sour green marbles. Thinking I knew it all, I'd wasted my time, and the time of the grapevine, because I had let it run according to common sense, doing its own thing, instead of keeping it pruned back for maximum fruit production.

Now, there's nothing wrong with a grapevine runner. It's healthy in growth, nice and green, and pretty to look at. But it's of no use for anything except decoration, because it's been allowed to run and do its own thing uncontrolled, without discipline to enable it to bring fruit to maturity.

There are two things the farmer can do to a grape crop that's coming along on properly disciplined grapevines. What he does depends on whether he's going for quantity or quality. The grape farmer who raises fruit for commercial grape juice is not too particular about the quality of an individual bunch of grapes. He's after quantity. But the farmer intending to have a blue-ribbon cluster for the county fair has to handle his crop in a special way. He watches the developing grapes very closely, and when they are approaching maturity, he cuts off every cluster from the vine except three. The discarded clusters look good, but they would be in the way for the very best to come forth.

The farmer watches the three clusters remaining on the vine, and after a while he cuts out one of them and throws it away. When the last two have come almost to full maturity, he clips the second best and throws it away, leaving the full strength of the vine with nowhere to flow except into the prize cluster. The day he takes that one to the county fair, first prize is in the bag. Why, he might even hear the judges say something like, "Well done, good and faithful servant."

The undisciplined Christian life is about as useful, about as productive of fruit, as the undisciplined grapevine. The disciplined life, on the other hand, produces baby Christians, the fruit of King's kids in action. "Heavenly obstetrics," bringing forth new younguns for the King, is the vocation Jesus gave His disciples. The *Manufacturer's Handbook* puts it this way:

> Go therefore and make disciples of all the nations, baptizing them in the name of the Father and the Son and the Holy Spirit, teaching them to observe all that I have commanded you; and lo, I am with you always, to the end of the age. (Matt. 28:19-20, NAS)

The word disciple means "disciplined one," "one disciplined in the ways of God, according to the Word of God."

"Oh, but I don't like to be disciplined," some aspiring King's kids say. "I'd rather be free to do my own thing, being led by the Spirit, of course."

In my early King's kid days, I didn't like discipline until I realized that the alternative was an unproductive life. Pruning is not particularly pleasant, but I've always been interested in results. I don't suppose the grapevine appreciates it when we cut off all its beautiful, green, luxuriant growth and chop it down to a scroungy-looking nothing. It looks, and probably feels, ruined—like you do when you tell your barber you want just a little edge trim and he practically shaves your head. But hair grows out, eventually, and when a properly pruned grapevine begins to produce fruit, it carries its grapes to beautiful maturity.

In the same way, one who is disciplined to produce a perfect crop in the name of Jesus is worth ten thousand ordinary pew warmers in anybody's church. The prize package, the blue-ribbon Christian, is always the result of discipline that has cut off second best to make room for heaven's best to come forth.

True disciples are King's kids who are willing to have all the second-rate stuff cut away. Just as there was nothing sinful about what was taken off the vine, there may be nothing particularly sinful about a lot of things that have to be pruned from your life if you're going to be a blue-ribbon disciple. Bridge clubs, fashion shows, horse races, ball games, and TV programs are okay. But time spent in these things instead of in the Word of God will keep you from being a fruit-bearing disciple for Jesus.

It's not a matter of heaven or hell. Jesus didn't say that worldly Christians would lose their salvation and spend eternity on the working end of a fire shovel. What He said was, "If you would be my disciple, you will have to live a crucified life, a life of fasting from indulgence in the things of the world so you'll have time to listen to me" (Matt. 16:24-25, my paraphrase).

It's a matter of our own choice. And Jesus doesn't want us to make a choice without thinking it through, figuring what it is going to cost us. Our truly sold-out allegiance to Him calls for such a high degree of commitment, such a perfect quality of love for Him, that it makes all ordinary human love look like hate alongside it. That's what Jesus was talking about when He said:

> If any man come to me, and hate not his father, and mother, and wife, and children, and brethren, and sisters, yea, and his own life also, he cannot be my disciple. (Luke 14:26)

If you choose to be His disciple, giving up the world and going all the way with Jesus, other people—worldly Christians as well as pagans—will call you a fanatic and other uncomplimentary things. But real King's kids don't let that faze them. They're glad to be maligned by men if that's what it takes to win the blue ribbon that says, "Well done, thou good and faithful servant."

The price tag that comes with a power-packed King's kid ministry includes the total giving up of everything that's second best if it's standing in the way. If you're not willing to pay that price, you're not entitled to complain about your miserable results.

You have to give up second best to get first best on any level of life. Jesus is heaven's best for each one of us if we will dare to believe it.

21

How to Live in Victory
over Secular Boob-Tube-Itis

God's Word is the chief instrument to show us how to live in
victory as sons of God:

> Thy word is a lamp unto my feet, and a light unto
> my path. (Ps. 119:105)

If we're not in the Word, we're in trouble, because we're
probably listening to some voice other than God's. Staying in
the Word keeps us tuned to God's wavelength, receiving His
signals. There is no substitute for spending time in the Word
of God.

There are a million reasons people offer as excuses for why
they don't spend more time in the Word. Every excuse I've
ever heard is a cop-out.

"Well, I wish I had more time to spend in the Word,"
people tell me. That's usually a lie. Everybody does exactly
what he wants to do in this lifetime. If they wanted to spend
more time in the Word, they would do it. It doesn't matter
what I might tell you to the contrary, I do what I really want
to do. And so do you. If you want to spend time in the Word,
you do it. If you want to read the daily scandal sheet, you do
that. If you want to stay glued to the tube, you do that. If you

want to give equal time to God, you do that, too.

Prior to our regeneration, we had no choice about any of these things. We were doing Slue Foot's thing automatically whether we knew it or not. But after we were regenerated, we were made able to choose the mind of Jesus to occupy our think tank. Then we could begin to do things differently.

Walking in Christ Jesus, choosing His mind and motivation to replace our own, involves some basic principles which are clearly stated in Paul's letter to the Colossians:

If ye then be risen with Christ, seek those things
which are above, where Christ sitteth on the right
hand of God. Set your affection on things above, not
on things on the earth. (3:1-2)

We seek the things that are above by staying in the Word which tells us all about the things which are above, things which God wants to put on earth as well as in heaven.

When I ask Christians, "How much time do you spend in the Word?" I invariably get the apologetic answer, "Not as much as I'd like to." When I check it out further, getting really nosey, I'm likely to learn a lot.

"Do you spend maybe an hour a day?" I ask them.

"No, but I honestly wish I could." They look sincere.

"Half an hour a day?"

"Well, not too often." They sound sincere.

"Fifteen minutes a day?"

"I couldn't say that." They are still sincere.

"Five minutes a day?" Their collars are getting a little too snug at this point.

"Well, sometimes I do that." I sense they are exceedingly uncomfortable.

"Not always even five minutes?"

"Not always. It's a busy life you know." Their eyes are giving a minute inspection to the cracks in the floor, and guilt is written all over them.

Five minutes a day once in a while is probably better than never cracking the cover of the Book, but it's kind of a scrawny diet. We'd get scrawny physically if we never spent more than five minutes a day at the grocery table. Limiting ourselves to five minutes at the heavenly grocery table *could* have a tendency to make us kind of peaked in the spiritual department, too.

It's interesting sometimes to quiz the same person about his boob-tube observation habits.

"How much time do you average looking at the boob tube every day, brother?"

"Oh, I'm not too bad in that department." Right away I can see he understands that TV addiction is not highly recommended, and he's comparing himself to a real addict.

"I understand that," I tell him. "Nobody is *too* bad. But to be specific, do you spend maybe five minutes a day on the average?"

The guy has to laugh out loud at that, so I set my stopwatch a little higher.

"An hour a day, maybe?"

"Yes, I'm sure I watch that much. Lots of programs are that long, you know. It's hard to interrupt—"

"Two hours a day?"

"Sometimes."

"Three hours?"

"Well, you know, a fellow has to keep up with what's going on in the world, and there's the late, late show. It helps me relax, and—"

Any scientist could tell you that if you spend an average of an hour or two or three a day with your nose in the garbage bucket and barely five minutes a day eating good food, you'll probably stay sickly. You won't stay sickly long, of course, because you'll drop dead with malnutrition.

What's true in the physical realm is true in the spiritual realm. We can't have it both ways. We can set our affection on things above, on staying on the heavenly wavelength, or we can keep in gear with all the latest secular boob-tube swill. We can take our choice. And the results of our ministry will be affected accordingly.

This is not legalism saying, "You've got to do it this way or die." This is not saying you've got to give up all your fun before God will accept you. But He gives us free will to choose to major in His Word to the exclusion of all worldly entertainment if we want to see things happen.

Getting rid of secular boob-tube-itis has worked wonders for those who have tried it. Their divided attention that robbed God of glory and His younguns of blessing has been brought together into a one-track mind that proclaims, "Jesus is all."

Where the name of Jesus is lifted up, God's promise is fulfilled:

> Now is the judgment of this world: now shall the prince of this world be cast out. And I, if I be lifted up from the earth, will draw all men unto me. (John 12: 31-31)

I'm willing to give up a lot for that, aren't you?

22

How to Live in Victory
over an Absence of Victims

In the beginning of my life as a King's kid, I tried all the wrong ways of witnessing there are. I'd trap people in a situation, clobber them with a few well-chosen verses quoted in a holier-than-thou condemning tone, and walk off and leave them shaken and bleeding while I moved on to the next victim. Oh, I was a menace, but I thought I was doing my duty.

Then I came across a Scripture that changed my attitude and my angle of approach. I found it in the Gospel according to Matthew where Jesus said, "I send you forth as sheep" (10:16).

That made me sit back and take inventory.

"Lord," I said, "I haven't been going as a sheep, so I guess someone other than you has been sending me. I've been charging out like a three-headed moose. Maybe I've been sending myself?" As I meditated on the habits of sheep, I decided that must be right, because a sheep never charges into anything. It's dumb and stupid—so stupid it will fall right into a hole, headfirst. That's why the shepherd has to carry a crooked pole—to fish dumb sheep out of trouble.

When I saw that I was out of line, I decided to try witnessing God's way.

One of the first things I realized was that it doesn't matter how stupid you are, if you don't open your mouth, no one will ever discover your stupidity. Anyone can get a reputation for being a knowledgeable person if he will just sit quietly and listen to everyone else. He'll be liked, too, because everyone wants to be heard.

Putting this into action, I decided that I would keep my mouth shut, just wait on the Lord to do His thing. Whenever I felt the urge to witness, I'd know that was my self, wanting to be heard. I started keeping my mouth shut and waiting for the other person to ask a question before I started spouting answers to questions no one was asking. Invariably, when I was obedient to wait for an opening, the fruit was forthcoming. I didn't have to do anything spectacular, I just had to watch it happen.

Recently I was on an afternoon flight from Dallas to Baltimore. I had just finished three days of juicy meetings, and I was all cranked up and ready to go. I boarded the aircraft and took my assigned seat. It was down in front next to the window. Soon the other passengers had boarded, the door was closed, and we were taxiing for takeoff. The seat beside me had remained vacant, and I took that as a pretty good sign that I wouldn't have an opportunity to witness to anyone in the course of that several-hour flight. Well, that was all right with me. I could sit back and praise the Lord for a while and take a nap to make up for some of the sleep I hadn't had while I was at the convention.

We had been aloft and droning along for some time when the stewardess happened to pause alongside the empty seat next to me.

"Excuse me, sir, but what is that?" she asked, pointing to the little pin on my lapel.

141

I was wide awake immediately, because she'd asked a question, and was waiting for an answer. All it takes is a question. I had thought that one of the paying customers would be my victim on this trip, but here was a stewardess instead.

What was on my lapel was a little sign-of-the-fish pin, the secret emblem of the FFJ, the Fanatics for Jesus. But I didn't go into all that. I said, simply, "That's the sign that the early Christians used to identify themselves to one another."

She shook her head.

"I don't understand," she said. Well, I thought at first that I was supposed to go into all the routine about how the letters of the word *fish* were an acronym for the words, Jesus Christ, Son of God, Savior, but the Lord was instructing me to keep it simple. I made it as simple as I could.

"It actually means that I belong to Jesus," I told the stewardess.

"Oh, that's pretty!" she responded, clapping her hands together. That didn't sound like a very theological reaction, and I was glad of it.

"Would you like to have a pin like this for yourself?" I asked her. "I just happen to have a few extra ones along with me on this trip."

She nodded agreeably, and I took the pin off and gave it to her. She pinned it to her jacket, turned to the other side of the aisle, and spoke to a big fellow slurping from a glass full of unholy spirits.

"Do you know what this means?" she asked him, pointing to her new pin.

He mumbled something incoherent, then tipped his glass up for another swig.

"It means I belong to Jesus," she said.

He almost dropped his glass at that. She had given him something to think about, and she moved on down the aisle.

That stewardess went the whole length of the plane, up one side and down the other, showing that pin to people and explaining it meant that she belonged to Jesus. Every time she said it, she looked like she meant it more.

It was a glorious experience for me. All I had to do was sit back and praise God while the pretty young stewardess did the legwork for me.

Nobody could hire an airline stewardess to do that kind of witnessing. But when the Holy Spirit wants the Word to go out, nothing can stop it. What happened was much more full of glory for the Lord than if I had been tied up with witnessing to a single seatmate. When the Lord is doing the reaping, sometimes the harvest is wholesale.

23
How to Live in Victory
in Seedtime and Harvest

One day I was on my way to a retreat at the Circle J Ranch at Worland, Wyoming, up in the Big Horn Mountains. Norman Grubb and Tommy Tyson were going to be there with me, and I was looking forward to a couple of weeks of pure glory.

I was sitting in the back seat of a car going across the badlands of South Dakota in sun that was broiling hot. The thermometer registered over a hundred in the shade. There was no air conditioner in the car. Half of me was already asleep, and the other half was slowly cooking itself to sleep. But in the midst of it all, I was questioning the Lord, who never gets drowsy.

"Lord, what is your process for getting people into the kingdom?"

For a long time I had been wondering why it is that some people come to Him so early in life and some come so late; why some come so easily and others insist on coming the hard way, or not at all. Why, for instance, did it take me forty-eight years to make it, while other people wore glory grins when they were still in knee pants? If I could find the answer to my wonderings and use it, I could have a lot more fruit from my ministry at the upcoming retreat and everywhere else I went to brag on Jesus.

Back in those days I was still trying to manipulate people and trap them into saying yes, even though the Lord had told me that was not the way to do it. I couldn't seem to get away from the old high-pressure salesman technique that guaranteed that if you could force a person to say yes to three things in a row, you could sell him anything. And yet that approach was not working. As a matter of fact, I could see that it was actually antagonizing people and driving them further than ever from the kingdom.

Well, as I alternately dozed and meditated about these things, leafing through my Bible, a verse in the sixth chapter of John caught my eye:

No man can come to me, except the Father which hath sent me draw him. (v. 44)

"Well, praise the Lord!" I shouted, suddenly wide awake. So that was it. All I had to do was tell the people, and the Lord himself would cause the response to His love to come upon them. He would draw them. Those few words took me completely off the hook. I saw that it's never my efforts that make someone come to Jesus. Neither is it a matter of a man's own efforts, saying, "Well, I guess it would be a good idea for me to get religion now and prepare myself for heaven." The Scripture made it plain that our salvation is always God's idea and not our own.

Another of the lessons Jesus taught me about witnesssing came from Matthew's Gospel. When I was reading it one day, three words lit up like neon lights:

Behold a sower. . . . (13:3)

"What do you mean, 'Behold a sower?' " I found myself asking. I had always beheld a seed. But one day, God said, "I want you to check the sower."

145

I was born in the country and knew that the seed grain, which represented the next year's crop, was so vital to the farmer's existence that he sometimes had to preserve it even when it meant he had to let his kids go hungry during the winter.

After a poor harvest year, I never heard of a farmer wasting seed grain by sowing it among thorns and thistles, or on rocks, or on unplowed ground. He would always see to it that the ahead-of-time preparation had been properly done so the seed would not be wasted. But if the sower happened to be a hired hand instead of the farmer himself, he might be careless with the seed. He might be so interested in getting rid of it as fast as possible, getting his day's pay and heading for home, that he'd plant it just any old place, whether the ground was perfect for it or not. But a man who was not a hireling, but a member of the kingdom team, would prepare the soil carefully before he let a single grain of the seed hit the ground.

In witnessing, the Lord seemed to be impressing on me, a sower *can* dump the seed out just any old place, the seed being the Word of God, and because God honors His Word, even such a careless sower will get some results. But when he is aware of the preciousness of what he is handling, he'll prepare the ground carefully in order to be sure of a maximum return. He'll be a careful sower instead of a sloppy sower.

Well, the Lord taught me something in that verse that I'd never thought of in quite that way before. I would be more careful about the work of preparing the soil where the seed was going to fall.

"But what constitutes the necessary ahead-of-time work of preparation?" I asked Him then. I knew how a farmer prepares a field for seed, but I couldn't see myself blasting rocks out of people or pulling thorns and thistles out of them to prepare their hearts to receive God's Word.

As it turned out, the Lord answered my question through another Scripture in Matthew's Gospel. It went like this:

Pray ye therefore the Lord of the harvest, that he will send forth the labourers into his harvest. (9:38)

That was it! *Prayer* is the work that has to be done ahead of time. If we'll do the praying, then the Lord of the harvest himself will see to it that the harvest of souls is reaped in the fullness of time. Intercessory prayer is our part in getting the job done. We're not told to send ourselves or anyone else as laborers to gather the harvest. The Lord will do the sending while we do the praying.

When we begin to realize our proper role in all this, we can forget about the results and let God take care of them. The results are not our business. We've just got to be faithful to pray, and He will take care of the victory.

And apparently there was still more I could learn about my role as a witness in His kingdom. One day He brought to my attention the words of Jesus, that He would make His disciples to be fishers of men (Matt. 4:19).

When I used to wade the trout stream, I learned that the less action, the better. I used my wrists, and the weight of the line carried a little old fly or worm, depending on the season and the appetite and habits of the trout, out to where they could have a chance at it if they were interested. I saw that if I wanted God to use me as a laborer in the harvest to catch a fish for the kingdom, I should disturb the water as little as possible, throw out some bait the fish was interested in, and wait for it to express an open-mouthed interest before reeling my line in. There was no way I could throw a meat ax at a trout and expect to have a fish fry. There was equally no way that I could grab lapels and expect to come up with a newborn King's kid.

When Jesus makes us fishers of men, He sends us forth as

147

baby sheep in the midst of wolves (Luke 10:3). And he tells us to be sly as serpents and harmless as doves (Matt. 10:16).

It was easy for me to act as dumb as a sheep, and to be as quiet as a lamb. When Jesus first moved into my life, I had stage fright like you wouldn't believe. I choked half to death whenever I stood up and tried to say my name. My knees got watery and I melted down in the pool. I used to get low marks in school because I couldn't stand up to recite. When I stood up, my mind took off; my voice faded to a croaky whisper. But after the Holy Spirit took over my life, including my tongue, I could talk to anybody. As a matter of fact, it gets harder and harder to shut me off when I have an opportunity to brag on Jesus.

But the secret in witnessing is not long talking or short talking. It's waiting on the Lord, letting Him make the opening. And when He has opened a door, no man can shut it. When the question comes to you from a pagan about how you can keep so calm when the world is falling apart around you, you can change your tactics from dumb to sly so Satan can't keep up with you. You're entitled to sneak up under rugs and behind furniture when your candidate has expressed an interest in things eternal. You can let him have it as the Spirit directs. And the harvest will come forth, because it's

Not by might, nor by power, but by my spirit, saith
the LORD of hosts. (Zech. 4:6)

His Spirit is like the wind. We can see the result of it but not the wind itself. And there's no way we can tell it where to blow. But if we're willing to move with the Spirit, we'll have season tickets for some great victories.

That's what the shepherd's staff is for.

24
How to Live in Victory
in Green Pastures

In the twenty-third psalm, God has given us a description of the process He uses in training King's kids. It's true that we are instantly transformed into new beings when we're born again, but after that new birth comes either stagnation or a growing toward maturity in this new dimension of life, depending on whether or not we're willing to cooperate with what He wants to do in us.

Let's look at what happens in the lives of those who choose to grow:

The LORD is my shepherd. (v. 1)

These first two verses of the psalm acknowledge Jesus as the Lord. King's kids in training take every one of life's circumstances and acknowledge Him to be in charge because once they have become new creatures, "all things are of God" (2 Cor. 5:18). Knowing that, King's kids never have to bog down in appearances or feelings; they can rejoice in the knowledge that Jesus is in control.

The first three words make a positive statement of fact, "The Lord is." Those who come to God must believe that He is, the Scripture says, and that He hears and answers prayer

151

(Heb. 11:6). The Lord is one, and at the same time, He is many things. He is my Savior, my everpresent help in time of trouble. He's my Strong Tower. He's my Rock. He's the Lily of the Valley. He's the Bright and Morning Star. He's the Lamb that was slain from the foundation of the world. He's my Healer, Baptizer. . . .

The Holy Spirit will carry you on and on with what God is to you when you begin to acknowledge that He is sovereign Lord. But if He's not sovereign Lord to you, if He's only a junior partner in your business dealings, in your living, then you've got problems. I learned, the hard way, that having a head man is God's arrangement, and He's the only one with qualifications to fill that position.

When the Lord is the Lord in our lives, we can say,

I shall not want. (v. 1)

These words of the psalm mean that I refuse to be caught lacking for anything in my life. It doesn't guarantee that I'll get everything I ask for, but that I'll have everything I need. Most of us would be in a mess if we got everything we asked for. But God is not afraid to say no when what we request is not His best for us. Sometimes He lets us have our way in order to teach us something.

Have you ever asked for something, gotten it, and wondered, "Now what in the world am I going to do with that thing?" It seems sometimes that God sorts out our requests and lets us have just enough of what we shouldn't have to make us more careful what we ask for in the future.

In the next verse, we come to the first step in the training of a sheep, or a King's kid:

He maketh me to lie down in green pastures. (v. 2)

On my own, after I'd become a King's kid, I thought I was supposed to run all over the beautiful green pasture, doing my own thing in perfect freedom. But the Lord said, "Down, boy. And stay down until I tell you to move."

Obedience is the first lesson we have to learn in becoming King's kids in action. We have to obey His instruction to wait when everything of self in us is protesting, "But I've got to get out there and get busy for you, Lord."

Getting "busy for the Lord," with all kinds of programitis, is one of the commonest ways of evading God's will. It usually means that we're doing our own thing, and God never honors that. We never admit it, of course. We churchmen are experts at camouflage. Nobody is ever busier for the Lord than we are. And we fool ourselves by keeping track of how many doorbells we've rung. Do we keep track of how many souls our doorbell ringing has won to Jesus? Oh, no. That would expose our programs as the losers' programs that programs without God will always be.

Programs are generally concocted with three points, and the points generally start with the same letter of the alphabet so they'll be easy to remember and fun to talk about. Everything in a program is always perfectly organized, from A to Izzard.

When we have the perfect program all written down on paper, and have drilled the routines into ourselves and our fellow laborers, we pray, "Lord, bless it," and then run out and fall flat on our faces. Everything gets all fouled up.

"Lord, why didn't you bless it?" we wail.

"Because it wasn't my idea in the first place," He replies. And that's the end of that. It is only after we submit ourselves to His leading and lie down when He tells us to, that we are ready for Him to use us in *His* program.

God has given us a number of persuasive checkpoints for determining whether we're doing our thing or doing His will. When a servant of God comes back from an assignment totally exhausted, we can know he's been out there operating his own program, under his own power. But when God's servant has been out there forty years and is still as

153

fresh as Moses was after the wilderness, we can know he's been operating in the power of God. We can tell it every time.

When I come home from a week on the road, all tired out, utterly exhausted in wind and limb, mama spots the cause the minute I puff and drag my way into the house.

"You've been out on your own, haven't you?" she says.

There's no way I can refuse to agree. We both know the signs. I don't have to say, "I'm finished, I'm bushed, I'm beaten"; it's written all over me. But when I come back as fresh as when I left—or better—mama says, "I bet Jesus was in charge of that mission." And we both know she's right.

Learning to lie down and do nothing is the hardest thing imaginable for a King's kid who's all fired up, raring to get out there and serve Jesus. Early in my Christian life, I did a lot of complaining about it.

"Lord, you're wasting my time," I'd point out to Him. "You must not understand how valuable I am to your kingdom."

It seemed as if He said, "I think I do."

Elijah complained to God one time in about the same way I did (1 Kings 19). He said, in effect, "Lord, it's a good thing you've got me on your team. Without me, why, you'd be out of business, because I'm the only one left who is faithful to you."

Did God say, "That's right. I can't afford to lose you"?

No way. What He said was, "I've got news for you, Elijah. I've got seven thousand more who have not bowed their knees to Baal. I can wheel them out of the crack any time I need them. And since you think you're all that indispensable, I'm going to have to put you on the shelf for a while. I'll prove I can get along perfectly well without you.

"I can use you if you'll be obedient, of course, but you've

got to learn to lie down and wait before you can walk in my victory. Before you can be led by my Spirit, you've got to get to the place where you're willing to obey me in spite of circumstances."

When everything in us is screaming, "Look, Lord! They're dying over there! Puh-leez let me go and minister," He has to say, "Down, boy," and He has to keep on saying it until we're willing to do it.

Before we can ever go out on our own, we have to learn to follow where He leads us:

He leadeth me beside the still waters. (v. 2)

In the natural, turbulent waters would look a whole lot more exciting and appealing to us, but a sheep is so dumb he can drown himself trying to wet his whistle at the edge of turbulent waters. We learn to obey the Shepherd as we consent to be led by still waters at first. A young sheep, just learning his place in the fold, can't handle big meetings or large campaigns without being clobbered by his own swelling self-importance.

He restoreth my soul. (v. 3)

The unrestored soul generally blocks the best God has for us because it goes by feelings instead of faith. Often when we say, "I don't feel led," to do a certain thing, that's our soul crying for attention, resenting the fact that it's not in charge of proceedings. The soul can't run out and do its own thing when it's submitting to the Good Shepherd, and its druthers die hard.

When the Good Shepherd restores our soul, He brings it into its proper relationship, subordinate to the Holy Spirit. Feelings have to be ignored, for the most part. Even feelings of blessings and the feeling of anointings are strictly second best, because they detract our attention from the leading of the Good Shepherd.

The soul delights in leading us captive into the trap of

self-hypnotic nothingness. But where the Spirit of the Lord is, there is no longer soulish enslavement to feelings, there is the release of spiritual liberty (2 Cor. 3:17).

Once the Good Shepherd has restored my soul to its proper place,

> He leadeth me in the paths of righteousness for his name's sake. (v. 3)

There is only one way to become righteous, and that is to become identified with the one who can be our righteousness inside us (1 Cor. 1:30). If I became righteous on my own, I'd have to glory in my righteousness. That's what I did back in the days when I had myself fooled into thinking I could somehow be in a partnership with God. I was trying to steal a little glory from Him. But God wants all the glory for himself, and He gives all the blessings to His people. When it comes right down to it, I need blessings every day, but I wouldn't know what to do with glory if I had a whole warehouse full of it. Glory belongs to God. No one else can handle it.

As I submit myself fully to God's leadership in the paths of righteousness, I don't find myself in a restricted kind of life. He allows me lots of choices.

"Lord," I tell Him, "here are two ways I can go in this situation. They look almost opposite to me. My wisdom is not good enough to sort them out; my trust has to be in you. I'm going to take the path that seems most reasonable to me, but I'll trust you to block it if that's not in line with your best will for me." I don't sit and shiver and quake, fearful that I might goof. I get the body in motion, because there's no way you can steer a parked car. If I keep moving, God can lead me.

Suppose I make a wrong turn? I've done that, more than once, and God has always been faithful to correct me. Often, I've had to make a wrong turn in order to find the right road. God never promised to make us goof-proof overnight. That's what the Shepherd's staff is for, to fish the sheep out of trouble.

The psalmist seemed to know that we might land in dire circumstances from time to time. The next thing he says is:

Yea, though I walk through the valley of the shadow of death, I will fear no evil. (v. 4)

Death is a shadow, an illusion. In addition, death for the Christian is graduation day, nothing to be feared. Paul knew that when he wrote,

Therefore we are always confident, knowing that, whilst we are at home in the body, we are absent from the Lord: (For we walk by faith, not by sight.) We are confident, I say, and willing rather to be absent from the body, and to be present with the Lord. (2 Cor. 5:6-8)

One day my wife's prayer partner, a woman with whom she had been praying every day for several years, went to the grocery store. When she returned home and drove into her yard, she felt a peculiar physical sensation. She telephoned her next-door neighbor and told her about it. Before the neighbor could hang up the phone and cross the yard between their houses, the woman had dropped to her living room floor, graduated to glory. That's a neat way for a Christian to graduate, feeling out of this world for a couple of minutes, then suddenly being absent from the body and present with the Lord. We don't have to be sick to die. God can stop our breath or our heart at any moment and take us right home.

My mother graduated that way. She took a nap one afternoon and woke up across the border.

King's kids can graduate with no fear of evil. I know that personally, because I've encountered certain death on a number of occasions since I've known Jesus. Facing positive destruction, I was amazed each time to find there was no fear in me. (You can read the details about these things in *How to Live Like a King's Kid* and in *How to Be a Winner*.)

In every case, when I was looking at the certainty of positive destruction of my earthly body, I experienced only joy. I knew what the psalmist knew. I feared no evil right in the midst of the valley of the shadow of death. The absence of fear always means the presence of the Lord, just as the psalmist went on to say:

For thou art with me. (v. 4)

The sheep and the Shepherd are walking together now, because the sheep has learned to pace his walk to that of the one who can keep him from all harm.

Thy rod and thy staff they comfort me. (v. 4)

The rod of correction that had to be used to force the sheep into submissiveness is no longer a torment to him, because now he finds it a great delight to do the will of God. The chastening that had been such a hard thing for him to take has brought joyful results. Read what God said about it through the letter to the Hebrews:

Now no chastening for the present seemeth to be joyous, but grievous: nevertheless afterward it yieldeth the peaceable fruit of righteousness unto them which are exercised thereby. (12:11)

David said, "I delight to do thy will, O my God" (Ps. 40:8), and the Good Shepherd brings us to the point where we can say it too.

When a properly submissive spirit has been cultivated within us, the corrective measures of God are always a comfort to us. If we have any feeling of uneasiness in the face of God's authority, that's a sure sign the spirit of rebellion is lurking inside us, waiting to go into action, doing its own thing. It is far more blessed to have our wills so in line with His that the rod and the staff are a comfort. They make us not afraid of getting into trouble, or revealing our imperfections, because we know His crooked pole can fish us out, time after time, and set us back on the straight path.

Don't ever feel that you must be a perfect Christian. It's not possible. But Jesus in us is perfect, and by the process of our dying to self and letting Him live His life through us, we will more and more resemble Jesus. The end result of this process is exciting. Look at what John wrote about it:

Beloved, now are we the sons of God, and it doth not yet appear what we shall be: but we know that, when he shall appear, we shall be like him; for we shall see him as he is. (1 John 3:2)

We will actually be like Jesus! That's shouting ground if I've ever seen any.

The next step in the Good Shepherd's training of the sheep is the preparation of a banquet table:

Thou preparest a table before me in the presence of mine enemies. (v. 5)

Why is the table prepared in the midst of my enemies? So I can invite them to come and eat with me! That's a pretty potent reminder that the Lord's ways are not our ways, that His thoughts are not our thoughts (Isa. 55:8).

When I first became a King's kid, I had an enemy. But I had committed myself to being a doer of the Word, and not a hearer only (James 1:22), and because he had despitefully used me, I made myself pray for him (Matt. 5:44). It wasn't exactly a joyful or a sincere prayer at first. It was one of dogged obedience. I'd say, "Lord, bless so and so." Even while I was praying, I'd be hoping He wouldn't do it. But eventually the grace of God got through to me, and I worked up to the point where I could meet the man on the street and not send flaming darts in his direction. As I followed the instructions in the *Manufacturer's Handbook*, the hate left me. And after I was baptized in the Holy Spirit, the impossible happened. Love took the place of hate.

Now, I'm not pretending perfection here. Paul confessed that he hadn't arrived all the way (Phil. 3:13), but he knew he was headed in the right direction, and we can know it too. Circumstances can set in and I can crank up an instant poor-me pity party. But it's soon called off as the Holy Spirit reminds me that I'm only a dumb sheep and that the Good Shepherd who loves me is in charge of everything that happens to me. For that, I can say, "Praise the Lord!"—and I do. That effectively douses any pity party and turns it into a glory party with the Lord himself providing the refreshments. A glory party is better than a pity party any day.

Do you remember all the bad things that happened to God's servant Job? Every kind of disaster you can name: his children were killed, his cattle were destroyed, he broke out in boils, and his wife told him to drop dead. As if that wasn't enough, his former friends turned into such creeps, he had no need for enemies. Instead of comforting him in his afflictions and distresses, they told him it was all his fault.

It's a long story, and you can read all about it in the *Manufacturer's Handbook* in the Book of Job. But what's relevant here is that in the end, God had Job pray for his "friends," and God sent the "friends" out to get the steaks for a party (42:8).

> And the Lord turned the captivity of Job, when he prayed for his friends: also the LORD gave Job twice as much as he had before. (42:10)

In the Shepherd's psalm, that kind of blessing is described in this way:

> Thou anointest my head with oil; my cup runneth over. (v. 5)

The Lord prepared a table for Job in the midst of his friendly enemies, and from that point on, Job's life was a constant party. Before Job died at a ripe old age, God had given Job greater riches than he'd had in the beginning, seven new sons, three beautiful daughters, and grandchildren and great grandchildren too numerous to mention. His head was anointed with oil, all right—oil representing the presence of the Holy Spirit—and his cup of blessings overflowed all over the place.

With all that happening, we can be sure of the truth of the last verse of the Shepherd's psalm:

Surely goodness and mercy shall follow me all the days of my life: and I will dwell in the house of the LORD for ever. (v. 6)

That verse was abundantly fulfilled in Job's life, as it will be in ours if we follow His directions. It's a glorious windup.

Where is this house of the Lord in which we will dwell forever? The house of the Lord turns out to be wherever the King's kid is, because God is in His Holy temple.

"Know ye not . . . that Jesus Christ is in you?" Paul asked the Corinthians (2 Cor. 13:5). Earlier, he had told them, "Ye are the temple of the living God" (2 Cor. 6:16). King's kids have to agree, "Yes, we are containers for Jesus, and we carry the treasure that He is in our earthen vessels."

The Scripture says,

We have this treasure in earthen vessels, that the excellency of the power may be of God, and not of us. (2 Cor. 4:7)

That's a perfect arrangement. Heaven's best. And if you need to stop reading at this point and crank up a hallelujah, feel free.

25
How to Live in Victory
in Dry Deserts

Once upon a time, Philip was preaching a great revival, having a city-wide crusade in Samaria. Thousands were getting saved, healed, and delivered. In the midst of all that, God caught Philip's attention and said, "I want you to leave this place to go to the desert" (Acts 8:26). That's bound to be the craziest set of instructions any big-time evangelist ever received on his tuning set. I imagine Philip shook his head a time or two and maybe even cleaned out his ears. But there was no mistaking the voice of God, and Philip didn't start sputtering seven reasons why he shouldn't go, he just took down his tent and went.

Philip might have wondered what he was going to do in the desert. Deserts have a habit of being kind of deserted. Maybe he thought he was supposed to preach at the sand fleas, and get them saved. But whatever he was supposed to do was God's business. Philip didn't doubt that God had something in mind, no matter how ridiculous it might have sounded to him.

Philip didn't have to be enthusiastic about his assignment; he just had to be obedient. He didn't have to feel an

162

anointing; he just had to go. And so he went, responding in faith to the Spirit of God.

Philip might have known what I have discovered: that the crazier a thing sounds, the more weird it looks to my common sense, the more likely it is to be direct from headquarters, and to contain a tremendous blessing for somebody. God never does anything the way I figure He will, and that's enough to keep King's kid living exciting. He always does everything in a far more interesting manner than what my think tank could possibly envision. And I get to be a part of the action, with a front row seat for everything as long as I'm keeping my antenna tuned to His wavelength by staying in the atmosphere of praise.

Well, when Philip got to the desert, he found it wasn't quite as deserted as usual. Coming down the pike was a little cloud of dust, and emerging out of the dust was a chariot with an Ethiopian riding in it. The Ethiopian was a black man, from another country, another race of people. I can imagine Philip shook his head wondering, "What am I going to do here, Lord? We probably don't even speak the same language!"

The black man had his nose stuck in a book, and he was so intent on his reading he didn't even notice Philip standing beside the road. But Philip didn't just keep on standing there, he got in motion and took off after the chariot. As he loped along in the dust, he overheard the black man reading out loud from the Book of Isaiah.

Hey! The guy spoke Philip's language after all. That put a little different complexion on the course of events, and as Philip speeded up and drew a little closer to the carriage, he heard the man mutter to himself, "Now all that sounds very interesting. But how can I understand what this means since there's no teacher around here to tell me?"

Well, Philip didn't wait for Emily Post to come along and

make proper introductions all around. He made a flying leap onto the running board of the chariot. When the startled Ethiopian turned to look at him, Philip swooped his hat off his head and announced, "Pardon me for eavesdropping, sir, but I just *happened* to overhear your last remark. It *happens* that I am a teacher. And by a strange coincidence, I just *happened* to be in the neighborhood today. I'd be glad to explain that passage of Scripture to you along with any others. I'm at your service, sir."

The black man lit up and moved over so the traveling evangelist could sit down beside him. Philip was glad to take the load off his feet, and he began to preach to him Jesus out of the Book of Isaiah (Acts 8:35). It's a fact that a King's kid can preach Jesus from any page in the Bible, because it's His book, and He's there, unmistakably, all through it.

All of a sudden, without any kind of invitation or altar call from Philip, the Word was quickened in the black man's heart, and he asked, "Why can't I be baptized?" He made it sound like he wanted to be baptized right then. Philip hadn't so much as mentioned baptism, but the Holy Spirit had spoken directly to the Ethiopian and told him what it was all about.

Now if Philip and the Ethiopian had been using their common sense, they'd have known that nobody in his right mind would expect to be baptized in the middle of the desert. They'd have known that they would have to wait until they could get back to town to the First Baptist Church where there was a baptismal filled with water instead of sand. But they weren't going by common sense that day; they were going by the Holy Spirit. Jesus had spoken of the Holy Spirit as rivers of living water flowing out of the belly of those who believed on Him (John 7:38-39), and sure enough, the Holy Spirit had taken care of every detail.

The moment the Ethiopian asked the question, his horses

pulled the chariot into a parking place alongside the most beautiful shimmering pool of water they had ever seen, right there in the middle of the desert. It couldn't have been a mirage either, because the Scripture says the two of them went down into the water (Acts 8:38). After they had come up again, the Ethiopian continued on his way to Africa, rejoicing and praising God all the way. It's a wonder he wasn't raptured before he got there, but God had something else in mind. The Ethiopian just happened to be on the queen's board of directors, and he couldn't wait until the next quarterly meeting to spread the good news of Jesus Christ. He started right in on it.

The gospel came to Africa because Philip was kook enough to do what God required of him. He was willing to go when it didn't make any common sense to go, and God was in full charge of the supernatural results.

I wonder what would happen if every modern King's kid was suddenly as sensitive and obedient to the leading of the Holy Spirit as Philip was that day.

Gideon was extremely hard to persuade.

26
How to Live in Victory
when You Are Good for Nothing

A submissive King's kid is the only kind God can use. All pride and self-sufficiency, all grandiose plans of our own have to be rooted out of us before He can do what He wants to do through us. I'll never forget one of the early instances in my Christian life in which God taught me that.

For a while after my baptism in the Holy Spirit, I was booked as a great healer. I thought that God had given me a "healing ministry." And other people thought so, too. Whenever I was scheduled to appear at a Faith at Work Conference, they would set up a special workshop for Hill the Healer.

It sounded beautiful. Some people even got healed, and I was not mature enough to handle this heady success without believing *I* had something to do with it. I forgot to give all the credit to Jesus, and after a while, I began to think no one could have a good conference without a Hill the Healer workshop. The longer I thought about it, the more indispensable I got in my own eyes.

The whole thing was deadly poison to my Christian growth. Before long, I was thinking things like, "I must be smarter than the average pagan. After all, I got smart enough to get saved."

Well, God loved me enough not to give up on me. In His mercy, He said, "Cool it." And He made me do just that. He closed every door. He canceled every appointment. Speaking engagements ground to a thudding halt. He put me on the shelf for three solid years, gathering dust. Those three years were longer than Moses' forty years on the backside of the desert. I thought they would never end.

I didn't take it lying down, I complained bitterly. I caterwauled, "Lord, you're wasting my talent. Think of my valuable time! I want to be out there, serving you. You need me, Lord. Remember the great things I've done in your name?"

He didn't seem impressed a bit.

I tried another angle.

"Look, Lord, the world is falling apart! If you don't use me, who's going to carry the message?"

"None of your business," He told me. "As long as you have any ideas of your own as to what you ought to be doing, I can't use you. Down, boy."

After my three years on the shelf, begun when I was operating by my self-sufficiency instead of by His Spirit, I learned to submit to Him. Finally, one day, after my complaining mechanism had about worn out from overuse, I came to the point where I said, "Lord, I think I have the message: "I'm not all that important; in fact, without you, I'm nothing at all."

"That's it!" He said. "Now you're ready to graduate." Somehow, I sensed that He was just as relieved as I was. Then I realized the truth that when I'm ready *never* to go, then I'm ready to go. And so He began to send me. As I read the *Manufacturer's Handbook*, I find the same pattern in the lives of some other King's kids.

Moses exhibited a little self-effort on his first assignment out. He killed an Egyptian (Exod. 2:12), and God had to put him on the backside of the desert for forty years to get that self-effort out of him. At the end of that time with the sheep, Moses confessed to God, "I don't have what it takes," and so he was automatically, perfectly qualified to serve Him.

When the angel of the Lord came to tell Gideon he was to lead God's people, he said, "I'm sorry, sir. But you've got the wrong boy. You must be after one of my brothers. Some of them are real leaders. Me, I'm the least in all my father's family."

I can imagine God's angel smiling as he said, "Yes, Gideon. That's right. And that's exactly why you're the one He can use."

Well, the whole thing sounded so ridiculous, Gideon shook his head and said, "I can't buy that. You must be some kind of a deceiver or something. Why, I bet you're not *really* an angel of the Lord. Can you offer me some proof of your identity?"

Back in those days, nobody had a driver's license or a social security card in his billfold. Proving one's identity called for a little doing. But the angel had his credentials ready just in case they were needed.

"All right," the angel said to Gideon. "Prepare yourself to be persuaded. Have you got any goat stew in the house?"

"Funny you should ask that," Gideon told him. "Because I just happen to have some left over from yesterday. I was counting on having it for lunch, as a matter of fact."

"How about bringing it out and setting it on this rock so I can have a look at it?" the angel said. Gideon knew enough to be hospitable to strangers, and maybe he thought the angel was hungry, so he brought out the bowl of stew and set it on the rock.

But the angel didn't start to eat it. Instead, he raised his power wand in the air and told Gideon to stand back. As Gideon was backing away from the rock with the bowl of stew on it, the angel lowered his wand. When it made contact with that bowl of stew, a great ball of fire jumped into the middle of the bowl. The next thing Gideon knew, the ball of fire had disappeared. So had the stew, the bowl, the rock, and everything else.

The angel dusted off his power stick, put it back in his holster, and looked at the dumbfounded Gideon.

"Okay, are you convinced now?" the angel asked him.

Maybe Gideon enjoyed the Fourth of July fireworks and thought he could get to see some more or something. Anyway, although he was shaking like a leaf, he stood his ground.

"That was a pretty neat trick," he acknowledged to the alleged angel, "but I'm still not persuaded that I can be a leader of anything. You'll have to give me some stronger proof than a ball of fire if you want me to believe any such ridiculous thing as that God can use the likes of me."

This time the angel didn't volunteer a trick of his own; he invited Gideon to lay out the test case. And Gideon proposed a test that had to do with water instead of fire.

"Look," he said, "I'm going to lay a sheepskin on the grass tonight before I hit the sack, and if you are *really* an angel of the Lord, fix it so that the sheepskin will be soaking wet with dew in the morning and the ground around it will be bone dry."

The angel said he would see what could be done about that, and Gideon turned in, dreaming of a powder-dry sheepskin. He didn't know a lot about mysterious fireballs, but he surely knew that when the dew wet something, it wet everything in sight. There was no such thing in his experience as dew wetting a sheepskin and leaving

170

everything around it dry.

Well, such a thing may never have happened before in all of human history, but it happened that night. When Gideon woke up in the morning and stumbled out into the yard in his bare feet and pajamas, his feet stirred up little clouds of dust from the dry grass. But the sheepskin was soaking wet with dew. Gideon picked it up and wrung a whole basin full of water out of it, more than enough for washing his face and brushing his teeth before breakfast. That was something else. God must have sent a uniquely tailored sheep-shaped cloud of dew and triggered it to unload exactly over the sheepskin.

All that was rather spectacular, but Gideon was extremely hard to persuade.

"If I'm really supposed to be a leader," he told the angel, "you're going to have to come through one more time. I want one more proof."

The angel sighed, shrugged his shoulders at the obstinacy of the little guy, swallowed patiently, and said, "What will it be this time?"

"Well," he said, "how about doing just the opposite this time? If you really are an angel of the Lord, instead of having the sheepskin wet, and the ground dry, let the ground be wet and the sheepskin dry."

"Nothing to it," the angel replied.

And the next morning, Gideon got his pajama legs soaking wet from the dew on the grass when he tiptoed out to check on the sheepskin. It was drier than his breakfast toast.

And so Gideon was finally persuaded. In spite of—or because of—his physical weakness, his lack of imagination, and every other shortcoming imaginable (including a hefty dose of lack of faith), he was to lead God's people. And he was to do it, not with a mighty army of strong and brave soldiers, but with a handful of nobodies like himself, pitifully equipped.

God entered the battle himself in a mighty way through a foolish-sounding dream He sent to the enemy soldiers.

They dreamed of a little round biscuit, tumbling down the hill into their camp. A biscuit is not ordinarily something to frighten an army. A biscuit isn't good for much other than sopping up red-eye gravy if you happen to have some. But when that weak little biscuit, that they understood to be Gideon, rolled into the enemy camp, they were all scared to death. They took off for home, leaving all their valuables for Gideon and his bunch to pick up in the leisure of God's victory. You can read all about it in Judges 6 and 7 in your *Manufacturer's Handbook*.

Human wisdom says, "Get out there, make it on your own, chalk up Brownie points for human achievement. Get a gold medal for all your human efforts. Take credit."

God says, "It's up to you. If you go the route of human strength, you'll fold up—second best. But if you let me have the glory, you'll last forever and have a ball all the way. And I'll let you bring a whole host of others along with you into glory land."

Gideons of the world, rejoice that His strength is made perfect in your weakness (2 Cor. 12:9), and that with Him all things are possible (Matt. 19:26). No matter how weak you are, you can do all things through Him who gives His strength to you (Phil. 4:13).

27
How to Live in Victory
over Husband-Wife Haggles

A long time ago, I had a religious wife. She went to her temple religiously every Sunday morning, doing the religious things that they did. She even wore a hat, or a little doily thing on her head that pretended to be a hat.

Slue Foot began to work on my wife after I had met Jesus for real, because he knows that family unity is vital to Christian growth. The home is the final testing ground for this whole spiritual dimension, and one night the battle was engaged. My wife came out with it:

"Look, you Jesus fanatic. I've had it right up to the eyeballs with this fanatical bit of yours. If you don't get out of *it*, I'm getting out of here. I'm fed up with all this ridiculous 'Praise the Lord,' and 'Thank you, Jesus' business."

Now, she had kind of hinted at these things before, but I hadn't taken her seriously. With a little practice, a husband can tell when a wife is just threatening and when she is in earnest about something. This time she meant it, and I knew it. We'd been sitting across the grocery table from each other for about twenty-five years at that point, and she came

173

through loud and clear.

I almost panicked. I didn't want to lose my wife. Jesus was going to have to come to my rescue on this one, or I was a goner.

"Lord, what do I tell her?" I wailed.

The answer I got came in the form of an understanding: "State your position to her as head of the house."

He directed my attention to the Scriptures describing the chain of command He has established for best results in kingdom living earthside:

> Wives, submit yourselves unto your own husbands, as unto the Lord. For the husband is the head of the wife, even as Christ is the head of the church: and he is the saviour of the body. Therefore as the church is subject unto Christ, so let the wives be to their own husbands in every thing. (Eph. 5:22-24)

Until that night I had never realized this chain of command and the reasons for it were laid out so plainly in the Scriptures. And here I was being told to explain these things to my wife. It made more than a little uneasy, because we had never talked about these things before, and I didn't know how she would take it. We had had a good working relationship, I thought. I paid the bills and mama did the cooking. I didn't interfere with her department; she let me run mine. She couldn't add two and two together, and I couldn't manage to make instant oatmeal, so it worked out fine. She'd never written a check; I'd never baked a pie. Without each other, we'd be lost. I'd starve to death, and she'd go to debtor's prison.

Slue Foot was trying to split us asunder. And it seemed that the advice I was getting from heavenly headquarters wasn't going to help matters all that much. For a while, I wasn't sure I understood whose side God was on and what exactly He wanted me to do. That called for another question:

"Lord, what do you mean, that I'm to state my position? What *is* my position?" I had never thought it through.

"Who comes first in your life?" was how He put it to me. And then I understood what He was getting at.

"Lord, give me the words to tell her," I prayed, and this is what He had me tell my wife:

"Look. I hope you don't go. I hope you don't feel that you have to leave." I was getting it straight in my own mind as I was telling it to her. "But let's get this one thing settled right now, once and for all: Jesus Christ is number one in my life, and you are number two."

Zonk! She looked as if I had hit her on the head with a chair. After all these years of thinking she was something really special in our household, she was confronted with the fact that she had to take second place. It was kind of rough, and I admit I felt sorry for what she was going through.

It was a tense moment. I was learning that you don't make apologies for God's Word. When you stand on it and tie your statements into eternal truth, God won't let you down. He'll back you up.

Immediately Slue Foot got on the defensive. The power of Satan began to leak out because the truth had been spoken, loud and clear.

"But where will I go?" mama asked, her voice trembling.

"I have no idea," I told her. "As far as I'm concerned, you're welcome to stay, but no more quibbling or argument about one thing: Jesus is first; you are second. If you have to go, you'll have to figure out the where for yourself. And *if* you go, don't slam the door when you go out. You just might want to come back sometime."

She just stood there, thinking about it.

In the midst of the impossible situation, God gave me a gift of faith that beat anything my intellect could have cranked up. I stopped holding my breath, because I felt the faith rise up in me that God would deliver us out of the sticky situation. He let me *know* that if our marriage came unglued, it wouldn't stay unglued forever. I understood by faith that my wife might go, but that if she did, she'd be back. As it happened, I got a brand-new wife without having to bother about divorce or alimony.

Part of mama's testimony now is, "I couldn't fight them, so I figured I'd better join them." So she didn't go. She hung around and got saved. She became a new creature in Christ Jesus. Our whole household is saved and filled with the Holy Spirit—my wife, my daughter, my granddaughter.

Two friends of mine were talking one night, and I learned that between them they had had seven wives, and not a good one in the lot. King Solomon did worse than that. He had a thousand wives, all of them pagans. But the Lord gave me only one, and made her perfect.

Two of God's people ministering together have ten times the power of one, especially in the home. The husband and wife agreeing together, and ministering together, are a channel for power that flows with no restrictions. Since my wife and I have done our best to remove all blockages to prayer together, when we get on our prayer bones alongside the bed and begin to intercede, we drive Slue Foot up the wall. A man and his wife praying together generate so much power that Satan will do anything to prevent it. He doesn't want prayer in harmony in the home. Outside the home, he's not so worried. If the home has fallen apart, the outside fellowship is only a phony cover-up, a cheap counterfeit of the reality of God which starts where we live.

Jesus sent them two by two for a purpose. The Scripture says, "Two are better than one" (Eccles. 4:9), and goes on to give some examples. In another Scripture, we see that one could chase a thousand, but two could put ten thousand to flight (Deut. 32:30). And it seems that there is ten times the power in two praying together than there is in one praying by himself. "If two of you shall agree on earth as touching anything that they shall ask," Jesus said, "it shall be done for them of my Father which is in heaven" (Matt. 18:19).

The geometrical superiority of two over one is demononstrated in nuclear physics. When two atoms are brought together, the binding energy increases to the tenth power. This same interlocking energy goes into action when two King's kids pray together. Slue Foot will do anything to keep them from it, but once they've broken through the barrier, watch out. Neighborhoods have been known to be saved by husband and wife interceding for them.

In the home, wives hold the key to the whole family of relationships of people to people. And God tells them plainly what this key is:

> Wives, submit yourselves unto your own husbands, as it is fit in the Lord. (Col. 3:18)

> Wives, submit yourselves unto your own husbands, as unto the Lord. (Eph. 5:22)

When I read these Scriptures to some unhappy wives, they get their hackles up:

"You mean I should submit myself to that loud mouth, that good-for-nothing, that drunken sot?"

They know the answer is yes before I tell them, so they have their excuses all ready:

"Well, but how about that other Scripture, the one that tells husbands to love their wives? I'd be glad enough to submit to him if he'd do his part, if he'd love me like it says." They hold their Bibles up under my nose and point out the verse:

> Husbands, love your wives, even as Christ also loved the church, and gave himself for it. (Eph. 5:25)

I always have to explain that wives shouldn't read the verses that are addressed to husbands. That's like reading someone else's mail, not recommended if you want to stay on the outside of the bars. Wives are to read their own mail, and to be obedient to what the Word says to them.

It's not helpful to the wife, or the husband, for her to point to what the husband is supposed to do. She should put her attention—and her obedience—on what *she's* supposed to do.

Husbands have to read their own instructions, when they get ready to do it. And they're more likely to follow them if the Holy Spirit is the one who does the pointing out, and not the lady of the house.

In my travels, I suppose I've asked thousands of wives this question: "Have you ever dared to try Ephesians 5:22? Have you ever tried submitting to your husband, just as he is?" Out of thousands of responses, I've heard maybe a dozen yeses, that's all. I can always pick the yes-answerers out of the crowd by checking out their glory grins.

Three wives at a coffee hour in Toronto were so glowing, we almost didn't need the lights turned on.

"The three of you look as if you're in on something special," I said. "Would you mind telling the rest of us about it?" They were glad to.

"We tried Colossians 3:18, just like it says," they announced. One of the glory grinners gave us the details: "We got together and prayed about it and asked God to give us the grace to try His chain of command in love. Without His grace, we could have tried it by gritting our teeth with an I'll-go-home-and-submit-to-him-or-else attitude, but we didn't think that was what God had in mind. We knew that attitude would make us worse than we'd ever been."

They said that when they put the nit-picking on the shelf

178

and began to praise God for their sorry husbands, exactly as they were, and tried submitting to them in all things, at first their husbands got worse. But soon, and suddenly, God changed the husbands into the creatures He had planned for them to be all along. The homes were transformed. One of the women giggled as she told how the experiment had turned out.

"We almost feel guilty," she said. "Our husbands practically worship us; our homes have become little corners of heaven."

You don't believe it happened? Honest doubt is good, because God will prove himself to you, given the opportunity. If you're a wife, you can check it out in your own home. According to my information, wherever wives have been doers of the Word according to Colossians 3:18, Ephesians 5:22, or 1 Peter 3:1-2, husbands begin to love their wives, and children begin to obey their parents. The whole family situation falls into place.

God never recommends a particular life style without providing the grace to make it work and the power to put it into operation. But He doesn't force our wills in these things. He lets us make the choice.

To the degree that a wife is sold out to Jesus, she will submit to her own husband. What if he's not saved? God doesn't say anywhere that a woman can cop-out of obedience to her spouse if he's still a pagan. She's to submit to him regardless of his spiritual state. Then, over in the first letter of Peter, wives have God's promise that if the saved wife lives with the pagan husband, she'll be the instrument through which he will be saved—if she doesn't motor-mouth him to death:

> Likewise, ye wives, be in subjection to your own
> husbands; that, if any obey not the word, they also
> may without the word be won by the conversation

179

[the word means *conduct,* here] of the wives; while
they behold your chaste conversation coupled with
fear. (3:1-2)

That seems to be God's clear answer to wives who ask,
"But my husband isn't saved. Should I submit to him?" The
Lord says "Yes, of course. Your submission is the very
means I have chosen to get him to receive my salvation."

One woman, considering these Scriptures for making a
perfect marriage out of a raunchy one, protested to me, "But
if I did that, we'd go bankrupt. He can't add two and two.
What about that?"

I told her she could pray, "Lord, if we go bankrupt, you'll
have to feed us. I know you can, because your Word tells me
you feed the birds on a regular basis."

"You mean I have to be that fanatical?" she asked.

"Be as fanatical as you have to get God's chain of command
operating in your household," I told her. "God might choose
to make a mathematician out of your husband, or He might
have your husband dump all the bills back in your lap and
say, 'Honey, will you please handle the checkbook?' If he
gives the job back to you in this way, you'll be engaged in
redemption check writing from that point on, not usurpation
of the role of head of the household."

The operation of God's promises goes beyond the natural.
It's kingdom living for King's kids, married or single. This
supernatural life has to work for one reason—because God
said it would. Is there anything too hard for God? The
natural mind says yes, but God repeatedly says no and
proves He's right when we trust Him.

Here's God's promise to wives who are obedient to
Colossians 3:18:

And whatsoever ye do, do it heartily, as to the
Lord, and not unto men; knowing that of the Lord
ye shall receive the reward of the inheritance: for

ye serve the Lord Christ. (Col. 3:23-24)

Try this promise for size, maybe even write it on a piece of paper and stick it on the front of your refrigerator or on your mirror until you get it in your gizzard. And remember that,

The Lord is not slack concerning his promise, as some men count slackness; but is longsuffering to us-ward, not willing that any should perish, but that all should come to repentance. (2 Peter 3:9)

One day recently, I was reading some of the Scriptures having to do with the proper chain of command in the home. This time, He was drawing my attention to the verses I'd always managed to ignore before, the ones addressed particularly to me and to other husbands:

Husbands, love your wives, even as Christ also loved the church, and gave himself for it; that he might sanctify and cleanse it with the washing of water by the word, that he might present it to himself a glorious church, not having spot, or wrinkle, or any such thing; but that it should be holy and without blemish. So ought men to love their wives as their own bodies. He that loveth his wife loveth himself. For no man ever yet hated his own flesh; but nourisheth and cherisheth it, even as the Lord the church: For we are members of his body, of his flesh, and of his bones. For this cause shall a man leave his father and mother, and shall be joined unto his wife, and they two shall be one flesh. This is a great mystery: but I speak concerning Christ and the church. Nevertheless let every one of you in particular so love his wife even as himself. . . . (Eph. 5:25-33)

"Wow, Lord!" I said. "How come you've never taught me anything about loving my wife before now? It's right here in your Word, but you've never said anything to me about it.

How come?" I pointed to the Scriptures just in case He had failed to notice them. His answer was a real put-down.

"You've never been interested enough to listen to me on that subject."

I had to admit it was true.

"You're so right, Lord," I said, hanging my head. "But why haven't I been? You know I want to be obedient to all of your Word—"

"You've had a bitter spirit against your wife," He told me. Before I could crank up an argument, He delivered a real sledgehammer blow: "The rebellion you've complained about in her is a reflection of the rebellion in you—against me."

I had to defend myself against that.

"But, Lord, I've thought I was in total submission to you." Even as I made my protest, I could feel chinks in my armor, places where the whole armor of God did not fit me but where Slue Foot still gave me a fit instead, places where I wasn't as sold out to Jesus as I'd let on to myself and others.

"Lord, I repent," I cried out, seeing that the fault was mine, and not my wife's, and not the Lord's. "Show me how to love the wife you've given me."

As soon as I said that, God had me where He'd been trying to get me, and He dumped so much glory on me I could hardly stand it. Being made righter with Him than I'd ever been before, I was set free to *be* the head of our house in a new way, because I was really submitted to Jesus as my head. And I was newly aware of Jesus showing His perfect love for my wife through me. He hadn't been free to do that while there was a blockage in my relationship with Him.

In the days that have passed since that revelation to me, I have seen clearly how the degree of a husband's fitting into his proper place as head of the house, loving his wife, depends entirely on the degree of his sellout to Jesus. And what incentive He gives us for that:

Likewise, ye husbands, dwell with them according to knowledge, giving honour unto the wife, as unto the weaker vessel, and as being heirs together of the grace of life; that your prayers be not hindered. (1 Peter 3:7)

His whole armor can fit us only when every inch of us is transformed into the likeness of Jesus. Our prayers get through unhindered only when we are rightly related to our wives and to the Lord, forming an unbroken chain. When these conditions are met, all heaven rejoices that we are learning to live in victory according to God's perfect plan.

28

How to Live in Victory
when Your Wife Tells You What to Do

You don't know a thing about my spirituality until you catch me offguard at home with my wife, daughter, or granddaughter. For instance:

My wife has a thing about clean curtains. Most wives have a thing about something, and her thing just happens to be in the clean-curtain department. Every other week, it seems, the curtains have to be freshly laundered and rehung. It's part of God's training process for me that she never mentions the curtain-hanging chore until I've come in from a hard day—on a veritable mountain top because I've lived the victory through the most enormous trials and temptations a man ever faced. Naturally, I'm feeling extremely religious, all prayed up. But my wife doesn't seem to realize what a spiritual giant I am. When I have my overcoat buttoned all up, my hand on the doorknob ready to go out to a prayer meeting, she delivers her announcement.

"Oh, by the way, King's kid, you and I are going to hang the clean curtains tonight."

Having given me the good news, she shoves a curtain rod into my gloved hand without even asking my permission.

Her nonchalant, "By the way, King's kid . . ." comes through like a general commanding an army.

Now if I grin and say, "I'm delighted to hear that," she knows I'm lying. But if I say nothing, I'm really doing well compared to the old days. I'm making measurable progress. How I react—or respond—is a true measure of my spirituality.

For years, this business invariably unraveled me. I had a lot to learn about walking in the Spirit. But the last three times it's happened, I have taken my hand off the doorknob, grinned as I unbuttoned my overcoat, and reached for the curtain rod with a hearty, "Praise the Lord! Let's go!" A glimmering of heaven has seemed to stream in through the windows in the midst of the whole operation. It seems that I'm getting better at it with practice, and I suspect that when this particular exercise no longer bugs me at all, even deep down, when I enjoy it so much that I actually look forward to the curtain-hanging episodes, they'll have served their purpose, and I won't get to help with this little chore any longer. I'll have learned my lesson.

Rejoice twice a day, when everything is going your way? Oh, no. Rejoice all the time, no matter what. Pray seven times a day, facing the east? Oh, no. Pray without ceasing—all the time. Give thanks when you feel like it? No, give thanks *in* everything and *for* everything. Never stop giving thanks, for this is the will of God in Christ Jesus for you (1 Thess. 5:18).

When we are constantly rejoicing, praying, praising, and giving thanks, no matter what, we are spiritual beings dwelling in the heavenlies right here on earth.

"But you're a hypocrite when you thank and praise God if you don't feel like it," people protest, picking up the first thing the enemy throws at them through their common sense. But if you don't praise God until you feel like it, you'll never get around to it, except, perhaps, on those rare occasions when everything is perfectly pleasing to you. On the other hand, if you'll begin to praise God regardless of how you feel, you'll soon be praising Him more and more, because your "sacrifice of praise" (praising God when you don't feel like it) gets you tuned to the wavelength where God dwells.

Feelings come from the soul. And Slue Foot can be counted on to toss you all kinds of creepy feelings, trying to get your attention. Praising God anyhow is the best way to drive him up the wall with frustration.

In the letter to the Hebrews, God gives us some instructions about bringing this sacrifice of praise to Him:

By him therefore let us offer the sacrifice of praise
to God continually, that is, the fruit of our lips
giving thanks to his name. (13:15)

Here we see that our praise to Him is to be continual, our lips in motion thanking Him all the time. Webster says that "continual" means "without interruption." That doesn't seem to permit any recess period for not praising God when we don't feel like it.

I have run into some Christians who still want to cop-out, saying, "Oh, yes, but it doesn't mean we are to praise Him out loud, Brother Hill." I have yet to find one of these yes-but-ers who can explain how silent praise, beginning and ending somewhere down inside us, can be called "the fruit of our lips." To me, the whole verse calls for praising God at all times, in all circumstances, and doing it right out of the front of my mouth whenever the situation will permit it.

In all things, we are to praise Him. Slue Foot can't survive in the atmosphere of heaven we invite when we praise God. That's why his favorite trick is to get God's people to stop praising when they don't feel like it. Then you will *never* feel like it, and you'll go down deeper and deeper, ending up in nit-picking about God's way of running the universe. You'll waste your time listening to your sick head which says, "Look at appearances," instead of to God who says, "Don't look at appearances. Be reprogramed in your thinking. Look at me!" And when we look at Him, we *have* to praise Him.

The two little verses of Psalm 117 have struck me as being worth chewing on all the time:

O praise the LORD, all ye nations: praise him, all ye people. For his merciful kindness is great toward us: and the truth of the LORD endureth for ever.
Praise ye the LORD.

If we meditate on that psalm for a while, and begin to be obedient to God's Word in it, we'll begin praising Him on the outside of us, and the first thing we know, even our insides will be continually praising God. We will never have to bog down when adversity comes.

"You mean adversity will come?" someone asked me.

"Of course it will come," I told him. "God never promised to keep His younguns out of trouble but to deliver them from the midst of trouble. Trouble will come, and it will be exactly the kind of trouble we need for our training at the moment. We can count on that."

29
How to Live in Victory
when You're Thrown to the Lions

There is no way you can get away from trouble if you are a trainee for kingdom living. There is no need for us to tag trouble as something destructive or negative or bothersome if we know our rights and privileges as members of the royal household and know God's methods for converting a mess into a message every time we praise Him.

God can't deliver us out of trouble until we get in trouble in the first place. An Old Testament character by the name of Daniel found out about it one day (Dan. 6).

Daniel was living in a foreign country where they had certain rules and regulations about how and when and where the people were to worship the gods they had made with their own hands. Daniel didn't pay a whole lot of attention to the rules for worshiping powerless idols; he just kept on worshiping his living God. He got by with it for a while, but then the authorities found out, and they came to him and said, "Danny, my boy, the report has it that you are not worshiping the gods of our country. Is that right?"

"I worship the only true and living God," Daniel told them.

"Don't be evasive," they barked. "We'll tell it like it is: If

189

you continue to worship any God other than ours—"

They stopped to shake their heads back and forth before they conveyed the rest of the dire news:

"Danny, my boy, we have a plan which is designed to convince folks who do these things that they are not acceptable in our country. This is the way it goes. If you persist, we will invite you to a lions' club luncheon, and you will be the lunchmeat."

Well, that didn't faze Daniel, and he continued to worship the one true God in the manner to which he had become accustomed. That didn't happen to involve hiding off in a corner somewhere, but standing in front of an open window, praising the Lord. Whether he felt like it or not. He wasn't intimidated in the least by the thought of the lions. His attention and direction and dedication to God overcame his fear of lions and everything else.

The authorities were as good as their word. When Daniel continued to worship his God, the committee pounced upon him and carried him in the direction of the den of lions. I can imagine what must have gone through Daniel's mind, what he might have been praying as they were on their way with him:

"Oh, Lord, please keep me out of the lions' den."

That might have been a pretty good prayer, but God had a better idea. He let Daniel be put in the lions' den—but He kept Daniel out of the lions! That was really all Daniel wanted anyhow. And being in the lions' den but outside the lions was a brand-new thing. It had never happened before. As a matter of fact, it was such a mind-boggling event that it really got the king's attention. He issued a new decree, saying that Daniel's God was the only true and living God and that all men should tremble and fear before Him.

Anytime a King's kid dares to trust God in the face of insurmountable obstacles, to praise Him no matter what, some pagan notices and turns into a King's kid. And that's exactly how God wants to use us. Whenever we come to a situation where it looks like there's a lion's den full of lions and we're on the luncheon menu, we're to dare to praise Jesus, to trust Him, and to know that we are complete in Him. No one can kill a King's kid until the King is ready for it to be our graduation day.

30
How to Live in Victory
over Unpaid Debts

The major roadblock to Christian growth and maturity, to victorious living among the children of God, is unforgiveness. God's Word over and over again stresses the importance of forgiveness, not only for our spiritual well-being (so that our souls can prosper), but for our physical well-being, too. Our bodies are so constructed that they can't harbor unforgiveness on the inside without showing it forth on the outside.

The first place it generally shows up is in the joints of the body, beginning with the knuckles in your fingers. Swollen, stiff knuckles are called arthritic knuckles. And if your arthritis happens to be from unforgiveness, chances are it will go away when you go and get reconciled to the brother who has bugged you. I've seen it happen many times. Here's how it works:

Our nervous system is an electrochemical system. Electrical impulses travel from the brain through the nerves in a liquid solution of electrolytes made of water and chemicals, very like the storage battery in your car. The proportion of water and chemicals is very carefully controlled to insure the proper voltage across the system. If we could build a computer half as intricate as the human brain which controls all these things, it would weigh about seventy-five tons. And the seventy-five-ton computer wouldn't begin to do what the soup-bowl-size human brain does.

When the perfect electrolytic solution is kept healthy, by constant forgiveness, continual cleansing of sin by the blood of Jesus, the bone marrow stays in good shape, the joints work smoothly, things go along perfectly.

When my brain mechanism detects a need for water in the system, it tells me, "You're thirsty." I go to the water fountain, get a drink, and the system has all it needs for perfect functioning. If I'm where I can't get a drink of water, the solution may be too concentrated for a while, and trouble can set in.

Turning a cold shoulder to the brethren can affect the mechanism, causing calcium deposits to clog the joints. So can blowing your stack.

Let's say you are burned up against one of the brethren, but instead of really letting him have it, you've chosen to smolder silently, holding it all inside. When that happens, you raise the voltage across your nervous system, your blood pressure goes up, and your whole energy level rises to prepare you for going into action. But instead of letting off steam, you absorb all that action energy within your system. The result: you blow a gasket. The middle joints of your fingers can become arthritic almost overnight. I've seen it happen. And I've seen it un-happen when the victim chose to go and be reconciled with his brother. Or his sister. Or his wife.

I had a pain in a shoulder joint one night, a pain I didn't need. The Lord brought to my remembrance that I had a resentment against my wife, so I had to go to her and ask her forgiveness.

"For what?" she wanted to know.

"Well," I said, "I had a resentment against you, and I need your forgiveness."

"I don't know a thing about it," she said, and just turned her back and walked away.

I had humiliated myself. I had humbled myself like a worm. And my wife didn't even give me a medal. But it wasn't *her* joints that were hurting, it was mine. And because I had gone to make things right, my ache went away. Forgiving and asking forgiveness is highly beneficial.

I know these things by firsthand experience. Anything that you can do wrong, I have already done wrong at least once in my life on planet earth. When Jesus washed me clean and took away my record and let me know I was forgiven, He let me know that I needed to go and forgive others in an active kind of way. That meant going and asking those slobs to forgive me, and that was a strain and a struggle for anyone with an ego like mine.

As an active alcoholic, I had said some very unkind things to a man one day, and going to him and apologizing was one of the hardest things I ever did. He was bigger than I was, and by rights, he could have busted me one in the nose. But I went, and as soon as I had asked his forgiveness, my arthritis flew the coop. It was a physical readout of my raunchy resentment inside.

I have seen the same thing happen to other people. Sometimes their hands are locked up in monstrous ugly knots, and the minute they become willing to go and be reconciled to their brother, those hands begin to open. That clears the channel for physical health to flow and for them to begin to be able to look God straight in the eye and receive eyeball-to-eyeball guidance from Him, with nothing in between (Ps. 32:8).

If we try to take off on a life of adventure as King's kids in training without removing the roadblocks in our life, it's a waste of time. If we hang on to unforgiveness and resentment, for instance, the gifts of the Holy Spirit will not operate freely in our lives, and we may find ourselves backed into a theological corner, concluding, "Well, these gifts are not for today—they were for way back when." We'll become dispensationalists, dispensing with the things of God that won't work for us because we've refused to be honest about our own guilt. When unforgiveness and resentment are festering inside us, causing all sorts of physical problems, it's useless for the brethren to pray for our healing. It won't happen until we've followed the instructions in the *Manufacturer's Handbook*.

In Matthew 18:23-35, God has given us the parable of the two servants to explain in detail how these things work out. This is the story of one servant who owed the king a lot of money and of another servant who owed the first servant a little bit of money. At first, the big boss was going to sell off the first guy and his family into slavery so he could collect what was owing to him, but when the servant begged and pleaded with him, the king forgave the fellow the whole amount of the debt instead. Then the forgiven servant went to the guy who owed him a little bit of money and demanded payment.

"Just a little more time, and I'll pay you off," the fellow begged.

"That's not good enough," the first servant said, grabbing the fellow by the neck as if he was going to choke the life out of him. "If I can't have it right now, I'm going to throw you in the pokey. You can rot there until doomsday if you don't come up with the green stuff you owe me. After all, I know my rights."

He was as bad as his word, and had his debtor thrown into

195

prison. Maybe he brushed his hands together in satisfaction, proclaiming, "That takes care of that."

But it turned out there was more to the story. When the king found out what had happened, and the friends of the second servant made sure that he did, he called the unforgiving servant in and took him to task.

"I forgave you a big debt. How come you couldn't forgive your fellow servant a little debt?"

I don't suppose the poor guy was able to come up with any satisfactory answer. None is recorded anyhow.

I had probably read this parable a hundred times without really seeing what the fate of the unforgiving servant was. In my mind, I had him thrown into the hoosegow with the other guy, thinking maybe they spent the rest of their days playing checkers together for recreation in the midst of an ongoing pity party. But that's not what the Scripture says. The king didn't say, "Throw him in jail." He said, "Deliver him to the tormentors" (Matt. 18:34).

Who are the tormentors, the torturers? Why, they're the boys in black, the bad spirits of depression and oppression as well as body ailments like arthritis, leukemia and other kinds of cancer. Such spirits will hammer you into the ground right up to your eyeballs. The depression they bring is like a big black heavy blanket smothering you day after day, and never turning back no matter how sunshiny the circumstances might be. The most faithful of the brethren can't pray such spirits off; they depart permanently only when you go and get your forgiveness accounts squared away.

According to Jesus, the same thing that happened to the unforgiving servant will happen to us if we don't obey His repeated commands to forgive one another. This verse follows the one in which the unforgiving servant was delivered to the tormentors:

So likewise shall my heavenly Father do also unto
you, if ye from your hearts forgive not every one
his brother their trespasses. (v. 35)

I don't know how it strikes you, but whenever I read that
verse, I'm led to put top priority on forgiving everybody I
know.

Before I understood this parable, I spent a lot of time
praying for people who didn't get better. I was trying to cast
out spirits that had a firm hold on their victims until they
went and did what they knew God's Word was telling them
to do. My prayers did an about-face when I realized that.
From then on, instead of praying for such people to be
relieved of the spirit of depression or oppression, I began to
pray, "Lord, put them in a position to receive your
forgiveness. Don't take this torment away, but keep on
tormenting them until they can't stand it a moment longer.
Force them to go and ask their brother for forgiveness so
you can bring them into wholeness."

That kind of prayer sounds tough, but it works, and the
end result is shouting ground. Nothing else will work, because when God delivers you to the tormentors, you cannot get out from under until you have paid the last farthing.

An unforgiving spirit that is not dealt with can keep you in
a perpetual pity party. "Poor me, just look what so and so did
to me." That kind of celebration keeps you in the icky soulish
realm and blocks the flow of energy God wants to send
through you to produce the life of health and prosperity. It is
a principle all through the Bible, that we are not in a position
to receive God's forgiveness for ourselves until we have also
forgiven those who have trespassed against us. If you're
tormented, if you have trouble staying in high victory, if the
prayers of the brethren for you don't seem to be producing
joy of the permanent variety, maybe you need to go and
forgive somebody.

197

What we pray in the Lord's prayer is something God hears
and answers every time:

> And forgive us our debts, as we forgive our
> debtors. (Matt. 6:12)

A whole host of other Scriptures repeatedly make it clear
that our forgiveness from God is dependent on our
forgiveness of our fellow men. Try this on for size:

> When ye stand praying, forgive, if ye have ought
> against any: that your Father also which is in
> heaven may forgive you your trespasses. But if ye
> do not forgive, neither will your Father which is in
> heaven forgive your trespasses. (Mark 11:25-26)

Another Gospel puts it this way:

> Therefore if thou bring thy gift to the altar, and
> there rememberest that thy brother hath ought
> against thee; leave there thy gift before the altar,
> and go thy way; first be reconciled to thy brother,
> and then come and offer thy gift. (Matt. 5:23-24)

If the King's kids don't follow these clear instructions to
keep their forgiveness up-to-date, from then on out, their
religious activities are strictly a cop-out to try to cover up
their guilt. And guilt will destroy them if they continue to
maintain a spirit of unforgiveness.

When we refuse to forgive others, we're inviting God not
to forgive us. We're saying, in effect, "Lord, I prefer to
carry my own guilt in my own bloodstream." That means
certain deterioration of our essential blood supply, and it
translates into deteriorating bodily health. The rate may
vary, but the effect is always the same. You get dead from
carrying guilt in your own bloodstream. The better way is to
forgive one another, confess our sins, and receive God's
promise:

> If we confess our sins, he is faithful and just to
> forgive us our sins, and to cleanse us from all

unrighteousness. (1 John 1:9)

When we keep our confession up to date, God gradually cleanses us from the unrighteous tendency toward reacting against other people and turns us around until we begin to respond to the needs of people instead.

Paul was talking about forgiveness when he wrote,

Let not the sun go down upon your wrath: Neither give place to the devil. (Eph. 4:26-27)

When the Scripture says that we are not to let the sun go down on our wrath, it seems to be indicating that we might have wrath sometimes. But when it comes, we're to get rid of it as quickly as possible. If we let the sun go down on our wrath, if we go to bed without having forgiven our brother, our soul is left open, distorted and distended by the demon of wrath. If we entertain that demon, inviting him to stay, he'll hang around, doing damage every moment. By the time we wake up in the morning (if, in fact, we've been able to sleep with all that excess adrenalin racing around through our hallways), we'll be worse off than we were to start with. The first demon of anger and resentment will have invited seven of his friends in to join in the merriment of making us miserable. And our last state will be infinitely worse than our first, according to Matthew 12:45.

Wherever possible, it's highly recommended that we make things right with all men before we go to sleep. If we've had an unpleasant session with a member of our family during the day, we can get them together for family devotions before we hit the hay. When we're on our prayer bones together before the Lord, there's no way we can stay mad at one another. I've tried it, and I can't stay upset at mama when we kneel by the bed and pray together. The resentment, the mean and bitter spirit, goes away in spite of me. We can't really praise God or intercede for someone and be ugly inside at the same time. The two things are incompatible. Keeping up-to-date in our forgiveness of one another is part of the pathway to keeping right with God.

The whole business of forgiveness is brought into sharp focus by Paul when he is giving his instructions about the spirit in which communion services are to be conducted. Look carefully at what he says:

> For as often as ye eat this bread, and drink this cup, ye do shew the Lord's death till he come. Wherefore whosoever shall eat this bread, and drink this cup of the Lord, unworthily, shall be guilty of the body and blood of the Lord. But let a man examine himself, and so let him eat of that bread, and drink of that cup. For he that eateth and drinketh unworthily, eateth and drinketh damnation to himself, not discerning the Lord's body. For this cause many are weak and sickly among you, and many sleep. For if we would judge ourselves, we should not be judged. (1 Cor. 11:26-31)

Apparently, communion wasn't having its intended effect on many of the Corinthians. "Many of you are sick, and many of you sleep in death," Paul was telling them, "because you take communion in the wrong spirit. You've perverted the whole thing, bringing baskets of food and jugs of wine to the church for a Sunday school picnic, but you're not sharing with everybody. Some are hungry while others are gorging themselves."

He accused them of eating and drinking unworthily, that is, without awareness of what Christ had done for them and what they ought also to do for one another. That was why some were left weak and sickly or maybe even dead after a communion service which should have been healing for all. In the face of all that, Paul didn't tell them to get rid of communion; he told them to clean up their attitudes and approaches to it.

When I read Paul's letters to the churches, I don't feel too bad, because I never find him saying, "Congratulations, children! You are perfectly beautiful Christians." More times than not, he's saying something more like, "Kids, you're acting like slobs. Why don't you grow up? Why don't you get with the things that are recommended to bring spiritual maturity?"

Many people have been marvelously healed in communion services taken in the right attitude with nothing in-between them and God or their fellowmen. If there is unforgiveness, the healing won't come, this Scripture says.

The prophet Isaiah recorded some communion-related truths about Jesus before He was ever born as the son of Mary:

> But he was wounded for our transgressions, he was
> bruised for our iniquities: the chastisement of our
> peace was upon him; and with his stripes we are
> healed. (53:5)

In one breath, Isaiah, prophesying by the Spirit of God, is saying that our sins were forgiven by Jesus' shed blood, and our bodies were healed by the stripes that He bore on His body. The first part of this verse is generally accepted by Christian churches today; the last part of the verse, where the verb is in the *present tense*, is often shoved aside. It is dismissed with a perfunctory, "Oh, but healing is not for today." The fact is, healing *is* for today, and is made available to us through holy communion if we are there in the right spirit.

"Let a man examine himself" before partaking of holy communion, Paul says. The best way to do that is not to pick up a shovel and go digging into your subconscious, searching for nuggets to toss into the ash heap, but to ask the Lord to do it for you:

201

"Lord, I want the benefit of all that you have died to give me. Please show me if there be any block of resentment, any rejection of another person, any unforgiving spirit within me. If I've buried it so deep that I can't find it, you dig it up for me, Lord." He will do it, and as we are willing to go and make things right, our unworthiness to partake of the communion will be replaced with a reliance on His worthiness, and we will be drinking health and not damnation to ourselves. Then we will not remain weak and sickly from buried guilt.

Suppose you're about to partake of communion and the Lord shows you that you have a resentment against someone who is maybe on his way to South Africa by airplane at the moment. There is no way you can go and be reconciled to him right then. In such cases, the Lord will accept your willingness to go as if the deed were already done. The slate will be clean in God's sight, and you can go ahead and partake of communion with no condemnation and no guilt. It will have its healing, cleansing effect on you.

Being out of sorts with the brethren can result in double vision. This is the divided mind James talks about:

Purify your hearts, ye double minded. . . . Humble yourselves in the sight of the Lord, and he shall lift you up. Speak not evil of one another, brethren. (4:8, 10-11)

According to an earlier verse (1:8), "A double minded man is unstable in all his ways." The double-minded man is a spiritual schizo, and God can't use him. God wants King's kids who are single-minded so they get signals directly from heaven and none from the other place. I've had people tell me, "I'm getting two voices." My advice to them is, "Go and get right with the person you're not right with, and you'll get rid of the voice you don't need."

Following Jesus' voice in the matter of forgiving one

another paves the way for a life of victory.

"Does this forgiving business have to go on forever" people sometimes ask me, "or does there come a point when enough is enough?" God must have figured His people would be asking questions like that, because He had His secretary record Peter's question along the same line and Jesus' answer to it:

> Then came Peter to him, and said, Lord, how oft shall my brother sin against me, and I forgive him? Till seven times? Jesus saith unto him, I say not unto thee, Until seven times: but, Until seventy times seven. (Matt. 18:21-22)

Peter seemed to think at first that there might be a limit to how many times he was expected to forgive the person he couldn't stand the sight of. It seemed to him that seven times a day ought to be a reasonable number of forgivenesses to expect. But Jesus didn't put his stamp of approval on that. And He didn't up the ante just a little and say, "Try a dozen times, Peter." He said that seventy times seven would be more appropriate. That's 490 times a day—once every minute for eight hours and ten times left over. That'll keep you so busy forgiving that you can't possibly build up resentment against anybody.

There will be no place for bitterness or resentment in heaven. I experienced something of that revelation in my pagan days. I was in London at Easter time one year, and having heard that Saint Paul's Cathedral had a beautiful Easter service, I found out the time and got myself there for the festivities. Glorious? Maybe, for some people, but certainly not for me. I was miserable the whole time, because my unsaved soul was so full of darkness, the presence of life and beauty was somehow oppressive and condemning to me. I could barely sit through the service because I was totally incompatible with the atmosphere of heaven. That's how I know, today, that the things of hell in me will have to be gone before I'm ever a candidate for glory in the here and now or in the hereafter. High victory belongs to those King's kids who act like it. The blessings of kingdom living will be yours when you're in good shape with the brethren and with God.

31

How to Live in Victory
over Miserable Attendance

Every schoolchild used to know that a pearl begins with an irritation, a frustration, an unwelcome visitor in the mechanism of an oyster. Instead of kicking the irritation out, the oyster begins to smother it with the milk of molluskan kindness, oyster glop, or "nacre," if you want to be technical. The oyster covers the rough irritation with layer after layer of the lustrous smoothness so it won't be so scratchy to his insides. And after a long time, what began as a worrisome intruder has become super smooth, extremely valuable, a pearl of great price.

What is it that prevents scrawny, little pearls from growing into big, valuable pearls? Impatience. Every time an oyster gets tired of pouring out smoothness and kicks the irritation out of his shell too soon, the world is robbed of a pearl of great price.

Patience is something that doesn't seem to come naturally to all oysters or to some members of the human race. The Lord is always saying, "Wait patiently," but Satan is shouting, "Use your common sense and get on with the game."

Over a period of years, I have learned that I can always afford to wait for the Lord. It has been my experience that I have repeatedly seen God do the greatest things when I was on the verge of giving up. The temptation is always there, but I pray, "Deliver me from temptation," and then He lets me stick around to see His victory in the midst of what looks like sure defeat.

Some years ago, there was a Saint Andrews Society for men in an Episcopal church in Baltimore. One spring, they conducted a weekend retreat to which they invited men from other churches in the city. Sam Shoemaker was the featured speaker, and we all got fired up because Sam knew how to stir men to action. There must have been forty men in attendance, and Sam recommended that we begin to have regular weekly prayer and fellowship meetings following the retreat. Our function was to zero in on the needs of the congregations we represented and lift them up to heaven so God could work on them.

Everybody within hearing range of Sam's voice responded to his suggestions with high-level enthusiasm. We didn't waste any time, but began meeting the following Monday morning in old Saint Paul's Church in downtown Baltimore. There were about thirty of us at the initial meeting, fifteen the second Monday, seven the week after that, and then we went on week after week with just two or three of us in attendance. It looked like the foot of the cross.

After a few months of that, the third man found something more comfortable to do with his time, and that left two of us—my buddy Ed Rinehart and me. Ed and I were in perfect agreement. Each week we'd agree that we were wasting our time, and we'd say we weren't going to bother coming back again.

"After all," we told one another, "we're not even members of this church. We're Baptists, and if the Episcopalians don't want to support their own activity, forget it. Why should we care?"

We were fed up with the whole thing, ready to shake hands on our agreement about disbanding the prayer meeting idea entirely. But for some reason, the Lord didn't sound fed up. He seemed to be saying, "Be faithful to the vision. Keep on coming."

The next week, Ed would arrive from one part of town, I'd arrive from another, and we'd bump into each other in the hallway.

"Oh, *you're* back again," we'd chorus.

"Yeah." That sounded a little sheepish, as if we felt guilty for not keeping our part of the bargain.

"I thought we weren't going to come anymore." If there'd been a window in the hallway, we'd have stared out of it, but since there wasn't, we had to eyeball each other.

"I couldn't help it."

"Yeah. Me, too."

Every King's kid knows that when you're looking to the Lord for your directions, and He puts it on you to go somewhere, you don't stay home. You go. And you don't talk about failure when you know you're hooked up with the one who makes us more than conquerors, just like Paul (Rom. 8:37). One King's kid plus Jesus is always a majority anywhere, Ed and I reminded ourselves, even when it looked as if victory had long since disappeared in a direction exactly opposite to the one in which we were headed.

The weeks went by. The calendar was heading into Easter time. Every Monday morning, Ed and I were faithfully praying in a basement room where we had been relegated as kooky diehards who didn't know when to quit. Upstairs somewhere, sounds of organ music would be echoing through the dim recesses of the deserted church building. Our meeting time just happened to coincide with a regular weekly rehearsal of the organist.

But one day when we gathered for our meeting of two people—plus the Lord—we were aware of a strange silence emanating from the same dim recesses that were usually vibrant with music. We figured that maybe the organist had gotten fed up with us, too. While we were in the midst of praying, there was a knock on the door. We might have thought it was Peter, fresh out of prison, except that *we* seemed to be the ones on the dungeon level that day. Maybe it was an archangel sent to set *us* free? Under the circumstances, it seemed worthwhile to stop speculating about it and find out.

Ed and I stopped praying and invited the knocker to come in. At that, a middle-aged man opened the door and joined us in our dungeon. In the twinkling of an eye, we had a fifty percent increase in the number of people in our crowd. It was enough to cheer anybody up.

"I understand there's some kind of a meeting that goes on here every week about this time," the man said.

"That's right, this is it," we said enthusiastically, offering him a couple of chairs.

He looked around, looking kind of mystified at how you could have a meeting with just two people, and sat down in one of the chairs. Trying to put him at ease, we explained that we were delighted to have his company, and then we waited for him to make the next move.

"Funniest thing happened," he said. "I'm the organist for this church, and I left my music at home today. First time in my life I've ever pulled a stunt like that. It's new music, too, special for Easter, and there's no way I can practice it without the notes in front of me. Anyhow, I thought that as long as I was here with nothing to do but leave, I'd step downstairs first and see what your meeting was all about.

Had a hard time finding you though—"

We could understand that all right. We were meeting where you'd expect to find a pile of coal and a furnace, with maybe a few rats running around in the corners. But in my spirit the place was beginning to take on the aura of the Bethlehem stable where a King was born. I was suddenly overjoyed to be there. And I was thankful for the heavenly coincidence God had pulled to help out with our attendance record.

After a few preliminaries in which we explained that the purpose of our meeting was intercessory prayer, I said, "But of course we don't know what we're praying."

That was a new thing to the organist, and he did a double take.

"You what?"

"We pray in the Spirit," I told him. Not being a charismatic, he had never heard that terminology, so I explained it to him.

"That means we pray in unknown tongues, in a language we've never learned. I admit it sounds goofy, but it's scriptural, and it seems to be highly beneficial when King's kids do it."

He tipped his head as if he was trying to shake something out of his ear, thinking he'd heard wrong. While his eyebrows continued to climb toward his receding hairline, we told him that we both knew God personally, and that Jesus is His first name. That was news to him. So was most of the rest of what we told him during the next few minutes. But he took it all in, and gradually his eyebrows began to relax a little. We may have been crazy, but at least we weren't acting dangerous.

"How amazing! You say that Jesus is God's first name and that you know Him personally. I've been playing organs in churches and cathedrals and directing choirs for over thirty years from coast to coast, and this is the first time I've ever heard that a person could know God personally."

"Well, now that you've heard of it, would you like to try it? Would *you* like to know God personally?"

I didn't have to try to talk him into it.

"I most certainly would," he answered immediately. "Can you introduce me to Him?"

At that point, brother Ed, who was a little on the emotional side, began to have some tears running down his cheeks. Without asking anybody's permission, he began to praise Jesus out loud. With that kind of atmosphere to work in, it wasn't long before there were three King's kids in the basement instead of just two. And when Ed and I laid hands on the organist and prayed for Jesus to fill him with the Holy Spirit, he put on an ear-to-ear glory grin that almost split his head in two.

With that, our meeting disbanded. God never told Ed or me to go back again. He had accomplished His purpose, and all it took on our part was a little patience.

Have you been impatient and discouraged at the size of some of your King's kid meetings? Have you thought about quitting because you couldn't see a big crowd? Consider this:

No matter how small a King's kid meeting looks to an outsider, there are always at least two persons in it, a believer and Jesus. He said He'd never leave us or forsake us, and that has to mean He goes along to all the meetings He asks us to attend. Generally, there'll be some other invisibles along with Him, because God's Word says that goodness and mercy will follow us all the days of our life (Ps. 23:6). Since they're present, that makes at least four. So there's no need to be discouraged over the size of a King's kid meeting. There's always more to it than meets the eye, and if God made the whole world out of things that were invisible (Heb. 11:3), He can accomplish His purpose that way still.

To every King's kid, He seems to be saying something that sounds a little bit like something in the letter to the Hebrews (12:1). The way it came through to me that day was something like this:

"Run with patience the race that is set before you, and I will do the rest. I will even provide the patience."

Can we live the victory in Jesus? What else?

Without the feathers, talons, or beak, the mighty eagle is a defenseless, sorry-looking specimen of birdhood.

32
How to Live in Victory
when You're Completely Worn Out

The best illustration I've ever found in the Scripture about the benefits of waiting on the Lord is found in the Book of Isaiah:

> They that wait upon the LORD shall renew their strength; they shall mount up with wings as eagles; they shall run, and not be weary; and they shall walk, and not faint. (40:31)

As I was reading that verse one day, the Lord seemed to direct me to get down the encyclopedia and read up on the habits and behavior of eagles. As I read, I learned some remarkable things. One particular breed of eagle is programed by God for a periodic, built-in, instinctive renewal program. In that program, every seven years the eagle turns in its good old equipment for a brand-new, better set of tools.

The eagle prepares himself for the reprograming by flying up to a high protected place on the side of a mountain, where it won't be disturbed for a while. It seems to know it's going to be there for quite a spell.

The first thing the eagle does on its secluded perch is to

open its bill and tear out all the big powerful wing feathers that enable it to fly. They are good feathers; they have helped him make a living for years; but he mercilessly rips them out by the roots, until the ground is literally covered with them. The beautiful eagle begins to look pitiful to the eye. But not nearly as pitiful as he's about to look. Because a little while later, the eagle proceeds to tear off its strong talons, the claws he's been using to grab enough groceries to live.

Stripped of flying feathers and grasping claws, the eagle has only one asset left—but not for long. That asset, a large and powerful beak, has got to go too. The eagle grinds it off to a nubbin on the side of a jagged rock. Finally there is nothing left of it but a big hole where the beak used to be.

Without the feathers, talons, or beak, the mighty eagle is a defenseless, sorry-looking specimen of birdhood. Thus unhandsomely equipped, he sits and waits on the Lord. And waits and waits. God has programed the eagle to be patient.

After a few weeks of faithfulness to his calling, there is evidence that something is happening. Strong, perfect new feathers are coming through to take the place of the old frayed and worn ones. New talons, bigger and more powerful than the old ones, not chipped and cracked from hard use, begin to emerge. A shiny new beak starts to sprout, much better than the old one which was nicked in places from its encounters with rocks and hard bones.

As the eagle waits on the Lord, he is utterly renewed. By himself, he contributes nothing except a willingness and a need to be renewed. When the long wait is over, the eagle flies off, bigger and stronger than ever, because he has given up everything of his own on which he had been relying, in favor of what the Lord had for him.

When I saw all that about the eagle, I was much encouraged about the apparent occasional doldrums in my own walk with the Lord. God has programed eagles to wait upon Him instinctively for a renewal of their strength. King's kids are given opportunities to do the same thing if they are willing to submit themselves to His way instead of insisting on the worthless do-it-myself perfection falsely promised by non-stop programitis that schedules everything—everything except waiting on the Lord.

33
How to Live in Victory
when You've Lost Your Job

One of the things God has taught me, over and over again, is that every time someone tries His recommended way, He keeps His promises, including these from the sixth chapter of Matthew's Gospel:

> Therefore take no thought, saying, What shall we eat? or, What shall we drink? or, Wherewithal shall we be clothed? (For after all these things do the Gentiles seek:) for your heavenly Father knoweth that ye have need of all these things. But seek ye first the kingdom of God, and his righteousness; and all these things shall be added unto you. (vv. 31-33)

A scientist telephoned me one day and said, "I'm out of work, and in a terrible state. Someone up at the Army Chemical Center told me that you are in the business of scientific things and you might know about an opening."

"What are your qualifications?" I asked him.

"Ph.D. in physics and math," he told me. He went on to explain about his ten years of experience with one outfit, five with another, and two with still another one. He was beautifully qualified for space travel, all right, knew a lot of biochemistry, but neither of these things fitted any job openings I knew about.

"Tell you what," I said to him when he had finished his recital of qualifications. "I know someone who can help you, all right. If you'll come down tomorrow, we'll have lunch together and we can talk about it."

When the scientist arrived at my office, he was a picture of dejection. And no wonder. He had a wife and five little ones, but no job. His savings were just about exhausted. I could tell he figured his family was getting lined up to starve to death in the near future if I didn't come up with something.

"Where is your friend? The one you said could help me?" he asked, looking anxiously around my office for a visible third party.

"Oh, He's here," I assured him. "But let's go down and have lunch before we talk." He looked hungry and seemed satisfied that my friend would probably show up at the eating place.

My friend was already with me, of course, but the scientist didn't know that yet. King's kids always have Jesus with them—they are portable prayer towers, temples of the Holy Ghost.

After the unemployed scientist had packed away a hefty meal, he was ready for my explanation about the someone who could help him. I began by telling him how it had been with me, how my life had been drab and empty in spite of "Who's Who" accomplishments. I told him about my training and how I had gotten in on the ground floor in the diesel engine industry and grown up with it, becoming an authority as well as a successful businessman. When I discovered that all the attainments and advantages and successes of life were empty nothings, I had tried suicide at the age of forty-five. But after I goofed suicide, Jesus moved in and made my life complete.

The man was listening all right, because he was definitely at the end of his own self-sufficiency.

"What do you have to offer me?" he asked, simply, when I had finished my testimony.

"Only one thing," I told him. "New management. Are you interested? Are you ready to ask Jesus Christ to move in and take over your scrambled life and affairs?"

He didn't tell me anything more about his qualifications; he just said yes. We bowed our heads over the table in the restaurant, and the distraught scientist gave his heart to Jesus. That put him in a position to receive the power of the Holy Spirit, so I laid hands on him and asked the Jesus who had just saved him to baptize him in the Holy Spirit. And He did. We had a baptismal service right there at the dining table in the restaurant.

When our prayer was over, the scientist didn't look distraught any more. He was shining like the sun, praising Jesus. It didn't seem to matter at that moment whether he had a job or not. Ordinary things had lost their importance for him because he was full of assurance that Jesus was in charge.

When he began to look upward to the promises of Jesus instead of downward to the dejection of himself, he began to grow in the likeness of his heavenly Father instead of in the likeness of Slue Foot. He lost his tormented look along with his torment, and got the soft look of a King's kid who knew that everything was in the hands of the one who has all power.

Two days later, the formerly distraught scientist telephoned me.

"Guess what!" he shouted, and without giving me time to answer, he hollered, "I've just been given the best job of my life! It's in my own profession! Biochemistry!" He calmed down just a little to deliver the explanation. "I just *happened* to call one of our local industries, and they just *happened* to have an opening for a biochemist. They said my qualifications were exactly what they were looking for!"

We had a hallelujah party right over the telephone.

Coincidence? Hardly. It was Jesus, meeting the man's every need out of His riches in glory. A more abundant life is what He came to bring us, not a chinchy bread line.

It's a deceitful religious notion that King's kids are supposed to live like peasants. If we know our rights and privileges, if we're in a position to receive His blessings, and if we're not hanging onto the second-best detrimental junk of self-sufficiency, the more abundant life is ours.

There's nothing attractive about a wheel-spinning Christian, a cringing Christian, a struggling Christian. That's what the world has to offer—spinning your wheels until they fall off, struggling until you fall apart. But when a real King's kid, an out-of-this-world sort of guy, is in the very center of chaos, he'll act like he's in the calm of the eye of a hurricane. He can stay there, utterly unruffled, if he praises his way in and stays put.

If you ever get off to one side of a hurricane, you've had it. But in the center, everything stays together. King's kids can stay in the center by praising, no matter what's going on out on the fringes. Folks will notice, and when they get tired of fighting a losing battle, they'll come crawling in, asking, "How did you get to this calm in the midst of chaos?" Then you can tell them, "It's Jesus. I'm praising His name." If they're desperate enough, they may try praising Him, too.

Jesus talked about a man in the midst of a hurricane once:

Therefore whosoever heareth these sayings of mine, and doeth them, I will liken him unto a wise man, which built his house upon a rock: And the rain descended, and the floods came, and the winds blew, and beat upon that house; and it fell not: for it was founded upon a rock. And every one that heareth these sayings of mine, and doeth them not, shall be likened unto a foolish man, which built his house upon the sand: And the rain descended, and the floods came, and the winds blew, and beat upon that house; and it fell: and great was the fall of it. (Matt. 7:24-27)

One man heard the word and did it—he built his house on a solid foundation. Another man heard these things and did them not. He only thought about them, turning them into vain philosophy that profited him nothing. Now, both houses looked good, but one was built on a foundation of solid Rock—Jesus—and the other was built on the shifting sands of philosophy. There was no solidity to it.

I was privileged to see this teaching in action back in 1938 when I was driving through New York State at the time when a great hurricane hit that area. It had rained for a number of days, and the ground was already soaked. Then the hurricane rains came in great torrents, and the rivers overflowed. The floods came up. The tree roots were lying in mud instead of in solid soil, and when the wind blew, everything went flat. All the waterfront houses that had looked so desirable to the eye were swept away by the flood waters. The only things that stood were those that were solidly anchored in rock.

This is a perfect illustration of what Jesus is talking about in the Matthew 7 Scripture. If we're not anchored to the Rock who is Jesus, winds of doctrine and floods of doubt can sweep us away. In the face of a storm, we panic and everything falls apart. But if we're rooted and grounded in Him, we're not wiped out; we're changed from one degree of glory to another as we look on Him (2 Cor. 3:18). The only possible response to that, in the hurricane or out of it, is

"Hallelujah!" Freely translated, that means, "Hot dog! This is it!" King's kids are designed to live in that kind of exuberant joy (1 John 1:4).

34
How to Live in Victory
over Fear

The spirit of fear frequently assails Christian people. Basically, fear is faith in failure. Fear is being positively certain that everything is falling apart and that we'll be buried under the rubble. This faith that's headed in the wrong direction comes from a spooky spirit, and King's kids don't have to put up with it for a minute. They don't have to tolerate spooks. And they don't have to encourage their presence by mouthing off about them all the time.

The first day I checked myself on this, I caught myself saying, "I'm afraid . . ." twenty-seven times in ordinary conversation. Until I started the inventory, I had no idea that I was providing such a comfortable environment for the spirit of fear to dwell in me. But my insides knew it. So did Slue Foot. No wonder I was always feeling the spirit of anxiety building up in me. I'd go to a prayer meeting and be prayed for, and all the anxiety would leave, but the next morning, the bad confession of my tongue would be inviting him in all over again.

I guess I would have struggled with this kind of defeat intermittently for the rest of my life if I hadn't come across the principle in the *Manufacturer's Handbook* which says,

> Let the words of my mouth, and the meditation of
> my heart, be acceptable in thy sight, O LORD, my
> strength, and my redeemer. (Ps. 19:14)

If I'm born again, if God is my redeemer because I know Jesus, then I had better watch my tongue if I want my system to stay tuned exclusively to the wavelength of the Holy Spirit. The Spirit within me was positive, affirming, "By His stripes, I am healed" (Isa. 53:5), but with my tongue I was saying just the opposite: "I'm afraid I'm catching cold." I knew that life and death are in the power of the tongue (Prov. 18:21), and I suddenly realized that putting the wrong negative confession on top of a right positive one was highly destructive business, like putting a paper clip into a wall socket: the lights go out, and your fingers light up.

When I became aware of the proper use of my tongue in such matters, I got rid of the spirit of fear once and for all. We have God's Word for it that the spirit of fear does not belong to His children:

> For God hath not given us the spirit of fear; but of
> power, and of love, and of a sound mind. (2 Tim. 1:7)

Since God has not given His children a spirit of fear, when the delivery man brings it, we don't have to keep it.

"Listen," we can say to the one who is trying to dump the spirit of fear on our doorstep, "I didn't order that merchandise. Furthermore, I don't have any use for it even if it's free. Take it back where it came from." Then we're entitled to ask for, and expect to receive (Matt. 7:7-8), the spirit of power, love, and a sound mind. We can always find a use for it.

With the good spirit in control, you'll be successful in turning the spirit of fear away the next time it comes knocking at your door. The power will be yours to cause the gifts to function (Acts 1:8); the love of God will manifest itself through you, the perfect love that casts out fear (1 John 4:18); and if your mind has been fuzzy, hazy, and confused, you'll find it sharp as a tack.

Fear is not part of the equipment of King's kids who are living in victory. Instead of fear, they live in obedience to God's instruction, "Fear not," which appears in literally dozens of places in the *Manufacturer's Handbook*.

One of these passages, spoken through the prophet Isaiah, goes like this:

> Thus saith the LORD that created thee, . . . Fear not: for I have redeemed thee, I have called thee by thy name; thou art mine. When thou passest through the waters, I will be with thee; and through the rivers, they shall not overflow thee; when thou walkest through the fire, thou shalt not be burned; neither shall the flame kindle upon thee. For I am the LORD thy God, the Holy One of Israel, thy Saviour. . . . Since thou wast precious in my sight . . . I have loved thee. . . . Even every one that is called by my name: for I have created him for my glory, I have formed him; yea, I have made him. (43:1-7)

With an all-powerful God who loves us like that, how can we fear anything?

> If God be for us, who can be against us? He that spared not his own Son . . . shall he not with him also freely give us all things? (Rom. 8:31-32)

As King's kids, we are entitled to put those verses in our think tanks and drag them up whenever fear comes knocking. The spirit of fear will vamoose—or suffocate in the atmosphere of heaven with which we surround ourselves when we're looking to Jesus.

"No one has told me that in fifty years," she whooped, "and I'd all but forgotten it was true." She started to dance a little jig.

35
How to Live in Victory
in an Old Folks' Home

Jesus tells King's kids that it's better to give than to receive (Acts 20:35), and I have found repeatedly that it's true. Not only that, but I have found it is impossible for a King's kid to give without receiving a pressed-down, heaped-up, double measure of King's kid victory in return.

One illustration of this principle in my own life occurred a few years ago when I was invited to speak at Union College in Lincoln, Nebraska. That had to be a miracle to start with, a charismatic Baptist being asked to speak to such a group as that. I knew my invitation was by heavenly appointment.

As it turned out, something else was going on in town at the time I arrived. All the usual accommodations for visiting tourists were filled to capacity. The folks who had invited me met me with an apology.

"A terrible thing has happened," they said. "The hotel has run out of space, and the only place we have to put you up is in the local old folks' home. We're awfully sorry to have to do this to you, Brother Hill, but—"

"Well, glory to Jesus!" I shouted, meaning every word of it. "Don't be sorry. That's wonderful!"

They backed up a little bit, and a questioning look crossed their countenances.

"We thought you'd be disappointed," they said, a little disappointed that I wasn't.

"Me? Disappointed? At where the King puts me? No way! This has got to be a special blessing. God wouldn't put me there for nothing, would He? He must have something utterly fantastic in mind." I was eager to learn what it was, but I could tell by the looks on their faces that the folks who had invited me didn't look at things the way I did. It seemed that I should explain an important truth to them.

"Look," I said. "Don't you know that God works *all* things together for good for King's kids—including being domiciled with the senior citizens?"

They shook their heads, took me to my quarters, and left me there, still shaking their heads. They'd obviously never met a real kook before.

After I got checked in, I went back down to the lobby and started looking around to see what I might scare up. King's kids are always out sniffing like a hound dog on a rabbit's trail, following the directions of the Holy Spirit. Sure enough, I spotted something right off.

Sitting on a couch, her feet flat on the floor, her hands folded in her lap, her eyes studying the worn carpet, was the most dejected-looking specimen of humanity I'd seen in a long time. I judged her to be in her eighties, at least, thoroughly discouraged from having no one pay attention to her or act like they cared whether she lived or died.

Talk about opportunity! Think of what Jesus had done for her! And she looked as if she had forgotten all about it. I could deliver a joyful reminder. Hallelujah!

Walking over in her direction, I said, "Pardon me, lady, but I believe that Jesus wants me to tell you that He loves you so much that He died on the cross *especially* for you." (I got that word "especially" that morning from sloshing around in the Word in the vicinity of 1 Timothy 4:10.)

That was all she needed. That old lady shot off that couch as if its sagging springs had suddenly been born again, catapulting her into the air.

"Hallelujah!" she shouted, and reached up to hug my neck. I had to bend down a little so she could get to it, and that felt so good, I shouted hallelujah right along with her. We almost cranked up a glory fit right there on the premises.

"No one has told me that in fifty years," she whooped, "and I'd all but forgotten it was true." She started to dance a little jig, lifting her skirts to show her high-button shoes.

"Oh, this is so wonderful!" she exclaimed. "But how did you happen to know enough to tell me Jesus loves me? Nobody *ever* talks like that nowadays."

"King's kids do," I told her.

She hadn't heard that term before, but she knew right off what it meant.

"Oh, like a child of the King of kings!" she said. Without waiting for confirmation from me, she shouted, "Glory!" grabbed my arm, and the next thing I knew, we were both prancing in circles around the furniture. Without question, she had forgotten about her apparent poverty and was living it up in her riches in Jesus.

Well, that kind of got things started for the weekend. The livened-up old lady asked me to escort her into the dining room at suppertime, and she introduced me to everybody. We *all* started praising Jesus then, and the place began to sound like a *young* folks' home. Before the weekend was over, we had real revival going on in every room. I hated to leave.

If ever I have occasion to return to Lincoln, Nebraska, I'll pick that retirement home to stay in over the fanciest hotel accommodations in the city. In the meantime, if I get bored

with ordinary fellowship meetings, I know how to get my
batteries charged up. It would probably work for you, too.
Just call on some old folks who have forgotten they have the
privilege of getting together in Jesus' name. *You'll* get a new
vision of the victory we have in Jesus. And *they'll* start to
live it, too.

36
How to Live in Victory
with Special Equipment

Spirit-filled King's kids have nine pieces of special equipment making a composite whole which is capable of ministering abundant life to those who lack it:

Now there are diversities of gifts, but the same Spirit. And there are differences of administrations, but the same Lord. And there are diversities of operations, but it is the same God which worketh all in all. But the manifestation [the showing forth] of the Spirit is given to every man to profit withal [to benefit the whole group]. For one is given by the Spirit the word of wisdom; to another the word of knowledge by the same Spirit; to another faith by the same Spirit; to another working of miracles; to another prophecy; to another discerning of spirits; to another divers kinds of tongues; to another the interpretation of tongues: But all these worketh that one and the selfsame Spirit, dividing to very man severally as he will. (1 Cor. 12:4-11) he will. (1 Cor. 12:4-11)

The first one of the gifts of the Holy Spirit is the gift of a word of wisdom, which might be defined as "knowing what to do next."

It's easy to distinguish between divine wisdom and worldly wisdom. Divine wisdom always works when we do it; worldly wisdom doesn't.

There are other ways to tell the difference also. Just as we have a yardstick in Scripture for distinguishing true prophecy from false prophecy, so God has given us an ice pick to clearly separate divine wisdom from the worldly variety which is totally different from God's type:

> If ye have bitter envying and strife in your hearts, glory not, and lie not against the truth. This wisdom descendeth not from above, but is earthly, sensual, devilish. For where envying and strife is, there is confusion and every evil work. But the wisdom that is from above is first pure, then peaceable, gentle, and easy to be intreated, full of mercy and good fruits, without partiality, and without hypocrisy. (James 3:14-17)

Godly wisdom is pure; it is not mixed with selfish motives. There is no self-love represented in divine wisdom. Because it is always pure, it contains no non-nourishing additives to gum up the works. It's all useful, no nasty residue.

God's wisdom is *peaceable*. A temporary kind of peace*fulness* can come from compromise, a selling out to the enemy for a temporary cessation of hostilities—a peace-in-our-time kind of thing—but something truly peace*able* is *able* to bring peace out of chaos, peace out of the midst of disturbed conditions, peace that passes understanding, peace that will not be broken but can endure forever.

Divine wisdom is gentle, easy to be entreated. It is never nit-picking, arguing, differing. It speaks with absolute authority, and is full of mercy and good fruits. From the description here in James, we can see that this first gift of the Holy Spirit contains all the fruit of the Spirit. Without the gift of wisdom, it's really not possible to deliver the fruit of the Holy Spirit to feed the hungry.

The wisdom that God gives is without partiality. It benefits equally all who receive it.

The gift of wisdom is without hypocrisy. It does not believe one thing and do another. Believing one thing and being incapable of carrying it out is a pretty standard sort of failing among people.

A person who knows he should pay a bill but doesn't do it is a hypocrite, according to the dictionary definition. We have to start with first things first. If we think we're holy, we have to pay our bills. That's not mere doctrinal religion—that's very practical Christianity. One who doesn't pay his bills is no kind of example for the kingdom of God.

When God appointed Solomon as king to rule over God's people, He said, "Solomon, my appointed king, what'll you have? You may request of me whatever gift you desire, and I will grant it."

Solomon could have asked for untold wealth, or power, or authority, but instead, he asked for wisdom to know how to minister to God's people. In asking for wisdom, he had proved himself trustworthy, so, in addition to giving him wisdom, God gave Solomon the greatest riches that were ever known on this earth. In every situation, if we seek wisdom from God, everything else needful will be supplied along with it. If Solomon had asked for riches in the first place, he wouldn't have been fit to be king of anything. You can read all about this conversation between God and Solomon in 1 Kings 3.

God provides all sorts of wisdom, and He says,

If any of you lack wisdom, let him ask of God, that

giveth to all men liberally, and upbraideth not; and
it shall be given him. (James 1:5)

Wisdom brings order and peace, harmony and right
relationship within the whole group because it contains all of
those elements which produce these things. And they are
manifested wherever King's kids are living in victory.

The second gift of the Holy Spirit in this list is the word of
knowledge. The word of knowledge refers to information
about a person's needs that you'll never get at other than by
this supernatural gift. God always has one more fact, one
more insight at His disposal that you cannot get at unless
He reveals it to you.

The gift of faith is the supernatural gift of the faith of Jesus
himself for the given situation. Paul wrote to the Galatians
about such faith:

The life which I now live in the flesh I live by the
faith of the Son of God, who loved me, and gave
himself for me. (2:20)

My own little measure of faith is the receptacle for His big
faith in me. As I read about the illimitable faith of God—He
had so much faith that He could just say the word, and
worlds came into being!—my little faith is augmented by His
big faith. That gift of faith rises up and fills the vessel,
replacing doubt with certainty, so that we can walk into a
situation and minister like a King's kid.

Notice the plural *gifts* of healing in this list. That's healing
for spirit, soul, and body—total wholeness. When we're
praising God and seeking to be in line with His will, we're
manifesting Him in His resurrection glory in terms of
wholeness of the person. When God says that it's His will for
us to "prosper and be in health" (3 John 2), He's talking about
wholeness. When He says that we are to be wholly
sanctified, and preserved blameless in spirit, soul, and body
(1 Thess. 5:23), He's talking about wholeness there, too.

The next gift mentioned in this list is the working of miracles. After the first five hundred healings and miracles happened in our Baptist church in Baltimore, we stopped keeping records. We got the message from God that healings and miracles are the expected atmosphere of a Spirit-filled church. They are the natural supernatural "signs following" confirming the preaching and believing of God's Word (Mark 16:20).

We have a regular healing service in our church on Thursday mornings. The pastor and his wife, after teaching the Word, letting it build faith in the people, invite folks to come forward to receive healing for themselves or others unable to be present for whom they have come as intercessors. Hands are laid upon them, special prayers given as the Spirit leads, praying with God's infinite intelligence instead of with our own limited variety, and the results are left to God. He never disappoints us when we hear the Word and then do it.

The gift of tongues, which we use when we pray in the Spirit (1 Cor. 14:15), and the interpretation of tongues are often referred to as the least of the gifts because they appear at the bottom of the list in First Corinthians 12. But I look at it like this. If you come to my house, I will not take you over to the corner and brag about the telephone that's sitting there. I probably won't even mention it. But if you want to make a call, it is a very handy instrument, much more convenient than making a trip to the other side of town or kindling a smudge fire to send a message with a blanket, Indian smoke-signal style. In the same way, while we do not talk about tongues all the time, we do recognize their vital importance as instruments for transmitting a message to God, by way of a language the enemy can't wiretap or our human minds confuse.

After telling us what the gifts are, God says,

Covet earnestly the best gifts. (1 Cor. 12:31)

Which are the best gifts? It all depends on the situation. The best gifts are the ones required to meet a particular need in the life of some needy person. The gifts are not for us to keep, they're for us to give away. God doesn't endow us with one particular gift, and only one, and that's it. He may give us a ministry gift, of course, one in which we seem to be generally more proficient than other members of the body, but when we go to meet someone's needs, we have Jesus within, and He contains all the gifts. When we transport Jesus to the point of someone's needs, He can minister through us in any way that He sees fit.

If we get the "what's in it for me?" approach out of our minds, we'll begin to make some progress in these matters. With themselves in their minds, people say things like, "I hope He doesn't give me that kooky-sounding tongues gift, because I don't want that one. I want the one that sounds pretty. I want prophecy."

I used to be confused in my pumpkin head until I learned to covet the best gift in the best way. In the beginning, Satan would grab my eardrum and beat on it with words to this effect:

"Now remember, you want the best gift, or you don't want any. You certainly don't want anyone to hear you sounding funny."

Well, it took a good while, but after God got me to understand what the gifts were for, I learned to covet the gift that sounded funny or the one that sounded beautiful, not according to my own particular druthers, but according to which one would best fit the need of the situation in which I was ministering at the time. Sometimes I needed all the gifts to help a person in need, and all of them were available to me for the asking.

The condition of Kings' kids after they've received the

power hookup is comparable to that of a milkman. He doesn't make milk, and he's not made of milk. He may not even like milk. He doesn't have to. He simply delivers the milk to folks that need it. In the same way, we are to go and deliver the gifts of the Spirit. And the best gift for a particular assignment depends on what the need is.

King's kids are to go out and act as if the gifts are theirs to deliver to the needy. I hear so many Christians say, "But I don't have a healing ministry." Well, I haven't read of anything called a "healing ministry" in the Bible, but I have read that Christians are to lay hands on the sick, and they will recover (Mark 16:18), and that we are to pray for one another that we may be healed (James 5:16). We are not supposed to wait for someone to give us a framed document that says "healing ministry" before we lay hands on sick folks or pray for them. If we'll do it, He'll take care of the credentials and the results. Go ahead and lay hands on the sick. If God doesn't choose to heal through you, you'll know it soon enough, because nothing will happen. But if something does happen—

It's that simple. Just do it and see.

In exercising any of the gifts of the Holy Spirit, we need to put aside all ordinary information contained in the standard-brand think tank and rely on the resources of God. We can pray, "Lord, I want your wisdom in this. Lord, I need your knowledge, your kind of faith to make this thing work." As surely as you ask, He will hear and give you what you need to deliver to the needy (Matt. 7:7).

Satan, of course, tries to discourage believers from using any of the gifts of the Spirit, because he knows he's a defeated foe when the supernatural power of God goes into action through a believer. One of his favorite points for attacking us is through the pride of life. Some years ago, I was teaching about the power gifts at a Faith at Work conference in Detroit, Michigan. On Tuesday, I had blown an opportunity to let God operate in power to meet someone's need, because Satan backed me into a corner, made me afraid I would goof it and spoil my Christian image. Well, afterward, I vowed that that would never happen to me again. I promised God that if my heart began to thump real hard, I wouldn't pretend I thought it was just indigestion, but I would get up and do what God was telling me to do, no matter how ridiculous it might look or how stupid I might feel.

Well, it happened. I was in a workshop with perhaps a hundred and fifty people sitting around in several big circles. We had been talking about the gifts of the Holy Spirit and how they function. The talk must have been rather persuasive, because suddenly a woman stood up and said, "I think we've talked about these things long enough. I want to see it happen."

I nearly swallowed my Adam's apple. Satan was cheering me on, as usual.

"Dumbbell," he sneered at me, "you've gone too far this time. You should have kept the discussion strictly theoretical, not pretended that these things really work today. You know that nothing's going to happen, don't you? You're going to make a fool of yourself, Hill."

I was scared to death that he was right, of course, but I was even more scared to go back on my promise to the Lord. So I met Slue Foot right on his own ground and agreed with him, in part.

"You're right," I admitted, hoping to disarm him with my honesty. "If it's up to me, nothing will happen. But if it's up to God—"

The battleground is not really in the center of the arena, it's in our think tank. We can believe the Word of God and act on it, or we can reject the Word of God and let Him lose the glory. The choice is always ours. Either people will go away believing the Bible is true, or they'll go away suspecting that it's really an ancient book written by many fallible people.

The reason King's kids don't live like it, is that they don't think like it. God's Word tells us that's so:

For as he thinketh in his heart, so is he. (Prov. 23:7)

And He tells us to have the mind in us that is in Christ (Phil. 2:5). Following His instructions, we can think Jesus and live like King's kids in any situation, looking to the power that is in Him instead of to our own limitations.

While a woman was acting like a King's kid, walking to the center of our circle to sit in the prayer chair, a man said, "Aw, I can't go for that stuff. The New Testament wasn't written by God. It was written by twelve Jews and a Greek."

"Well," I shrugged, "that's all right with me. If twelve Jews and a Greek are the best that God could get in the way of secretaries, that shouldn't bother anybody. I happen to have a secretary of Polish descent, but I hired her to put it on paper, and as long as she writes it the way I dictate it, she's got a job. I imagine God's secretaries were pretty competent, too, or He wouldn't have hired them."

Well, I won't go into detail about the specific needs of the woman in the prayer chair, but God met them all. The upshot of the experiment in faith was that a whole bunch of folks in that group became believers because we were not afraid to act in faith that God's promises are all yea and amen in Jesus.* When King's kids go into action, pagans can be counted on to change their stripes in epidemic proportions.

---

* For several dozen exciting, true case histories of things that happened when King's kids took God at His Word, see the author's *How to Live Like a King's Kid* and *How to Be a Winner*.

37
How to Live in Victory
over Educated Idiots

Some learned theologians have written profound papers
on the subject of the gifts of the Holy Spirit explaining that
the gifts are not for today. I can't help calling them Educated
Idiots, because they can stand in my presence, while I'm
worshiping God in an unknown language, and insist that
such things don't happen today. In every case where I've
pinned them down about it, I've found that they had one
thing in common—they had never tried it for themselves.
They were nonspiritual people trying to pose as spiritual
experts.

There are other educated idiots who say that the gift of
tongues *is* for today but that Satan is the giver of the gift. All
of us should pray for those who teach this devilish doctrine,
because one day they will stand before the throne of grace
and God will ask them, "How come you, my devoted
servants, had the audacity to give Satan the credit for my
gift of tongues?"

I don't know what they will answer, but I know I don't
want to be in their shoes.

If we don't understand a thing, we don't understand it.

That's not a crime, and we can't be blamed for it. But lack of understanding is not the same thing as rejection. A child may not understand electricity, but that doesn't have to keep him from enjoying the benefits of a turned-on light bulb after the sun has gone down. God hasn't called anyone to pose as an expert in an area in which he has no practical experience.

Let's look for a minute at some of the things the gift of tongues is good for. First, God tells us in the Book of James what an unruly member the tongue is:

> The tongue is a fire, a world of iniquity . . . it defileth the whole body, and setteth on fire the course of nature; and it is set on fire of hell . . . the tongue can no man tame; it is an unruly evil, full of deadly poison. . . . Out of the same mouth proceedeth blessing and cursing. My brethren, these things ought not so to be. (3:6, 8, 10)

In my own life I came to a point where I was absolutely desperate about my need to have my unruly member, the tongue, tamed somehow, by somebody. I prayed, "Lord, I'm ready to quit this church life. I'm just not cut out for it. I'm a menace; I mess up everything I do. I'm going to have to wear a muzzle to church or make a dash for home before the service is over, so I won't be tearing somebody to ribbons with my tongue. You're going to have to tame it for me; I just give up. That's all there is to it."

Well, He heard my desperation and came to my rescue. Not long after I gave up trying to tame my own tongue, He gave me His gift of tongues, and from that day to this, the more I pray in tongues, the less likely I am to use it for Slue Foot's business. As a matter of fact, the next time I walked into a group after receiving God's gift of tongues, I felt an amazing thing happen. I opened my mouth as usual; my tongue was poised to squirt its usual poison, but nothing came out. It was as if God put His hand over my mouth and stopped me from pouring out all that garbage.

That was a whole lot better than the way I used to try to handle it. In the past, I would sometimes try to catch those stinky words after they got out of my mouth, but I could never grab fast enough. Like the psalmist, I asked God to set a watch over my mouth, and He heard and answered with His gift of tongues:

Set a watch, O LORD, before my mouth; keep the door of my lips. (141:3)

When I back off from speaking in tongues in my private devotions, I find in me the tendency to join in with the gossipers and backbiters again. You never get rid of a habit, a bad one or a good one. It's always part of the computer, programed there inside, but you can replace it with something else. And the control of my tongue is in the hands of the Holy Spirit. Anything that tamed my tongue from the menace it was to an instrument that glorifies God has to be a gift no man can describe as the "least." For me, it was more like the most. Without it, I'd still be bad-mouthing the brethren from morning till night. With it, my blabbermouth is tamed. When my gift of tongues is in operation day and night, I find myself wanting to praise God instead of wanting to cut up the brethren.

"Do I have to speak in tongues?" people often ask me.

"No, you don't," is my standard reply. "You can minister death with your tongue as long as you can stand it. When you're ready to minister life instead, come and we'll pray for you" (Prov. 18:21).

The Lord has other purposes for this wonderful gift of tongues. His Word commands us to pray without ceasing (1 Thess. 5:17), and I found it impossible to do this with my own limited human intellect and vocabulary. Restricted to the English language, I quickly ran out of words of praise. I sounded exceedingly repetitious, and that got kind of boring after a while. Besides, how could I keep praying in English when I was engaged in a consultation with somebody about manufacturing processes? Well, the gift of tongues gave me an unlimited language, and since that kind of praying by-passed my mind, I could keep on praying down in my gizzard while my mind was actively engaged in matters concerned with the engineering business.

Another use of the gift of tongues is in the greatest ministry there is, the ministry of intercession. God showed me something about that nearly twenty-two years ago. I said, "Lord, I don't understand all about this prayer in the Spirit, and I'm sure I don't need to. I'm thankful that it has tamed my tongue. But if it's all the same to you, would you mind pointing out some of the other advantages of it?"

He answered in terms of a Scripture that had always puzzled me before. Now it was made clear:

And it shall come to pass, that before they call, I will answer; and while they are yet speaking, I will hear. (Isa. 65:24)

I heard a missionary tell an instance in which that very thing happened in his life. He had just gotten back from the Congo.

"Demon power is so strong in that part of the world," he said by way of introduction, "that demons are visible most of the time." Then he went on to tell us about what happened one day when he was going down a trail to visit a remote village. Suddenly, right in front of his eyes, a gigantic serpent slithered across the path. As he stopped in his tracks to let it pass, a voice that seemed to be coming out of the snake's mouth hissed at him, "I'm going to destroy you this trip, missionary. I'm going to destroy you."

"Praise Jesus," the missionary had said. "Greater is He that is in me than he that is in the world. Go away, Slue

Foot."

And he did go away. For a season.

When the missionary reached the clearing where the village was located, he was tired from his trip. He swung his hammock between two trees so he could climb in to rest for a while. You never sit or lie on the ground in that part of the world on account of all sorts of poisonous bugs, spiders, scorpions, and such.

Just as the missionary was getting settled in the hammock, a native boy on the other side of the clearing shouted at the top of his voice:

"White man, jump!"

The missionary had been in the jungle long enough to know that he should move first and ask questions afterward, so he took a flying leap out of the hammock. Only he didn't have to ask any questions after he had jumped clear. The answer was directly under the middle of the hammock, coiled to strike. A deadly cobra.

In his spirit, the missionary knew that he had been saved from agonizing death because some intercessor somewhere was praying for him. God had seen to it that someone was on his knees in his behalf, and before he called, God had heard the prayer of the unknown intercessor, and He had answered.

The missionary's account was a pretty good incentive for the round-the-clock prayer groups that keep at the business of intercession in the only time-tested language the devil can't wiretap.

It was mind-blowing to me to learn that God can use any of us as a channel of lifesaving intercession for someone half a world away if we're available for praying prayers that don't originate in our own think tanks.

People are not bashful about showing their ignorance of the gift of tongues. Someone came up to me the other day and said, "You're not supposed to speak in tongues unless there's an interpreter."

The Scripture doesn't say that. It says,

How is it then, brethren? when ye come together [that is, when you assemble for a meeting, like a church meeting], every one of you hath a psalm, hath a doctrine, hath a tongue, hath a revelation, hath an interpretation. Let all things be done unto edifying. If any man speak in an unknown tongue, let it be by two, or at the most by three, and that by course; and let one interpret. But if there be no interpreter, let him keep silence in the church; and let him speak to himself, and to God. (1 Cor. 14:26-28)

That passage makes it plain to me that if there are three messages in tongues and no interpreter, that's the end of that for that particular session.

Others pass by the gift of tongues claiming, "Well, Paul says that's the least of the gifts." But Paul didn't say that tongues was the least of the gifts.

Except for Paul telling us that he'd rather prophesy than speak in tongues without an interpreter, I can't see that the gifts are rated in importance at all. It won't do to say that tongues is least because tongues and interpretation of tongues are last in the list in 1 Corinthians 12:8-10. To begin with, love (charity) is mentioned last in the faith, hope, and love list in 1 Corinthians 13:13, and yet the same verse says that love is the greatest of the three. For another thing, tongues is not mentioned last in some lists in other places in the Bible (1 Cor. 14:26; Mark 16:17-18). All nine of the gifts just happened to be the very best gifts you could have, because they're from God, part of the Holy Spirit package He gives to those who believe in Jesus.

245

Can you imagine standing before God's throne of grace some day and having Him ask you, "Brother So and So, what was the worst of my gifts in your estimation when you used to talk about them down on earth? What was the one you used to criticize so much?"

You'd want to shrivel and hide in a hole in the ground, and you'd be bound to try to get out of the truth.

"Who, me, Lord? Me, criticize anything you had given me?" You couldn't look Him in the eye when you were asking it.

His finger would be pointing to some marks on a page.

"The record says right here that you blabbed maliciously about my gift of tongues."

You'd probably swallow your Adam's apple and pray for the gold pavement to get a crack in it so you could slither out of sight. But it wouldn't happen.

You might start to mumble something about Professor So and So telling you that these gifts were not for today, but that cop-out would only prolong your agony. All along, you'd had the Word of God on the matter, that He is the same forever, that He changes not, and that His gifts are without repentance, meaning He doesn't take them back once they're given. And you'd hate to confess that you had not believed the Word of the Creator of the universe.

Just thinking about the possibilities of such a confrontation ought to be enough to make you embrace all the gifts, no matter who looks down on them. It ought to make you ready to stop being ignorant about spiritual gifts and to believe what the only authority, the Word of God, says about them:

> He that speaketh in an unknown tongue edifieth himself. . . . I would that ye all spake with tongues. . . . I thank my God, I speak with tongues more than ye all: yet in the church I had

246

rather speak five words with my understanding,
that by my voice I might teach others also, than ten
thousand words in an unknown tongue. (1 Cor.
14:4-5, 18-19)

Here Paul says that the one who speaks in an unknown
tongue edifies himself, that is, he builds himself up
spiritually. Do you suppose Paul was against that? We need
all the edifying we can get.

Paul says he wishes that everybody spoke in tongues, and
he thanked God that he spoke in tongues privately more than
any of the rest of them. He seems to be giving tongues a high
recommendation here.

But, Paul says, *in church*, that is when the people are
gathered together, he would rather say five words from the
pulpit that the people could understand than ten thousand
words they couldn't understand. He was doing his
tongues-praying in private, praying ten thousand words
there to edify himself, cranking himself up into a dimension
of power so that when he did go into the pulpit, he would be
equipped to bring God's message by the Holy Spirit, loaded
with power.

I had a pastor once who was quite a pulpiteer. He planned
his sermons very carefully, made sure that each one had the
Sanhedrin-prescribed three points and a poem, and had his
notes all precisely written down, with the in-between words
carefully memorized. When he preached, everybody said,
"Wasn't that wonderful!"

It sounded pretty, all right, but I don't think God was ever
impressed, because I never saw Him doing anything in the
way of signs following to prove the man was a believer. But
you should see the signs now! Since God has filled that pastor
with the Holy Spirit, and given him fourteen Spirit-filled
deacons along with it, they get together in the back room and
pray their thousands of words in an unknown tongue. Then

the deacons lay hands on the preacher so he will be loaded with power when he steps into the pulpit, and wow!

One morning recently he stood before the congregation, geared for glory, opened the Scripture, read a verse, put his hands in the air, prayed in tongues, an interpretation came, and people didn't wait for a sermon and an altar call. They got up from their seats and streamed forward to be saved, healed, baptized in the Holy Spirit. This happened in a Southern Baptist church in Baltimore, and I understand it happened back in Solomon's day, too.

Solomon's church was a pretty sizeable outfit, thirty-eight thousand members on the roll and most of them on the active list. According to an account in 2 Chronicles, four thousand of them were on the praise-the-Lord committee, better than ten percent of the congregation. It was their job to praise God without ceasing, all around the clock.

When Solomon's folks all came together for a worship service one day, the trumpets and various other instruments fell into harmony with the praisers. This tuned all circuits to the state of resonance, inviting maximum power flow, and God did the rest. The glory of God came down and literally filled the temple. The priests didn't get to say another word, because God himself ministered to the people by His Spirit. (2 Chron. 5:13-14).

If you are denying God the right to control your tongue as well as the rest of you, feel free. But you may be held accountable. It's one thing to be ignorant of the gift of God; it's something else to know about the gifts and reject them.

My daughter Linda is a King's kid and has been for several years. She didn't understand much about the gifts of the Spirit at one time, however, and she said to me, "Dad, I really don't see that the gift of tongues would be of any use to me. I don't think I need it."

I had learned not to pressure people, that's the Holy

Spirit's territory, and so I told her, "Okay, Linda. It's up to you. If ever you decide you want it, it's there for the asking."

Linda works as a secretary for a couple of neurologists, and she sees people every single day who are in desperate condition, needing all the help that medical science and God can give them. Linda had been an intercessor for their needs, praying with everything she had that God would help the patients. Then one day, someone brought an extremely ill elderly person to the office, and as Linda prayed, she saw a miracle of healing take place. She told us about it that night at our prayer meeting and said, "I just realized that that kind of thing ought to happen more often, shouldn't it?"

We agreed with her that the life style of King's kids is to be a powerfully healing contagion wherever they are.

"You know," she said, "I see now why I need *all* the gifts of the Spirit—so I can minister on God's terms without any restrictions." We were willing to be channels for God's power, so we laid hands on her and prayed. As we prayed, I saw her new prayer language being funneled into her.

"You've got it!" I announced.

She shook her head and said, "I don't feel like it."

We assured her that feelings were unreliable, soulish, to be put aside as of no account where spiritual things are concerned, and she went home. The next morning, she telephoned the news. On her way home the night before, she had suddenly begun to sing in the Spirit, the Spirit providing new words and a melody she'd never heard before.

You'll never know if these things are true if you stay "religious" about them and keep on nit-picking about them. Why not try them on for size and see how they work?

38
How to Live in Victory
over Depression

One day I was speaking at a FGBMFI breakfast meeting in Ontario, Canada. We were winding up the meeting along about three o'clock in the afternoon, and I happened to notice one man standing apart from the rest. He was tall—and tormented. After the meeting had officially closed, and the benediction had been pronounced, I walked over to the man and asked him a question.

"Have you ever met Jesus as your Savior?"

"Yes, many years ago."

"Have you received the baptism in the Holy Spirit?" I could see that something was missing in his life.

"No, I haven't," he said, and then added, "but I've been prayed for many times." He was the most discouraged-looking specimen of humanity I had ever seen, and so I did something I very seldom do. I almost always wait for someone to ask to be prayed for, but I sensed an urgency in this man's case.

"I would like to pray for you," I said.

"Well," he told me, "I'm a Baptist minister, and I think I should have the power of the Holy Spirit, but—"

250

He never finished his sentence, just reluctantly lowered himself into the prayer chair. As I laid hands on him and prayed in tongues, I saw Chinese-looking word characters being poured out of a bucket right into his head. I wound up my prayer and told him about it.

"You have a new prayer language," I announced. "God has installed it complete—it looks like Chinese word characters or some other oriental language. All you have to do is speak it out."

I could hardly wait to hear what it sounded like, but the man got out of the chair thoroughly disgusted.

"They've told me that so many times," he said, "but I've never received any of it." As he was turning to leave, looking more dead than alive, a woman came up and asked me to pray for her. She wanted to receive the baptism, too. She sat down in the prayer chair, but instead of praying for her myself, I asked the Baptist pastor to pray for her.

"A lot of times," I told him, "a person will receive his new prayer language when he is meeting the needs of someone else."

The fellow drew back. He didn't want to have anything more to do with this kooky business, but I took his hands and almost forcibly placed them on the woman's head. Well, I guess he thought he might as well get it over with and be on his way, so he opened his mouth and prayed. An oriental-sounding language poured forth from his lips. I couldn't understand a word of it. Out it rolled, volumes of it.

The dead look went out of his eyes, and his whole face turned on. When the woman came up for air in *her* praising of the Lord, he told us both exactly how it was with him. Tears were in his eyes, and his voice was choked with emotion.

"Last night in bed," he said, "I told God that if He did not manifest His gifts in my life within twenty-four hours, I was going to commit suicide. I was so sick of my powerless, ineffective ministry that I refused to live one more day unless He did something spectacular to meet my needs."

As the three of us stood hugging one another, I understood why God had me almost force prayer on that brother, why He showed me those oriental characters so clearly, and why the woman came up for prayer at precisely the right moment. God had ministered in the whole situation for great good, just as He promised (Rom. 8:28).

Our think tank says such things can't happen, but we're going way beyond the limitations of intellect when we're ministering in the Spirit. When we pray with our understanding, we're using our heads. That's all right as far as it goes, but it's limited to what our heads can understand. The standard prayer of unbelief we used to pray went like this: "Lord, heal him if it be thy will." We would say, Amen, and rush to the nearest telephone to call the undertaker. Such a prayer stemmed from perfect understanding—that no healing would take place. When we pray in the Spirit, we open the door for miracles to take place, because God doesn't know anything about limitations.

Sure, it's all right to pray with your understanding (1 Cor. 14:15). But when you're interceding for someone who looks desperate and you don't know why, feel free to speak to God in the language He supplies. It just might get the job done. He said it would:

> Likewise the Spirit also helpeth our infirmities: for we know not what we should pray for as we ought: but the Spirit itself maketh intercession for us with groanings which cannot be uttered. And he that searcheth the hearts knoweth what is the mind of the Spirit, because he maketh intercession for the saints according to the will of God. (Rom. 8:26-27)

Praying in the Spirit is an avenue to victory that common sense knows nothing about.

39
How to Live in Victory
over False Prophets

Daring to stand up and let the Spirit speak through us in prophecy is one of the ways King's kids can cooperate with what God wants to do among His people.

Any time you stand up to prophesy, or do anything else for the Lord, Satan is present to jeer.

"You're blowing it," he'll chortle from the sidelines. "You're really making all that up out of your own think tank, and everybody knows it." He is always there to scare you half to death, to try to run you out of the country with your tail between your legs, to make you back off for fear of ruining your religious image. But if you stand fast in the Lord and speak His truth anyway, the prophecy will come forth perfect and beautiful. Slue Foot is the one who will have to run. King's kids never have to run if they're obedient to the Spirit.

Sometimes people come to me and say, "Brother Hill, I had the first words of a message, but I was waiting to receive the whole thing before I stood up."

That's not faith, that's fright. The author of fright is Slue Foot himself, who says if you don't have every word letter-perfect, all rehearsed, don't dare open your mouth.

Don't listen to Slue Foot. If the power of God is on you to prophesy, you'll generally know it by the thumping in your chest. If you have the first three words—or even the first one word—don't sit and wait for somebody else. Stand up, speak out, deliver the words you already have, and the Holy Spirit will feed the rest of the message to you in perfect time.

Slue Foot is always wanting to back King's kids into a corner and say, "Don't you dare do it until you're perfect at it," and he can make them forget that they're supposed to covet to prophesy (1 Cor. 14:39). King's kids learn by doing. They don't wait for university-level perfection while they're still kindergarten age. They aren't afraid to move a muscle, because they know God will forgive them for their mistakes. When we're green, we're supposed to keep trying. That's the only way we'll ever learn.

The yardstick, the measuring stick for true prophecy, is spelled out in Paul's first letter to the Corinthians:

He that prophesieth speaketh unto men to edification, and exhortation and comfort. (14:3)

True prophecy builds up, corrects, and comforts. It always brings the hearers closer to Jesus. If you hear a prophecy that says, "Thus saith the Lord, you have been disobedient children. Therefore I'm going to bring the fire down and consume you," you can know it's someone's opinion and not a word from God. Any prophecy that doesn't check with the yardstick by being comforting, edifying, or correcting is false prophecy. The Spirit of God never condemns.

Being the incomplete and imperfect vessels that we are, we are practically guaranteed to goof now and then. But God doesn't throw us away just because we are fallible creatures. He says, "Come on back and get some more training. Get the judgmental selfishness and resentment out of your system so you can be a clear channel for me instead of a foggy one."

When we encounter a prophecy which is a mixture of God's word plus the vengeful spirit of one who is prophesying, we don't throw the whole thing away because it's contaminated by the prophet. We exercise our God-given discernment, hold fast that which is good, and let the rest go by. King's kids are imperfect functioners, younguns in the Spirit, who are certainly guilty sometimes of mixing the opinions of men with the word of God in prophecy.

"Despise not prophesyings," the Word says. But it also tells us to check out what we hear in order to prove all things:

Quench not the Spirit. Despise not prophesyings.

Prove all things; hold fast that which is good. (1 Thess. 5:19-21)

When I prove all things, that means that I don't accept anything from anyone that doesn't check out with the written Word of God. God tells us that He is the same yesterday, today, and forever (Heb. 13:8). That *has* to mean, among other things, that He never deviates from the truth of His written Word. There's no eraser on God's writing stick. What He has written, He has written, and it stands forever.

When we are told to "hold fast that which is good" we have to assume that there may be some things that are not good, some things that we will be expected to throw away. That seems to suggest a spiritual parallel to some of the ordinary, everyday things we are accustomed to doing all the time. For instance:

When I go out to buy a dozen ears of corn, some Golden Bantam roasting ears, I take them home expecting to throw ninety percent of my purchase away. I know in advance that I'll chuck the husks into the garbage can, enjoy a thin layer of calories, and then throw the cob away. But I'm not disgusted at the inedible, unusable part. I expected to have the peelings and the bone left over for my compost heap. Same thing with my breakfast boiled egg. I don't complain that the shells are scratchy to my throat, I just eat the insides and leave the shells on my plate.

The same principle is applicable to a lot of teachings that come my way. I strain out what I can use, the part that is in conformity to the Word of **God,** consume the vitamins that will help my spiritual growth, and throw away the cobs, husks, and silks, along with any active worms I happen to discover in the process. I don't have to argue with the teachers about what they're teaching, or to tell them what's useful to me and what's wormy.

It was hard for me to learn that I didn't have to straighten out everybody whose doctrines didn't agree with mine straight down the line. If you didn't think exactly as I did, you were naturally wrong, and I had to correct you. Furthermore, if you didn't receive my correction the first time, you got a further blast of it shortly. I kept up the bombardment. But I've learned better. And today, if I don't agree with you, I'll pray for increased understanding. Who knows? I might suddenly find that you're right after all. Meanwhile, I haven't had to nitpick us both to death to prove anything. The new approach makes for peace throughout the fellowship, and that's highly recommended.

Another checkpoint for true prophecy is recorded in Deuteronomy:

> And if thou say in thine heart, How shall we know the word which the LORD hath not spoken? When a prophet speaketh in the name of the LORD, if the thing follow not, nor come to pass, that is the thing which the LORD hath not spoken, but the prophet hath spoken presumptuously: thou shalt not be afraid of him. (18:21-22)

In other words, if it doesn't happen, God never said it would. This has to do with the kind of prophecy that foretells coming events, not with the word of God in prophecy that is for immediate comfort rather than future information.

If a prophet's utterance doesn't come to pass, proving that it wasn't of God, don't condemn the prophet. Don't shoot him or stone him or throw him in the den of lions. Pray for him, because he's still very much in the flesh.

How about prophecy that another person claims to receive for you? Watch out!

A man called me one night not many months ago and said, "Brother Hill, I have a word direct from the Lord for you."

"Hallelujah!" I shouted. "I appreciate that. I always enjoy hearing from the Lord. What is His word for me today?"

"Well," he said, "the Lord told me to tell you that you're supposed to send me a check for $50,000."

"Hallelujah! Thank you, brother," I exclaimed. I mean, after all, when God says I'm supposed to give someone a cool fifty thousand, He must be arranging to make that much—or more—available to me.

"Will you send it today?" my informant wanted to know.

"God is the only one who can answer that," I said. "I don't happen to have fifty grand in my hip pocket at the moment or lying on top of my dresser, or even stashed in my checking account at the bank, but if God tells me to send it, I'm sure He'll show me where it is."

In any prophetic utterance of this kind, I'm entitled to hear directly from God as well as from the prophet. And I always get the confirmation—when the prophecy is from God. In that particular case, it didn't seem to be, because I have yet to hear from the Lord about it, and the fifty thousand hasn't shown up as a bulge in my billfold. It was probably a case of a man prophesying in a hopeful fashion and blaming God for it. I was open to the Lord's will in the situation, and even prayed about it:

"Lord, if this is from you, give me a real eagerness to send the check. I'll trust you for the wherewithal." The eagerness never came.

I had learned long ago that God always provides the means for His will to happen. I had learned, too, that I wasn't to condemn the prophet. I thanked him, and I praised the Lord. The man had good motives—he wanted to build up his church—but he seemed to have misread God's message. The fact that he thought God had told him to get the money out of me didn't bother me. But since I had no personal directive from heaven, I knew I wasn't supposed to send it to him.

It is necessary to check these things out, not to jump into something like that until you get a double witness. Many a life has been completely scrambled because someone took the word of a so-called prophet and acted on it without confirmation.

God says,

In the mouth of two or three witnesses shall every word be established. (2 Cor. 13:1)

Are King's kids supposed to exercise that kind of judgment? Of course:

But he that is spiritual judgeth all things, yet he himself is judged of no man. (1 Cor. 2:15)

King's kids judge everything in terms of the Word of God. If something doesn't agree with the written Word, forget it. If it passes that test, next we judge it by the confirmation of the Spirit within us, and then by the mouths of two or three witnesses. If all those line up, we know that we have a green light for full speed ahead. If they don't line up, it's a pretty good sign that the "prophet" was out of line.

The spiritual man has the mind of Christ, the next verse tells us, and he is to judge everything from the standpoint of

258

God:

> For who hath known the mind of the Lord, that he
> may instruct him? But we have the mind of Christ.
> (v. 16)

Human judgment always leads to condemnation; God's judgment always calls for blessings. The human spirit judges other persons in terms of a penalty. God's Spirit judges the other person in terms of his need for more of His grace, blessing, and deliverance.

Where we judge by means of the gifts of the Holy Spirit—word of wisdom, word of knowledge, and the gift of discernment—our judgment reflects God's real outlook. When we're judging from God's standpoint, we don't come under condemnation nor does the person being judged. When God is in charge, everyone benefits.

Judgment by pagans is another matter entirely, because

> The natural man receiveth not the things of the
> Spirit of God: for they are foolishness unto him:
> neither can he know them, because they are
> spiritually discerned. (1 Cor. 2:14)

When I am in charge, everybody loses—even me, ultimately. That's how the human spirit works. It says, "What's in it for me?" and fouls things up for everybody, including himself.

Judging as a spiritual man is such a reversal of our former method of operation, it seems weird at first. King's kids don't always enter easily and naturally into the new way of doing things, because they have old habit patterns of seeking self-gratification, but after awhile, the Spirit of God makes us outgoing in spite of ourselves.

It's amazing that God can do anything with any of us, considering the raunchy raw material He has to work with. It's always been like that. Look at three of the major leaders in the Bible—Moses, David, and Paul. They had one thing in common—they were all murderers. But God still used them.

Amazing grace is the major ingredient in the formation of a King's kid. He fashions us as vessels for His treasure out of the rebellious children we were before we said yes to Jesus and became King's kids in training. In the training process, we have the Spirit of God within us to teach us, teachers on the outside to encourage us and break the Bread of Life to us, groups in which we can share fellowship with one another, and the whole pagan world to romp around in to fulfill our assignment of heavenly obstetrics, bringing others to Jesus. Just offhand, I couldn't think of a better arrangement for victory, could you?

I learned to live like royalty.

40

How to Live in Victory
when You Don't Know
the Answers

Years ago, as a young engineer, I joined a British concern and was invited to England for training with the parent company. At my first state dinner in a British mansion, with a butler, footmen, and ladies-in-waiting, I was almost overwhelmed.

When we went into the huge dining room, my eyeballs nearly popped out of my head. At each place setting at the long banquet table, there was enough hardware to take care of any three families that I'd ever known. At my place alone, there must have been fifteen forks and six knives and ten spoons and enough glasses and goblets to start a crystal shop. Someone told me it was from Oliver Cromwell's private collection—museum pieces, irreplaceable.

Pretty heady stuff for a country boy.

Where I grew up, each person had a knife, a fork, and a spoon. If I took my fork and used it to dig fishbait worms, and bent it in the process, I had to straighten out the tines before supper.

Naturally, I was utterly unprepared for using the array that was spread before me in the British mansion. Well, I had learned that you can pick up a lot just by watching other people, and so I tried following the actions of the fellow across the table from me. When he picked up a particular fork, I picked up my corresponding fork and took a bite of the same thing he took a bite of. I put the fork down where he did, when he did, picked up my spoon corresponding to the one he picked up and tasted what he did. I drank when and what he drank, and agonized my way through a sumptuous meal I couldn't enjoy for worrying about which implement to use.

In time, I learned what went with what. I learned to live like royalty, handling the hardware with perfect confidence, just as the lords and ladies did. If you hadn't known the difference, you might have thought I was one of them.

I could fool anybody, and I needed to, because I was in training to represent my boss, a British nobleman, in his worldwide industrial operation. Really, I was being trained to be a phony.

God has us in training to be real King's kids—nothing phony—to live together with Him in His family forever, not as understudies, but as real members of the royal family. Just as my eye guided me in handling the hardware, one of the ways King's kids are trained for heavenly living is by looking to the Lord, letting Him guide us with His eye. The Bible says He will do this for us when we are in training:

> I will instruct thee and teach thee in the way which
> thou shalt go: I will guide thee with mine eye. (Ps.
> 32:8)

We get this eyeball guidance when we are ready to learn, when we are willing to be eyeball to eyeball with Jesus, looking unto Him and not to ourselves or to anyone else for our guidance and instruction.

I've seen the principle in action in field trials—competitions among hunting dogs. A retriever is trained to flush the birds

264

out so the hunter can shoot them, and then to bring the dead birds back to the hunter. Most importantly, however, the retriever is trained to be absolutely obedient to the hunter, not even to rely on his own judgment but to wait for his master to give the signal before he makes any motion.

A well-trained dog will sit during field trials, hearing the birds hitting the ground over in the brush, sniffing, knowing they're there, just dying to race out and stir them up, but knowing he isn't free to do that until the hunter gives him the go-ahead by moving his eyes from the dog to the birds. The judges are watching and waiting, alert for one false move that could disqualify the dog or cause him to lose points on his score.

I've seen a dog sit literally shaking, his muscles tensed, revved up with the power to get going, the only motion coming from the tears rolling silently down his furry cheeks because he's so eager to stir up the birds. Everything and everybody is motionless—judges, hunters, and dogs. The tension is tremendous, because if there is the slightest physical motion, the birds will sense it and be gone.

After what seems an eternity to the dog who has his eyes riveted on the hunter's eyes, the eyeballs of the hunter move from the dog to the birds. That silent signal means *go*, and the dog is off like a shot. All the waiting tension is turned into a fantastic burst of forward energy.

The guidance system of God works something like that. We have to keep our eyes on Him to get the signals. If we're looking in some other direction, we'll miss the signal. We'll risk being too early or too late. King's kids in training can't afford to look anywhere other than to the trainer himself.

Sometimes the Lord chooses to guide us through a still small voice that we hear only when we're really tuned in to Him. The prophet Elijah got his guidance from God by such a voice one day (1 Kings 19:12-13), and King's kids today can receive His guidance in the same way. It has happened to me.

A while back, I was involved with my engineering company in bidding on a project which called for the delivery of an atomic energy plant to the South Pole. We were bidding in conjunction with a large manufacturer, and I assumed they had carefully examined all parts of the proposal.

Now, you don't just design such a plant, manufacture the components, wrap it up, and tell a truckline, "I have a package for you to deliver to Antarctica. Will you pick it up, please?"

The South Pole hasn't gotten around to building many highways yet, and the place is just plain inaccessible except for a few weeks out of the year. Everything has to be airdropped in packages that can be pushed out of an airplane in flight and land on the bull's-eye without cracking up and without damage to the contents. The navy would airdrop personnel later to unwrap the packages and set the thing up.

It was a rather tall order. It took some time to work out the design, specifications, cost analysis, and everything necessary in order to make a reasonable bid. In the nature of things, it had to be a fixed-bid proposition. We couldn't up our price later on if things got tough; we'd be stuck with whatever was written into the proposal.

We spent weeks on the thing, and then came the day when I was to sign the contract, committing us to our part in the transaction. When I picked up my pen to put my John Henry on it, I was interrupted by a loud awareness that said clearly, unmistakably, "Don't sign it. Recheck the specifications."

As there was no one visible in the room with me, I assumed the instructions were coming from the Holy Spirit.

I knew enough to listen to Him, but what He was telling me to do was clearly impossible. I told Him so.

"Look," I said, pointing to the contract specifications which were so complex they filled a book a couple of inches thick, "I've spent weeks on this thing already. It has to be in the mail tonight. Today is the absolute deadline."

He wasn't persuadable.

"Don't sign it. Recheck the specifications."

"But, Lord," I argued, thinking He sounded like a broken record. "I simply don't have time to recheck all that fine print. If there's something wrong, you'll just have to show me where it is." That should settle it. If He couldn't show me, I'd be free to sign the thing and be done with it.

I laid my hands on the book with its thousands of minute details, prayed that the Lord would show me the trouble, picked the book up in my hands, and let it fall open.

I looked down, and some words on the page to which the book had opened flew up at me. It was a real killer clause, stipulating that the contractor would, *at his own expense*, be required to correct any malfunctioning of the equipment *on the job site*.

Wow! That was one of the most underhanded provisions anyone could sneak into a purchase specification contract. It didn't even say that the malfunctioning had to be our fault. Improperly trained personnel could cause a thing to goof even if it was perfectly constructed to start with.

One application of the sneaky clause could have wiped us out. At the time, the navy had an informal price tag of a cool million on the ticket for taking a man to the South Pole and back, to say nothing of what it would have cost us in incidental expenses, such as extra-thick long johns, fur-lined boots, earmuffs, and all that.

"Thanks, Lord," I said, with gusto, and then I called in my secretary.

267

"Prepare an addendum," I told her. "Tell them we take exception to paragraph so and so on page such and such. Amend it to say that we will not be responsible for any malfunctioning that is not our fault and that we will replace any faulty equipment, not at the job site, but F.O.B. Baltimore."

She typed up the alteration, I signed the bid, mailed it, and we got the contract. When the equipment was built, we had it dumped at the South Pole, and all was well—for a while.

Then, a few months later, I had a telephone call from the contract officer who asked me, "Are you ready for some bad news?"

Well, I didn't know if I was ready right then or not, but I shifted my praising the Lord into high gear, and within a few seconds, I was ready for anything.

"Are you ready to send personnel to the South Pole right away?" he asked.

"Not necessarily," I replied. "Why do you ask?"

"Your contract calls for it," he needled me. "We've just had a call that something has gone wrong with the mechanism you built for us, and your contract calls for you to correct it at the job site, at your expense."

It was hard for me to keep from praising the Lord in a very loud voice.

"Sir," I said, managing to hold my hallelujahs to a low level, "if you will read the proposal I signed, you will find that you are mistaken. We took exception to that sneaker in the contract and agreed to replace any faulty mechanism F.O.B. Baltimore."

The guidance of the Holy Spirit, by a supernatural word of knowledge, had saved us from bankruptcy. It made me realize, all over again, how absolutely vital it is for King's kids to consult the King if they want to live in victory.

41

How to Live in Victory
over Ignorance of Spiritual Gifts

In his first letter to the Corinthians, Paul recognized that Christians didn't know all they ought to know about the gifts of the Spirit.

The first verse of chapter twelve is sort of revealing. I'd have thought Paul would have spoken to that highly spiritual church at Corinth saying, "Brethren, I know that you are thoroughly familiar with the gifts of the Spirit." But that's not what he said. He wrote,

Now concerning spiritual gifts, brethren, I would
not have you ignorant.

There must be a tendency toward ignorance about the gifts in all of God's churches and among all of God's people or He would not have thought it necessary to put such an admonition at the beginning of the teaching on gifts of the Spirit. Ignorance of spiritual gifts blocks us from the high privilege of living up to our inheritance in Jesus.

What causes ignorance? One of two things: lack of knowledge or unteachableness. Once you're aware that there is a better way, you have to be unteachable in order to miss it. And these Corinthians apparently were unteachable like so many are unteachable today. Once you've been confronted with facts, and turn away from these facts and maintain your religious doctrine, then you remain ignorant by choice, not by accident.

"Stop being unteachable," God was saying to the Corinthians—and to us.

"Am I unteachable?" I asked the Lord. "If I am, I didn't know it."

"That's just it," He said. "The whole human race is basically unteachable, but doesn't know it. It relies on its head, forgetting that the whole head is sick, just as I said in Isaiah 1:5."

Relying on our own heads, we listen to the "authorities" and wind up believing that the gifts are not for today. But the Scripture says God doesn't change, that He is no respecter of persons, and that His gifts and promises are given without repentance, that is, He won't take them back. Instead of quoting people who say these things don't happen anymore, it's better to stop being ignorant and quote God's Word, which says they do:

For I am the LORD, I change not. (Mal. 3:6)

God is no respecter of persons: but in every nation he that feareth him, and worketh righteousness, is accepted with him. (Acts 10:34-35)

The gifts and calling of God are without repentance. (Rom. 11:29)

The Amplified Bible makes that last one unmistakably clear:

God's gifts and His call are irrevocable—He never withdraws them when once they are given, and He does not change His mind about those to whom He gives His grace or to whom He sends His call. (Rom. 11:29 TAB)

Apparently God knew a long time ago that twentieth-century Christians would have a tendency to let their think tanks confuse them about the gifts of the Spirit. But though He does not want us to be ignorant, He leaves us free to make the choice:

But if any man be ignorant, let him be ignorant. (1 Cor. 14:38)

That verse came as a big relief to me. All my life I had wanted to persuade everybody, but here God says, "Relax, Hill. Leave the willfully ignorant fellow alone. You can keep on praying for him, but forget about trying to straighten him out. That's territory that belongs to my Holy Spirit, because nobody else can do it."

Reading the Bible one day, I saw that Paul had had some of the same troubles. He tried to get Barnabas straightened out, and he got so disgusted with John Mark, they quit traveling together. Everywhere Paul went, he was trying to straighten out somebody, and he was always landing in the pokey. In those days, even the finest pokeys didn't come equipped with central heating, innerspring mattresses, and color TV. They were more like miserable holes in the ground. And Paul began to get the point.

"After all these years of quibbling," he said, "I have learned something. All I need to know among you is Jesus Christ, and him crucified" (1 Cor. 2:2).

We are to lift up Jesus, according to God's Word, and not get all bogged down and divided asunder by dogmas and doctrines of men. We are to show forth the gifts of the Spirit to the glory of God, for the kingdom of God is to be found in demonstration of power, and he gives us a handhold on that power through the gifts of the Holy Spirit.

Two verses written to help dispel our ignorance of spiritual gifts have been widely misinterpreted by some theologians. In them, God is asking seven questions:

271

Are all apostles? Are all prophets? Are all teachers? Are all workers of miracles? Have all the gifts of healing? Do all speak with tongues? Do all interpret? (1 Cor. 12:29-30)

These theologians have answered these questions with seven nos. But when Jesus answers the same questions, we hear different answers.

"Do all speak with tongues, Jesus?"

"All believers can," He says.

"Do all have gifts of healing?"

"All believers can," He says again. We find His answers in the Gospel according to Mark (16:17-18).

If you happen to be a believer who hasn't yet spoken in tongues, keep your ears open when you're praying. You may be surprised one day. And start watching what happens when you lay hands on the sick.

Do all interpret?

They can. When the assignment is given to you, you'll know it, because nine times out of ten, your heart will start pounding at an accelerated rate. When it does, that's your signal to open your mouth and let the words come out.

Satan will invariably be on hand to needle you about exercising any gift of the Spirit:

"You're going to goof it," he'll rasp in the midst of a demonic chuckle.

"You know it," I tell him. "Unless Jesus is in charge, I'll always wreck everything, but I'm willing to risk my corpse-like dignity to do what He wants me to do. Get going, Slue Foot." When we come against him with the truth, he has to take off.

"Are all apostles?" can be answered, "Why not!" On occasion, when God wants to use me in that capacity, I'm an apostle—one who is sent forth—a troubleshooter sent to help the church.

272

"Are all prophets?" God will prophesy through anyone to meet the need of a particular occasion. Where no *persons* are willing, He has even been known to use a four-legged creature. (Read Numbers 22.)

"Are all teachers?" Certainly, when we need to be. We have a built-in teacher, the Holy Spirit, who can speak through us to teach when He wants to.

"Workers of miracles?" Why not? Each of us contains *the* miracle worker himself within us.

I'm surprised that this list of questions doesn't contain one more: "Do all raise the dead?" because Jesus has already answered that question in the affirmative, too:

> Verily, verily, I say unto you, He that believeth on me, the works that I do shall he do also: and greater works than these shall he do; because I go unto my Father. (John 14:12)

A no answer to each of these questions is ignorance, a dead end. A yes leads to vital Christianity, the result of believing that Jesus within us makes all things possible as His strength is manifested through our weakness. The one we contain is unlimited in power.

You may be the only one on the spot to do a particular thing. Is God out of business because you're the only King's kid available and you're not equipped to meet the need? How foolish. Even if we don't have a specialized ministry in these things, we have the one within who can minister whatsoever is needed to whosoever has the need. He *is* the victory over everything the world can throw at us.

Don't let your religious head think of a fragmenting kind of God who gives a sliver of something here and a niggardly slice of something there. The total package of all the gifts is transported by the believer who has Jesus within, carrying all the gifts to be dispensed according to the needs of the needy. A sick person could use prophecy, but not nearly as well as he could use a gift of healing, because while you're prophesying to him, he could be getting dead.

How do you know what the other fellow really needs? You won't know, except by the Spirit, and all nine gifts instead of just one are required on occasion. We are to think of our ministry as the total ministry of a total person, Jesus himself, who came—and comes—to make people totally whole.

"Well, then," people ask me, "if King's kids are supposed to function in this way, what's wrong? Why do the pastor and his assistant do all the ministering, and the brethren just sit back and let them do it?"

Spiritual pride and doctrines of devils are two answers to these questions. They come out in the form of excuses:

"I can't do it perfectly, so I won't do it. I might spoil my image. And anyhow, these gifts are not for everybody." That the gifts are not for everybody, or that they are not for today are devilish doctrines.

Whom are you going to believe? God or the misinformed theologian? I'm not interested in what people say, no matter how many degrees they have or don't have, if what they say contradicts what the Word of God says in black and white. King's kids who want to live in victory would do well to stick with the Word of God. Then they'll make some progress.

Be a doer of the Word. Check it out for yourself. Read it and do it, and if it doesn't work, you'll know that it's not for today. But if it does work, you'll be off for high adventure in Jesus. And you won't have to wonder, "Is it true?" You'll know how it works because you'll have seen it in action.

All you have to do is act on the Word. Give the gifts away. That's the way it works. If you sit around, hoarding them for yourself, the chances are you'll bog down like the Dead Sea. Where there's all intake—gimme, gimme, gimme—and no outlet, there's stagnation. A stagnated sea, filled up with wiggletails, is good for fertilizer and not much else. Stagnated Christians are an impossibility where the gifts of the Holy Spirit are in motion. They're the best giveaway ever invented—benefiting everybody.

"But I'm not worthy!" is another cop-out I've heard a lot. "I don't have what it takes," is another. These are the best things a King's kid could ever know about himself. No one said you were worthy, or that you have what it takes. That's the blessing of King's kid living. We don't have to be anything to enjoy the benefits and pass them on to others, because Jesus is everything for us.

> He is made unto us wisdom, and righteousness, and sanctification, and redemption. (1 Cor. 1:30)

He contains all we need, and He is in us, so that if any man wants to glory, he'll have to glory in the Lord (1 Cor. 1:31). That's what King's kid living is about. God does it all, so He gets all the glory. We receive the blessings, but they are not for our amusement or amazement or entertainment; they are for us to give away as fast as possible.

When you say, "What's in it for me?" the old possessive attitude blocks the power of God. When you say, "What's in it for someone else?" the outgoing love of God that's shed abroad in our hearts by the Holy Ghost which is given to us (Rom. 5:5) begins to minister life to others—and to us. The spiritually dead are raised, and the blind are given sight, the deaf hear, and the captives are set free.

When I was a new Christian, I fell into the trap of thinking I had to do everything so carefully, so perfectly, that I ended up doing nothing, afraid I'd blow my beautiful religious image. Then one day, someone said to me, "Hill, don't take life so seriously. You're not going to get out of it alive anyhow."

What a relief that was. And we all need to realize that if we're going to live the King's kids way of life in victory.

42
How to Live in Victory
over Iffy Doctrines

A few years ago, I had an emergency phone call saying that Jim Christian, the scheduled speaker at a CFO camp, had had a slight heart attack and would be unable to attend the meeting. Would I fill in for him?

As it happened, the July week of the conference was the only free week I had left in the whole year, and so I was pretty certain God had reserved it for that Michigan camp.

When I arrived, I learned that the lady with whom I was to minister during the week was a modernist and a Universalist. She preached that everybody was going to be saved, so it didn't matter how they lived, or what they did, they were scheduled for heaven.

If I had known who my co-laborer was to be that week, I'd have probably been too stupid to accept the invitation. I'd have had doubts that God could take care of himself and of me in such a situation. Sure enough, after the first session, an acute reaction set in in me.

"Lord," I called out, "I can see this week is going to be a total loss. The lady is contradicting everything I say!"

When I said, "Jesus is the way, the only way," she

countered with, "You don't *really* need Jesus. He is nice to have around, but everybody's going to be saved anyhow—with or without Him."

Her teaching was straight from the pit, and I was in a tizzy, but Jesus seemed calm about it all.

"Is this the one thing I can't quite handle? Have you really run into something that's got me stuck?"

"Lord, I don't really think so," I confessed. "It just seems that way."

"Well, then," He seemed to say, "why don't you just sort of wait on the Lord, like you've been preaching, and keep on praising me and see what I will do?"

"Lord, have mercy," I cried, having a temporary setback in my awareness of His ability, proving that I haven't arrived, but that I'm still in training myself. After a time, however, I managed to choke out, "Praise the Lord," a few times and it seemed to help.

The week went on—Tuesday, Wednesday, Thursday. . . .

Everything I said, the Universalist lady said backward, but it didn't bother me because I had gotten back on the wavelength of praising God, no matter what. If I hadn't been praising, I'd have been shot down for sure. As it was, I heard the lady dish out lies over the same pulpit where I was spouting God's truth, straight from His Word. I didn't argue with her; I just kept on praising God anyhow. And because my mind was staid on Him, He kept me in such peace about it that anybody looking on might have wondered if I was even aware that she was contradicting me at every turn. I was having a ball, experiencing the wonder of the truth that adversity plus praise spells victory in Jesus. I didn't know what He was going to do about her, but I could tell He was doing something in me all along.

We had about two hundred college kids attending the retreat at that particular camp, and when Thursday night came along, they invited me to share privately with their group after the big meeting of the evening.

"We've got a question for you," they said for openers. "Is Mrs. So and So right when she says everybody is going to be saved, or are you right in saying that some may not be saved because they have never received Jesus personally? Who's right? Is she? Or are you?"

"Lord, this is the big question to them. What's your answer to it?" I asked Him. "Remember, Lord, it's your act. I'm out of it. What's your answer?"

As soon as I'd finished asking the question, the answer came loud and clear from heaven, right into my mind. I didn't hear voices or angel wings, bells, sirens, or train whistles. I didn't even smell any incense or get any goose bumps. I wasn't looking for any of those things; I was looking for wisdom. And what came very clearly into my understanding, I spoke forth just as I received it:

"What difference does it make who's right?" I asked the kids. "This is not a theological debate. The point is, if you know Jesus Christ personally, you have a guarantee of positive results. You are definitely going to be where He is, because you have God's written Word of guarantee. Now, if you don't know Him personally, He does not guarantee that you will arrive at the preferred destination. *If* you do—for the sake of argument, let's assume that the Universalist lady might be correct—you might get there by way of a very painful, bumpy detour trip, dropping down in potholes, floating around for centuries.

"Somebody's concept says that there's an in-between dimension where you will spend a few million years being cleansed of your sins instead of a this-day being in paradise with Jesus that's specified for King's kids when they leave the planet earth. The roundabout way sounds second best to me. I'm not willing to gamble on a future as lengthy and important as eternal life and maybe miss heaven's best in the process. I want a straight route, myself.

"Which do you want, kids, a positive, no-doubt salvation, via a direct hookup with Jesus, or a possible roundabout circuit, 'iffy all the way,' that's guaranteed to get you into big trouble? Do you want a certain route or a maybe route?"

"Oh," they chorused unanimously, "we want a for-sure route, of course. We're not interested in anything iffy."

"Well, then, get hooked up with Jesus," I told them.

Everyone who hadn't been saved already got saved on the spot, deciding in favor of Jesus, the guaranteed way. Satan had meant to use the Universalist lady's presentation for evil, but God used it to point up the goodness of the best.

If there wasn't any doubt in the picture, if Universalists were persuaded their way was really the best one, they wouldn't have to be so nervous about their doctrine. They wouldn't have to be trying to push it off on other people.

King's kids don't have to be pushy. They need simply to present the facts, including the fact that Jesus said, "I am *the* door. Anybody who wants to go to the Father has to go through me."

The kids in the camp didn't want to gamble, so they responded to the invitation of Jesus to "Come unto me, and I will give you rest."

The whole week was a new proof to me that I don't have to go around trying to straighten people out from the doctrines of devils. When I used to try that on a regular basis, I was the one who got straightened out. I was laid out horizontal every time. But now I know that Jesus can handle everything all by himself. He always emerges a winner, and He seems to do it more quickly if I don't get in His way.

The presence of the teacher of deception gave the kids a chance to think things out, to make a clear-cut choice for a guaranteed road to glory as opposed to a possible road that might get you there or might not. Maybe they'd never had that made clear to them before. It was good for their education to have before them such a direct confrontation with truth and deception. Jesus is very specific when He says, "I am the way, the truth, and the life, and if you want to enjoy the benefits of having God as your heavenly Father, it's through me or not at all" (my paraphrase of John 14:6).

Are there any other ways? Jesus says not. Back in the days when I was still hung up on trying to be reasonable, I tried a lot of other ways and found that none of them worked. Then I tried Jesus, and His way has worked so well for me that I highly recommend it to everybody who will listen. So far, I haven't had any complaints from the takers.

Life is too uncertain for us to waste any time fooling around, and God says He is not slack concerning His promises toward us. He will fulfill them all, and in the meantime, He is longsuffering toward us, patient beyond belief because He is not willing that any should perish (2 Peter 3:9). He permits us to consider all these other offers, but He never puts His stamp of approval on any of them. He just keeps on pointing to Jesus and saying, "This is the way, walk ye in it (Isa. 30:21), and demonstrate my kingdom in power. Then you won't have to argue with anyone. You'll be living in victory."

43
How to Live in Victory
over Angels of Light

The world is full of deceivers, but if we are careful to keep ourselves submitted to the proper authority over us, whoever that might be, we are less likely to fall into the traps of the enemy.

Back when I came into the fullness of the Spirit in my own life, I said, "Lord, I don't want to function outside of the chain of command you have designed for my protection. What is your perfect order for the Christian spiritual life?"

For an answer, He led me to the last couple of verses in Acts 2, showing His arrangement:

And they, continuing daily with one accord in the temple, and breaking bread from house to house, did eat their meat with gladness and singleness of heart, praising God, and having favour with all the people. And the Lord added to the church daily such as should be saved. (vv. 46-47)

It looked to me from this as if the home churches reported to the home base church, keeping the proper line of authority. And so I said, "Okay, Lord. That's your Word, and that's the way I'm going to do it."

281

There was at that time a small handful of us in our Southern Baptist church who had met Jesus as Baptizer in the Holy Spirit, and to say that we were not appreciated by the bulk of the brethren is to put it mildly. They said the things that had happened to us did not happen in the twentieth century. They were totally sold on a principle of dispensationalism that dispensed with the things of God that they didn't like, things with which they felt uncomfortable. Oh, they acknowledged that God still saves today, but they believed that He was powerless to do anything else. Well, we knew they were wrong about that, of course, because of what we had read in the Bible and because of what we had experienced in our own lives, but we hung in there, according to God's instructions:

> Not forsaking the assembling of ourselves together, as the manner of some is; but exhorting one another. (Heb. 10:25)

Fellowship multiplies the power to dispose of the enemy when you're praying together. Those who are unaware of the tricks of the enemy to separate them from other believers and encourage them to do their own thing are likely to be destroyed by that enemy.

Growing up under authority can be a painful business. Babies do not always appreciate the application of authority when they are growing up, but it's still good for them. It's essential if they're ever to reach maturity.

I still remember the hand of authority that my dad applied to my seat of learning one night when I was about a year and a half old. He had to do it only one time. My seat of learning absorbed the message: "You do not rebel against your dad." I never did after that. I learned a lesson. Now, I didn't always *like* what he told me to do, but I always did it. If he had not been wise enough to put me under his authority, I would have gone into total rebellion instead of into the partial variety. That's how we're built.

And so our charismatic prayer group, not wanting to fall into deception, put itself under God's rules, to do it His way.

"Lord," we said, "we're going to meet in the club basement because you seem to have led us in that direction, but we're going to stay in submission to authority. We're even going to invite our pastor to attend the meetings." We did, too. To say that he was less than enthusiastic about our invitation is to understate the matter considerably. Not only did he turn our invitation down flat, but he let us know that if something wasn't Southern Baptist, it wasn't fit for a sick dog and we might just as well forget it.

He didn't forbid our meeting, though, and so we met, scheduling our meetings after the church's Sunday night service so we would not interfere with the denominational program. If our pastor had told us to stop meeting, we'd have done that, but he never said anything like that to us. We couldn't take any credit for our continuing submission, because we weren't smart enough to do that on our own, but we were sensitive to the leading of God's Spirit, and that's what He was requiring of us. God was leading us into a kind of automatic recognition of the chain of command He had set up. And following His directions, we prospered.

After about five years, as God added to our number, there were about twenty-five of us meeting on a regular basis. And we were seeing great results in terms of the operation of the gifts of the Spirit. We were all becoming fluent in our heavenly languages, we were getting insights by way of the gift of wisdom, the gift of knowledge, and discernment. There were even miracles of healing and other signs and wonders manifested among us. It was altogether beautiful.

Things were going so well, in fact, that after a while some of the group decided they did not need a pastor, especially one who did not believe that the gifts of the Holy Spirit were for today.

"We're just going to concentrate on our own little fellowship in our homes," they said. "The home church is where it's at today. God is finished with the organized, denominational church."

Have you heard that lie? It's right out of the pit, coming straight from the mouth of the father of lies. God is *not* finished with the organized church. He's using it. If He is ever finished with it, He'll be the one to say so, not us. Not only is God using the organized denominational churches, but He is also permitting Spirit-filled people to be instruments of His blessing in such churches when they stay in the proper chain of authority and don't act as if they know it all.

Well, eventually about half our prayer group had split off and become part of various little groups without a pastor, without any divine command, without any overseers. At first, everything seemed to continue to go well with them. But then it happened. The deceiver appeared, and they fell for his line. I became aware of it one night when I was the first one to arrive at our after-Sunday-night-services prayer group. While I was praising the Lord, waiting for the other members to arrive, a stranger walked in and introduced himself.

"God sent me here with some good news for you people," he said. "I am a prophet of God with a message for today."

"Well, that's interesting," I told him. "We're relatively new Christians, so we're very much interested in God's message for today. What do you hear Him saying?"

He answered in a very important tone of voice, and I could feel the appeal to my pride in every word:

"God has just shown me that you people are on the verge of a new spiritual breakthrough."

His approach is one of Slue Foot's favorite door-openers. He appeals to your ego, makes you think you're going to become great in the eyes of all the world. And right away, a bell rang somewhere deep inside me.

"Look out for this clown," the Spirit of God seemed to be warning me. "Watch out for his bag. Check his merchandise very carefully. Beware!"

If I hadn't kept myself submitted to God's already constituted authority, I'd have fallen for this deception because it had in it everything to engender rebellion. I could hear my soul asking, "What's in it for me?"

But my spirit reminded me that I should be looking for what was in everything for God—

About then, some of the other men began to come in for the meeting, and as the stranger was introducing himself around, I noticed something very peculiar about his appearance, something which I could have seen only by the gift of discernment, one of the perfect gifts of the Holy Spirit. There was a band of black light right across the man's face, like a shadow over his eyes. At first I thought it was just a natural shadow, caused by the lighting system in the room, and then God brought to my mind the Scripture that says that Satan comes as an angel of light, to deceive the very elect if possible, and I recognized the shadow for the darkness it represented.

I was glad I was saturated with the Lord and that I was not in rebellion that could trip me up and blind me to truth. I knew I'd be kept safe from deception. Otherwise, I'd have been clobbered for sure.

After the group had sat down to begin our meeting, including the ones who had left their churches, the stranger among us introduced his subject the second time.

"Folks, God has some good news for you."

"Fine. Let's hear it."

"In these last days, God is revealing some new truths by His Spirit."

Well, we couldn't say that wasn't true, because it probably was. Most of the fellows present nodded in agreement. Supersalesmanship teaches that all you've got to do to make a sale is to get a person to say yes three times in a row, and you've as good as got his signature on the dotted line. I stuck my antenna up a little higher. I was already suspicious of the man because of the black light and the appeal to my ego. Now my suspicions were heightened because what he was saying sounded so logical, so reasonable. I'd learned to be on the alert every time something appealed to my human reason. Such things are likely to be from Slue Foot, geared to the soul level, the ego.

"Be careful, Hill," I was saying to myself.

Then came the man's second statement.

"God is not limited by His written Word, the Bible," the man intoned, rather matter of factly.

Well, we had to agree with that, too. God has chosen to bind himself to His Word, but we certainly can't say that He is limited by anything.

The supersalesman had two yeses going for him already, leading us on.

"Therefore," he continued, trying to lull us into thinking that the next statement would be equally true—and here was his stinger—"the new truth that God is revealing today by His Spirit might be contrary to His written Word."

"Whoops!" I said, but not out loud. Satan had unmasked himself for sure with that one. "Devil, you're a liar," I said under my breath, and I never heard another word the man said.

I knew that God has never been known to operate contrary to His written Word. If I bought the lie of the deceiver, I'd have succumbed to the spirit of deception. The first thing that happens to those who buy that lie is that they begin to challenge the Scripture. "Is that true? Is this true? Which portion of Scripture should I get rid of? Which part should I demythologize and rationalize away?" They begin to get "religious," they begin to get theological, and the first thing you know, they're absolutely finished, wiped out as far as any faith in the Word of God is concerned.

Jesus said, "My sheep hear my voice" (John 10:27). If our hearing is tuned to the frequency of the voice of the Shepherd, we don't fall for the line of any false prophets. If something is not strictly according to the written Word of God, it may sound good, but I can't use it.

The visitor to our prayer group was hawking one of the deceptions very prevalent today, leading a lot of God's people into the deepest kind of error. He was associated with the Manifest Sons of God movement that teaches a doctrine called "sinless perfection." This doctrine says, "You are sinlessly perfect. Why, you're the Manifest Sons of God, and God's sons cannot commit sins. Therefore, you may do anything you want to do. If it feels good, feel free to do it." That's basic situational ethics, another doctrine of devils, and people have followed it into grosser and grosser deceptions.

After about twelve members of our group had fallen for the Manifest Sons business, they began to criticize me for my stand against it.

"Brother Hill, you're not loving," they said. "You're rejecting this man and his teaching."

"I certainly am," I told them. "And I intend to continue to reject anything that goes contrary to the written Word of God. It's not for me. I renounce every word of it."

As time went on, the people who had fallen for the false prophet began to accelerate their criticism of the church. This is another sign of an offbeat doctrine, destructive criticism of the established churches.

"The organized church is no good," these people said. "The pastors are just in it for the money. Actually, they're thieves. They're making fat pocketbooks for themselves." The spirit of criticism was having a heyday. After a while, they lifted another Scripture from its context:

Come out from among them, and be ye separate,
saith the Lord, and touch not the unclean thing; and
I will receive you. (2 Cor. 6:17)

Here God was talking about one thing, but they interpreted His words according to the evil desire of their own hearts.

"Do away with your churches and your pastors," they said, perverting the very Scriptures that were meant to keep them on the right path. They began to meet in small groups, without qualified teachers, and fell down, down, down, into worse and worse error until they were engaged in perversions just like the Corinthians were at one time.

All the saints have prayed for them, but no one has been delivered yet. Homes have been broken up over this thing, families smashed. One man who got involved and stayed involved was utterly destroyed.

"God told me to quit my job," he said, "and sit in the middle of my living room and He'd meet my every need." He and his wife and several little children sat and waited. The furniture people came and took away the furniture. The rug people came and took away the rugs. The electric people came and turned off the electricity.

We tried to counsel with him.

"Brother," we pleaded, "are you sure it's the Lord's voice you're hearing?"

"Oh, yes, it's loud and clear. Unmistakable." He wouldn't be budged.

Eventually, the mortgage people came and put him and

his family out on the sidewalk, Social workers came and scattered the little children into different foster homes. Charlie just sat, smiling sweetly, saying, "The Lord is leading me."

Over a three-year period, I saw that man fall into deception like you wouldn't believe. One day he came to a retreat in North Carolina, stood up in a chair, stripped to the waist, and shouted, "Don't touch me. I'm Jesus Christ. The power of God will kill you if you lay a hand on me."

I had a spare bed in my room, so I took him in to see if I could help him out. But it was too late. The fellow was so deceived, he didn't know what he had said. He had tried to fight this thing off, he told me. One night a bunch of devils had waked him and told him to go to a witchcraft meeting. "No, I'm not going," he told them. But suddenly it was as if a big bunch of snakes began to writhe and coil around inside of his head. The biggest snake of all untangled himself enough to say, "You *are* going." The man got up and dressed and went to the Manifest Sons meeting in an apartment on the other side of Baltimore.

That was the night someone in the neighborhood called the police. Afterward, the police captain reported, "Law enforcement officers are accustomed to seeing ugly things, but when we walked into that apartment and found so-called Christians, men and women, naked on the floor, barking like dogs, our stomachs flipped."

One of the men, a young fellow who had been active in Christian work with young people, ran out of the apartment and up the street screaming at the top of his voice, "I am Jesus Christ! Bow down and worship me."

"We'll do better than that," the policeman told him when they caught him and shoved him into a patrol car. "We'll set you up in your very own empire."

They delivered him to Crownsville State Hospital and

locked him up in the violent ward, frothing at the mouth with demons.

This kind of thing can happen when King's kids step into deceptions through a rebellion against God's chain of command and rejection of any part of the Word of God.

God has said that we are to abide in Him and that we are to let His words abide in us (John 15:7). He has also said, "Keep your hands off my servants" (Ps. 105:14-15). But for the grace of God, I would have fallen into this deception, because it's such an ego builder, makes you such a great guy to say, "My pastor is a dummy. He doesn't even speak with new tongues. Who needs him?"

But God says, "You'd *better* need him."

I was blessed to stay in line with God's opinion on this. I went to my pastor and told him, "I want you to know that I appreciate you. You don't believe the same things I do, but I want to stay under your command so I won't get shot full of holes."

That was pure grace, because I don't ordinarily do such things on my own.

God tried to warn His people against deceivers, speaking through the letters of John where we find,

> Beloved, believe not every spirit, but try the spirits whether they are of God: because many false prophets are gone out into the world. Hereby know ye the Spirit of God: Every spirit that confesseth that Jesus Christ is come in the flesh is of God: and every spirit that confesseth not that Jesus Christ is come in the flesh is not of God: and this is the spirit of antichrist, whereof ye have heard that it should come; and even now already is it in the world. Ye are of God, little children, and have overcome them: because greater is he that is in you, than he that is in the world. They are of the world:

therefore speak they of the world, and the world heareth them. We are of God: he that knoweth God heareth us; he that is not of God heareth not us. Hereby know we the spirit of truth, and the spirit of error. (1 John 4:1-6)

This checkpoint makes it plain to believers everywhere that anyone who denies the truth of the written Word of God is denying the Word who came in the flesh. We won't fall for the lies of Slue Foot if we are aware of what the Scripture says about these things.

In the past, I've gone to a number of persons caught in these devilish doctrines and tried to show them the error of their ways. Invariably I've met a response that said, "Brother, when you have reached our level of understanding, then you'll see it the way we do."

I hope I never reach their level of understanding which is down in the sub-sub-basement where Slue Foot is. Having done my best to set them straight, I can rest, knowing that my responsibility had ended, according to Brother Paul:

If thou put the brethren in remembrance of these things, thou shalt be a good minister of Jesus Christ, nourished up in the words of faith and of good doctrine, whereunto thou hast attained. But refuse profane and old wives' fables, and exercise thyself rather unto godliness. (1 Tim. 4:6-7)

The old wives' fables referred to in this Scripture would include such things as superstitions, good works by human methods, and any teachings that insist, "You're really a good guy."

Satan's craftiest trick is to mix a little bit of a lie with a whole lot of truth. He did that in the Garden of Eden, and rationalizing away the Word of God, they fell for it. He did it in the wilderness, but speaking the Word of God in power, Jesus mowed down the temptation. He does it with us, and we fall to destruction or stand in victory according to our knowledge of and obedience to His Word.

God said that He would send a spirit of deception, and if we chose to believe a lie, He would fix us so we wouldn't know a lie from the truth. Paul says it this way in his second letter to the Thessalonians:

> The coming of the lawless by the activity of Satan will be with all power and with pretended signs and wonders, and with all wicked deception for those who are to perish, because they refused to love the truth and so be saved. Therefore God sends upon them a strong delusion, to make them believe what is false, so that all may be condemned who did not believe the truth but had pleasure in unrighteousness. (2:9-12 RSV)

This is an exceedingly serious state of affairs. Doing our own thing is too expensive. It's better, far better, to ask God to take out of us the spirit of rebellion and enable us to submit to His divine order of things so we can live in the victory He bought for us.

44

How to Live in Victory
over Devilish Deceptions

Before I met Jesus, I dabbled in everything witchy or
twitchy on the market. I fell for everything weird or
eccentric or esoteric because of my squirrelly mind. I was a
good Buddhist. I could become one with a lotus blossom.
Transcendental Meditation was kid stuff. I got into
contemplation, which is way beyond meditation. I could pop
into my own navel, fuzz and all, for a visit. I thought that was
way-out stuff, but it was bound to be a shallow trip, and
when I came back out, I was the same dreary slob I was
when I went in. That is the read out on all religions and
philosophies. Religion and philosophy can only change your
mind. But Jesus can give you a brand-new life.

Writing to Timothy, Paul recorded a warning that men
would succumb to such foolishness in the end times:

Now the Spirit speaketh expressly, that in the
latter times, some shall depart from the faith,
giving heed to seducing spirits, and doctrines of
devils. (1 Tim. 4:1)

That wasn't Paul's own opinion; it was the Holy Spirit
speaking to God's people, telling them what to watch out for.

One of the doctrines of the devil making the rounds today is that everyone is going to be saved, that nobody is going to be left out of heaven. This false doctrine used to be called Universalism; its modern label is Ultimate Reconciliation. For their scriptural backup, its adherents quote Paul's letter to the Philippians:

> Wherefore God also hath highly exalted him, and given him a name which is above every name: That at the name of Jesus every knee should bow, of things in heaven, and things in earth, and things under the earth; And that every tongue should confess that Jesus Christ is Lord, to the glory of God the Father. (2:9-11)

That's a perfectly good verse, but it doesn't prove what the Universalists say it does, because nowhere in it does it say that every heart will believe that God has raised Jesus from the dead, and that's a vital part of salvation according to God's formula:

> If thou shalt confess with thy mouth the Lord Jesus, and shalt believe in thine heart that God hath raised him from the dead, thou shalt be saved. (Rom. 10:9)

It's true that everybody will be under enforced subjection to the King of kings when He comes the second time and rules the world with an iron rod, but if there's no belief in the heart to match the confession with the mouth and the bent knee, the conditions for salvation are not met.

On one occasion, some folks said, "Lord, Lord, look what we did in your name. We healed the sick, we cast out devils, we did many wonderful works." But Jesus said to them, "I never knew you: depart from me, ye that work iniquity" (Matt. 7:22-23). Freely translated, that's "Down the tube, children." In another verse, God reminds us that not everyone who says, "Lord, Lord," will enter the kingdom, but only those who have done the will of His Father in heaven (Matt. 7:21). Doing God's will is not a matter of good works, as so much of the world seems to think. The Bible makes it plain that "doing God's will" means that we believe, or trust in, the one He sent (John 6:28-29). Doing good works can never be the way to salvation, because the blood of Jesus is the only antidote for sin that God accepts. Our righteousness? It's filthy rags, He says (Isa. 64:6).

Another deception prevalent today to divide men from truth is a teaching called Unity. It says that the Christ is in everybody. We can look around us and know that's not true. When I was in Unity, I had to admit, "Well, if Christ is in everybody, they don't show it." All of my friends, top management people, were skillful connivers, just like I was.

Christian Science is still another doctrine of devils, begun by Mary Baker Eddy who was a rebellious teenager. She drove her daddy crazy because she wouldn't go to church. He was a preacher, and finally he said, "All right. Stay at home, then. Do your own thing." Soon afterward, she started her own religion, in full rebellion against Jesus himself.

All of these devilish doctrines know something about corrective exercises that can put mind over matter so that psychosomatic ailments don't sock you in bed forever, but there is in them no wholeness, no salvation. They insist that everybody is a good guy, down deep, that there's no such thing as sin or disease, and they laugh at the blood of Jesus. But no matter how much they sneer, it doesn't alter the truth that there is no remission of sin without the blood of Jesus. And if your sin remains in your own blood system, it will wipe you out, sooner or later.

Why is it that people are unable to see the error of these ridiculous things? Paul suggested an answer when he was writing to Timothy:

Speaking lies in hypocrisy; having their conscience
seared with a hot iron. (1 Tim. 4:2)

A conscience that has been seared with a hot iron would be
calloused over, not sensitive to the gentle moving of God's
Holy Spirit.

The world is being deceived by a multitude of things. You
don't see anything wrong with Yoga lessons? It's just a little
exercise for your body? You find no harm in practicing a
little TM to improve your mind or in reading your horoscope
"just for fun"?

I've got news for you. You'll never see anything wrong
with them until it's too late.

When you sit in your Yoga position, chant your TM
mantra, play with a Ouija board, or let the stars tell you
what to do tomorrow, you're opening your soul for a
full-scale invasion of Satan's work crew, the boys in black,
the demons. I've heard it in testimony after testimony. You
may wind up having to go to a nervous house for some time to
come, maybe forever. They may have to lock you in a padded
cell and take away all sharp instruments for fear you might
fall in with Satan's plans and destroy yourself. Suicidal
tendencies, the shrinks call them, and they're standard
equipment of the spirit of destruction.

Satan's workers encourage you, "Do your Yoga. It's good
for you. Stick with your TM. It'll enlarge your mind." But
God says,

Bodily exercise profiteth little: but godliness is
profitable unto all things, having promise of the life
that now is, and of that which is to come. (1 Tim.
4:8)

I'm highly interested in the life which now is, but I'm far
more interested in the one which is to come, because it will
last longer, like forever. And if bodily exercise is okay, but
godliness is better both for now and for later, godliness is
what I'm most in favor of.

296

Another of the ungodly ministries making the rounds right now—even among Christian groups—trying to show people how they can improve themselves and their human relationships without Jesus, is called "self-awareness." The whole self-awareness thing has been Satanic ever since it first came out. The first self-awareness was born in the Garden of Eden when Adam and Eve ate the no-no fruit. Immediately afterward, self-awareness of their nakedness set in, and they had to hide themselves from God. He helped them all He could, making fur snuggies for them to take the place of the fig-leaf variety which were sort of scratchy. But He had to excommunicate them from Paradise. And they regretted that day the rest of their lives.

There's no such thing as self-awareness in the animal kingdom. There's no four-legged creature that's aware of itself. I happen to have a couple of Chihuahuas. I can hold them up to the mirror, and when they look at themselves they seem to be thinking, "I wonder what that is." Their mirror image is a total stranger to them; they don't recognize themselves.

No cow ever mooed, "I am a cow, but I am tired of giving milk. I think I'll quit." If she did, she would cease being a cow and become a people.

Self-awareness is a trick of the enemy to make people exalt their own self-importance instead of the name of Jesus. King's kids can't afford to fall for anything like that.

God says,

Abstain from all appearance of evil. (1 Thess. 5:22)

If a thing looks evil or looks good but is called evil in the Word of God, King's kids are to leave it strictly alone. It's easier to stay away from something entirely than it is to indulge and have to explain later on, because once Satan has got something to throw at you and spread the word around about your "Christian character," it'll be hard for you to live it down.

Witchcraft and the occult are blocking many Christians today from experiencing the best that God has for them. God warned His people against these things way back in Moses' day:

There shall not be found among you anyone who makes his son or his daughter pass through the fire, one who uses divination, one who practices witchcraft, or one who interprets omens, or a sorcerer [fortune teller, The Living Bible], or one who casts a spell, or a medium, or a spiritist, or one who calls up the dead. For whoever does these things is detestable to the LORD. (Deut. 18: 10-12 NAS)

In addition to refraining from doing those things that are in themselves evil, God recommends that we refrain from doing other things which are perfectly all right for us, but which might create the appearance of evil in someone else's sight and thus be a stumbling block to him. In other words, it's not enough for us to *be* right in our actions, we ought to *look* right so as not to cause offense to anyone looking on. That is real liberty—to be free to choose *not* to do something I'm entitled to do, for the benefit of my brother. Jesus said, "If you want to come out on top, become a servant to all. Let your self rights be nonexistent" (Mark 10:43-44, my paraphrase).

I'm not pretending that I have arrived at this point, but I see what God is driving at. And as we pray for one another along these lines, we'll all get better at doing what the Word says.

Paul understood these things. Romans 14 is all about them. You can open your Bible and read the whole chapter for a little further instruction here. In essence, Paul was saying, "Everything is legally okay for me, but considering in love its effect on someone else, I'll not do anything that will cause my brother to stumble. I'll avoid every appearance of evil, even avoiding things I know are okay but that are evil in his sight."

How do we decide what appears evil? How do we know whether or not it is evil if it is not in that list from Deuteronomy? We can look at the thing in the light of Jesus' presence within us. If you can ask Jesus to go arm in arm with you to a place you want to go, it's probably all right for you to go. If you'd hesitate to invite Him along, going there is probably less than God's best for you.

If you don't like that checkpoint, try this one for size. Anytime you ask whether it's all right for you as a Christian to do a certain thing, you'd better assume that it's *not* all right. If there's any question in your mind about it, it's likely to be a poor second best to what God has in mind for you.

The enemy uses lots of tricks to get us to settle for second best, because second best blocks the best in terms of the glory of God and the blessings to His people.

How will you know if you're really functioning in the way that God provides for being in the center of His will? A further scriptural checkpoint is laid out in Paul's first letter to the Thessalonians when he writes,

> And the very God of peace sanctify you wholly; and I pray God your whole spirit and soul and body be preserved blameless unto the coming of our Lord Jesus Christ. Faithful is he that calleth you, who also will do it. (5:23-24)

When you are functioning in the way God prescribes, you will know the very God of peace throughout your whole being. There'll be no struggle, no striving, no stretching to make it work. When you are in the center of His will, you are at perfect rest. You'll see what Slue Foot is up to, but you can wait in peace for your marching orders.

Jesus within is the overall commander. He is watching the enemy, waiting for the fullness of time to act. At exactly the right moment, He'll give you the green light, saying, "Now's the time. Walk in and possess the land." When you wait for that instruction and act on it, you'll see the enemy dissolved ahead of you.

God is light, and in Him darkness cannot exist. The powers of darkness have to disappear when the energy of the Spirit, which is light, comes on the scene. Until then, we can wear ourselves out trying to put out the darkness, because only light can make the darkness flee. And it always does a thorough job. This proves that the warfare is not up to us. It's not our battle. "The battle is mine," saith the Lord (2 Chron. 20:15), and what He says is always true.

If there is anything other than peace pervading your whole being, there is some area of struggle left, some area where Satan is trying to get to you to make you prove something, or be something, or do something. Don't let him trick you.

The God who is the God of peace is the one, this Scripture says, who will sanctify you wholly. That means you don't have to worry about doing it yourself. God will do the sanctifying for you by His presence within you. He will *be* your sanctification (1 Cor. 1:30). Your spirit, soul and body will be properly related, properly balanced, and properly functioning on account of Jesus within, who is wholeness.

Notice that we are to be preserved blameless. Being blameless is not the same as being sinless. God doesn't make me goof-proof. I will make mistakes and have to confess them as sin. I will still need the blood of Jesus Christ to cover all my sins. But as I make a deliberate choice to stay tuned to His wavelength, setting my affection on His kingdom, instead of on TV—twisted vision—I experience more and more of His kingdom on earth. And choosing to dwell in that kingdom, keeping my mind stayed on Him, I can be a more useful channel for His grace to His people.

Fortunately, I had my praising-the-Lord antenna in the air.

45

How to Live in Victory
over Snowed-In Highways

Heading home after taking part in a School of Faith in a Methodist church in Asheville, North Carolina, I decided to detour to spend the night with Brother Joe Petrie at Sandy Ridge. After dinner with the Petrie brethren, I felt an urge to stroll through a cornfield behind the parsonage. It was a beautiful, crisp autumn evening, and my heavy winter topcoat gave me welcome warmth. As I walked along the rows, I found myself pulling ears of corn and shelling them into my pockets.

Being in a high state of praise, I knew I was in the Lord's will, so I didn't question His motives, but I asked myself, "Now why am I filling my pockets with chicken corn? I don't expect to be a chicken—"

"Do it anyhow," the Spirit seemed to say.

After I had shelled half a dozen or so ears, and my pockets were pleasantly bulging, I went in and rejoined the rest of the folks around the roaring fire for fellowship and prayer. One of the prayers was that God would set His angels watch roundabout me and give me safe journey the next day.

In the morning, I ate breakfast, hugged the brethren

goodbye, and started out, praising the Lord for His great love and abundant provision for all my needs. About half an hour later, snowflakes the size of turkey feathers began falling. It looked like all heaven was shaking the stuffing out of all the bed pillows in creation.

After two hours, everything on the highway ground to a halt in the deepening blanket of snow. Traffic was completely locked in by a howling blizzard that showed no sign of letting up, ever.

For the first two hours of the standstill, I feasted on chewy chicken corn from my overcoat pockets and crisp winesap apples from the back seat basketful I had bought the day before. It was just about as sumptuous a feast as anyone could want under the circumstances. My car heater was going full blast to keep me warm, and providentially, I had filled my tank with gas the night before and had new snow tires put on my car the preceding week.

I praised the Lord for all those things, but as the morning wore on, and it got to be one o'clock in the afternoon, I began to look at other appearances. Out of my snowy windshield, I could see the shadowy outlines of big tractor-trailers jackknifed, smaller trucks and cars hopelessly tangled. The wind howled, my fuel gauge was plummeting, several hours passed, and still the storm raged. I began to be impatient, tired of getting nowhere.

The natural man in me insisted I not sit there, but that I *do* something. Temporarily forgetting that I was to reckon my natural man dead (Rom. 6:11), I let him order me around. That always results in misery. I turned my collar up around my ears, pulled my hat down as far as it would go, sucked in a deep breath, threw my weight against the car door to open it against the wind, and fell out into the blizzard that about tore my socks off. Fighting my way up the road about five hundred yards or so, I discovered the impossibility of

304

anything getting through on that highway before the spring thaw. Not even a skinny tapeworm could make it.

Utterly discouraged, I turned around, fought my way back, and crawled into the driver's seat. It was a good thing I'd left my motor running, because my hands were too numb to turn the key. I wondered if I'd thaw out before I turned into a permanent rigor mortis icicle. I wished I'd told my wife what kind of funeral service I would like to have over my remains when they found me. Maybe I could write down some instructions—if my hands ever thawed out enough for me to use them.

Slue Foot was making the most of his golden opportunity, rubbing defeat into all my pores.

"Yep," he taunted, "you'll sit here until your gas is gone, and then you'll slowly freeze to death along with the rest of those poor slobs out there." He cackled as he delivered the next installment of his good news. "But you won't be lonesome—your chicken corn and apples will freeze right along with you."

He was so right. Being reminded of the chicken corn, I fumbled a gloved handful to my mouth and started gobbling grains like so many martyr pills.

"Lord," I grumbled, "don't you care anything at all for me? I deserve better treatment than this. Why, look at all I've done for you—"

Hearing myself broadcasting on Slue Foot's dismal frequency woke me up to the fact that it didn't have to be that way. If I could get my eyes off the circumstances and back onto Jesus, I could live in the heaven of God's victory instead of in the pit of Satan's defeat.

"Forgive me, Father," I hollered above the raging wind. I knew I needed to get into the Word, fast, for a potent antidote to the poison my pity-party planning had been pumping through my veins. But my Bible was in my luggage in the trunk of the car. I wasn't about to be stupid enough to get out in the blizzard again to get it. That was rough, because in my misery, I couldn't even think of any comforting verses.

The Lord saw my need, however, and began to put into operation a remarkable chain of events. By a strange coincidence, I accidentally bumped the lock on the glove compartment of my car. By a strange coincidence, the glove compartment accidentally fell open.

By a strange coincidence, a paperbound copy of the Book of Acts that I had never seen before tumbled out. And when I picked it up, by a strange coincidence, the book fell open to the account of Paul and Silas in prison, singing hymns and praising the Lord at midnight (Acts 16:25-26). While they sang His praise, by a strange coincidence, suddenly the prison doors were opened and they were set free.

There were more strange coincidences in the account, but that was enough for me. I had learned long ago that a coincidence is something that God causes to happen, but He chooses to remain anonymous. I had also learned that God's principles always work when God's people try them. I knew beyond a doubt that the Scripture in Acts was God's message for me.

"Lord," I said, "you're on. I'm game to try it if you are. And I understand, unless you've changed the ground rules, that I can expect to be set free from the prison of this storm in a supernatural way, just as Paul and Silas were."

He didn't tell me no, so I had His full permission to leave off the "poor little ole me" lament I had been composing for my pity party. I cranked up a joyful noise instead, singing hymns out loud and praising Him for the circumstances in which I was incarcerated. Then I asked Him to deliver me from them.

I continued to praise Him, feeling better and better every

moment. As I praised Him, I braced myself for a mighty earthquake that would swallow the snow, clear the highway, and spirit me out of the traffic tie-up.

It didn't happen. That's not how He chose to handle things that trip. Instead of being rocked by an earthquake, I became aware of a still small voice I'd have missed if I hadn't had my praising-the-Lord antenna in the air. It spoke softly but very distinctly from somewhere in the back of the car, saying, "I believe there's an opening up ahead. Follow me."

Immediately after the voice spoke, a tiny little car, like no car I'd ever seen before, came from somewhere behind me and began to weave its way right through the impossible, impassable jam of cars and trucks. The driver motioned for me to do likewise.

That was clearly preposterous, impossible. I could hear my common sense saying, "No way, you fool. You've already checked it out. There isn't any opening." But since I'd learned on many previous occasions that the Lord moves in ways my common sense can't get a handle on, I shifted into gear and took out after the tiny car.

I don't know how it happened. We would be approaching a complete roadblock, and suddenly we were past that one and coming up on another one. Did God narrow my car down to three inches in some places, lift it over obstacles in the road, or lift the obstacles out of the way so my car could get through? I never knew. I only knew He had to change the dimensions of something for the miracle to happen, upgrade, downgrade, through mile after mile of stalled vehicles. I didn't look to the right or left of me. If I had, it would have been curtains for us all. I just kept my eyes on the tiny car, going everywhere it did.

Suddenly, the little car vanished. And just as suddenly, I didn't need it anymore. I found myself on a turnoff that was covered with snow but free of cars. Clearly visible road signs pointed me to an untraveled route back to Joe Petrie's church with a fresh word of testimony for the evening service about the angelmobile God had sent to my rescue.

Angels? Why not? The Scripture says,

> But to which of the angels said he at any time, sit on my right hand, until I make thine enemies thy footstool? Are they not all ministering spirits, sent forth to minister for them who shall be heirs of salvation? (Heb. 1:13-14)

I don't ordinarily look for angels. I'm not a kook or a spook in that department. I'm a scientist, very practical, but I'm glad that God has ways and means that transcend the natural. If Jesus has made His angels to be ministering spirits to the heirs of salvation, it's natural that He should send one to help me out when I'm in trouble in a spot where no ordinary two-legged critter can get to me. And if He chooses to send the angel my way in a tiny four-wheeled vehicle, should I insist on a more conventional helicopter? Maybe the next time, He'll do it that way, who knows? That's His business. My business is not to look at circumstances but to keep my eyes on Him if I want to enjoy the benefits of victory in every kind of weather.

46

How to Live in Victory
when You Don't Know What to Do Next

Several years ago I had an interesting experience that might have involved another angel driving a four-wheeled vehicle. Only this time I got to see the angel.

It happened back during the space program. I was scheduled to fly to Bermuda from New York City on Sunday morning, and as the Lord arranged it, I arrived in New York a day early, so I could speak to a Saturday morning breakfast meeting of the Full Gospel Business Men's Fellowship International. The Lord doesn't waste time; somehow He also scheduled me to brag on Jesus at a Saturday evening meeting, this one to be held on Long Island. I didn't have to know the details of time and place, because someone would be coming to the breakfast meeting to take me to Long Island. That person would have all the necessary information.

Well, when the breakfast meeting was over, I received a brief phone call. The brother who was to meet me had been stricken with some kind of ailment and would not be picking me up after all. Thank you and goodbye. Before I could interpose any questions, I heard the click of the receiver.

309

Someone was obviously in a hurry. I was left having no idea where I was to go, or what I was to do.

There I was, marooned in New York City at one o'clock Saturday afternoon. Everyone had left the breakfast meeting, leaving me stranded. What to do? Well, I had learned to praise the Lord and do the next thing, getting the vehicle in motion so God could put His guidance into operation. It was cold outside, and if the Lord had outdoor plans for me, I had better be prepared. I went to the checkroom to get my overcoat.

Mine was the last coat hanging there. The place was empty except for Jesus and me. It seemed all right to ask Him a question out loud:

"Lord, what do I do next?"

"Keep praising me and come along," were the words that dropped into my think tank.

I didn't ask, "Come along where?" I just looked for a door to go through. Before I saw a door, I spotted a little man wandering around in a state of confusion. The fellow couldn't have been more than five feet high, and he looked bewildered, with a rather out-of-this-world expression on his face. His dark features made me think he might be an Italian or some other kind of foreigner. Maybe I could help him.

"Are you looking for someone?" I asked him.

"I not know," he said, and continued to look around, perplexed. "Lord sent me here," were words I understood out of a whole paragraph of broken English. "Someone want go Valley Stream, Long Island?"

Lights started flashing inside my top ten inches.

"Valley Stream is where I'm supposed to go," I told him. "But I don't know exactly where. And I don't know who is supposed to pick me up."

He started explaining a lot of things, some of which I

310

understood. It seems he had never been in New York City before, that he was a Catholic brother who had been in ministry in South America for years. But when he arrived in New York City that day, the Lord told him to go to Schrafft's restaurant in Manhattan to pick up a man who needed to go to Valley Stream, Long Island.

"Maybe I'm the one," I told him, "because there's nobody else here."

"Praise the Lord!" he said.

"Praise the Lord!" I echoed, and we started down the stairs.

"Never drive New York before," he told me on the way out of the building.

"Wow!" I said.

"Lost," he confessed.

"That makes two of us," I admitted. We were in perfect harmony.

When we got into the car the Lord had provided for the occasion, we forgot our problems and began to rejoice over the miracle of God's bringing the two of us together out of the millions of people in New York City.

How we got on the right road is a rather long story, but as we began to approach Long Island, he asked me, "Where you want going?"

"I have no idea," I said. "I'm supposed to speak at some Pentecostal church out here tonight. Do you know of any Pentecostal churches in Valley Stream?"

He thought for a moment or two, then said, "Brother So and So has church. That one?"

I didn't have any way of knowing, but it was worth a try. After all, I didn't know any place else to go.

The whole thing added up to the fact that Brother So and So's church was the one where I was supposed to be. That was occasion for another glory fit. But there was more.

After the service, the little man had a new question.

"Where you sleep night?" he asked me.

I shrugged my shoulders. "Don't know yet. No one has told me."

As people were leaving the church, several of them had said, "I hope you have a good night." I was hoping their hopes would be realized, because it looked as if I'd have to find a park bench somewhere, and I didn't imagine that would be too good.

It just happened that the little Catholic brother had an extra bed in his room, so he took me along to it. The room was tiny as a cell, just big enough for the two of us and his fat Italian Bible. We got to praying together, and the first thing I knew I was reading his Bible, without knowing a word of Italian. It was a real hallelujah party.

The next morning, he drove me to the airport, and I flew to Bermuda.

Was the little man an earthling? Or a ministering angel out of Hebrews 1:14? I don't know, but when I get through the pearly gates, that's one of the first things I want to find out. Meanwhile, I'll join Paul in saying,

> O the depth of the riches both of the wisdom and knowledge of God! how unsearchable are his judgments, and his ways past finding out! (Rom. 11:33)

But even though His ways are past my present finding out, I find they're designed to get me where I'm supposed to go.

And now, King's Kids let's pray together in one accord: Lord Jesus, I've decided to sell out completely to you. From now on, I'm your very own container. Possess me. Invade me. Diffuse yourself throughout my being. Cause me to become incandescent with your Spirit. Help yourself to me totally—and if I'm not entirely sure I mean all this—just do it *anyhow*. For your name's sake. Amen